Korea under Japanese Colonialism, 1910-1945

———◆———

A Historical Overview

Korea under Japanese Colonialism, 1910-1945

A Historical Overview

Professor Samina Sultana, Ph.D.

© Copyright 2024 by BengalGeek™ - All rights reserved.

Published by BengalGeek™ LLC: www.bengalgeek.com

The content contained within this book may not be reproduced, duplicated or transmitted without direct written permission from the author or the publisher.

Under no circumstances will any blame or legal responsibility be held against the publisher, or author, for any damages, reparation, or monetary loss due to the information contained within this book, either directly or indirectly.

Legal Notice:

This book is copyright protected. It is only for personal use. You cannot amend, distribute, sell, use, quote or paraphrase any part, or the content within this book, without the consent of the author or publisher.

Disclaimer Notice:

Please note the information contained within this document is for educational and entertainment purposes only. All effort has been executed to present accurate, up to date, reliable, complete information. No warranties of any kind are declared or implied. Readers acknowledge that the author is not engaged in the rendering of legal, financial, medical or professional advice. The content within this book has been derived from various sources. Please consult a licensed professional before attempting any techniques outlined in this book.

By reading this document, the reader agrees that under no circumstances is the author responsible for any losses, direct or indirect, that are incurred as a result of the use of the information contained within this document, including, but not limited to, errors, omissions, or inaccuracies.

Dedicated to

My Late Father and Mother

Contents

........♦........

FOREWARD..vii
ABSTRACT ix
ACRONYMS xix
PREFACE...xxiv
The Opening of Korea   (1870–1910)...xxviii
CHAPTER 1:   Korea Becomes a Japanese Colony 1
CHAPTER 2:   The Colonial Period (1906–1918)................................17
CHAPTER 3:   Japanese Economic Aggression 31
CHAPTER 4:   Development of the Nationalist Movement.................87
CHAPTER 5:   The Economic Domination (1932–1945) 143
CHAPTER 6:   Development of Foreign Trade 216
CONCLUSION 261
WORKS CITED...271
ENDNOTES..279

FOREWARD

♦

I am thrilled to share a book my mother wrote during her Ph.D. program, which she completed in her 60s. The book delves into Korea's history during Japanese colonial rule, which lasted from 1910 to 1945, the same period as World Wars I and II. With the guidance of her professor Mofakkar Ahmed and a lot of research, she has produced an engaging and informative piece of work.

The manuscript has undergone rigorous editing, including spelling checks and re-writing, while still preserving the original work's essence. Two of my son's friends, along with the professional editing assistance of Sterling Rich and Mallory Wiper, have ensured that the book meets the highest standards of American English specifications.

We have intentionally preserved some spelling discrepancies to maintain the authentic associations, official names of companies, businesses, associations, and other entities are presented as they are officially named. This book has been a great source of education and inspiration for us, and we believe it will be for you too. If you have any questions or concerns, please don't hesitate to contact me at www.bengalgeek.com.

—*Uzma Nishat*

ABSTRACT

......◆......

The purpose of the study is to describe and explain Korea's economic structure and development from 1910 to 1945 under Japanese colonialism. At the end of the 19th century, the corruption, internal conflicts among the ruling factions, and exploitation of the peasants in the feudalistic society of the Choson Dynasty reached their maximum. So, the Western capitalistic nations began to visit the "Hermit Kingdom" for trade. Meanwhile, Japan was the first East Asian country to overthrow its ancient feudalism and move towards capitalism. Japan also wanted to have a trade relationship with Korea but was unsuccessful. Without retreating, Japan ventured to use military strength to force Korea to open the ports to Japan. A treaty of "friendship" was made at the gunpoint of some Japanese warships. Meanwhile, China negotiated a Korean commercial friendship treaty with the United States to gain some power over Russia in the political race and for Japan to have hegemony in Korea.

In modern diplomatic terms, a Sino-Korean trade treaty agreement between China and Korea reaffirmed Korea's subordination to China. The agreement granted China the legal authority to interfere in Korea's internal affairs. Meanwhile, Japan eagerly awaited to take control of Korea's trade and affairs. However, instead of taking advantage of the foreign powers' conflict, Korean political leaders became embroiled in an internal power struggle, which ultimately left Korea vulnerable to Japanese invasion. Due to its superior geographic position and strategic preparedness, Japan gained an invasion advantage over other competitors.

Chapter 1 sheds light on Japan's policy to annex Korea, which prompted the governor-general (G-G) to start arresting members of patriotic organizations. Despite their efforts, the arrests were unable to stop the independent-minded Korean people, who began organizing protests against the Japanese. Traditionally, the Confucian literati protested and submitted a petition to the emperor but failed to achieve their goal. Some of them even committed suicide as a form of protest. The literati leaders then organized the "Righteous Armies" (RA), which was manned by the peasantry and disbanded members of the Korean army (1907). The guerrilla bands were placed in mountainous areas and received support from local people. However, guerrilla activities declined after Japan annexed Korea, and they shifted their fight to Manchuria and Russian maritime territory (RMT), where they continued their resistance.

During the period of Japanese colonialism in Korea, the transportation and communication system in Korea was developed by the Japanese for their own benefit. The railway system was expanded through the use of forced labor of Koreans who were paid very little. The Japanese acquired Korean land at lower prices and controlled education, making the Korean people learn the Japanese language, which was made compulsory. Japanese and Korean students had separate schools. Ironically, Koreans were more progressive in Japan than in their own country as they had to go to Japan for higher studies, and some even for elementary school. However, Korean graduates found it hard to get jobs as the better jobs were reserved for the Japanese. Girls were not educated, especially in rural areas, but later on, more girls started attending schools during the latter part of colonialism. This helped them achieve self-confidence, and they also began participating in sports and politics.

In Chapter 2, we will explore the early stages of Japan's economic dominance over Korea, which began with land occupation. To facilitate this, the Japanese conducted a survey that enabled them to acquire land through their citizens and companies. As a result, Japan, also known as the governor-general, became the largest landowner in Korea and subjected the peasantry to extreme torture. Thus, Korea was exploited by Japan as a colony. Despite the resistance of the "Righteous Army" and the suicides of patriotic individuals, Japan's annexation in 1910 allowed them to exploit Korea in all aspects of life. The Koreans had to endure this until 1945, after the end of World War II, to finally become free from Japanese aggression.

Japanese capitalism was led by landowners, bureaucrats, and feudal lords who oppressed peasants and civil rights leaders. After the Sino-Japanese War (1894–95), the Korean government lost its power and could not take advantage of the conflict between Japan and Russia. Japan dominated the Korean markets and attracted Korean consumers with their cheap prices. When the Japanese Residence-General (R-G) was established, the Korean government made regulations to allow foreigners (i.e., Japanese) to own land and real estate. This deprived Korean peasants of their land under the so-called "report system."

The Korean farmers were made poor and landless by the Japanese survey system. Many farmers, who used to till their hereditary land, lost their land as a result of the survey system. They were either not informed about the system or were not aware of its implications. The survey was hastily done to take the land away from the Korean farmers, and the Oriental Development Company became the largest private company owner. Japanese capitalists and private companies were allowed to take over the land, along with the Japanese Residence-General, who became the largest landowner in Korea. The survey resulted in a significant increase in the amount of land owned by Japanese companies or landowners.

It is worth noting that 58% of the forest land in Korea was owned by the Japanese. As a result of the economic conditions faced by Korean farmers during that period, many of them migrated to Manchuria, Russian Maritime Territories, and Japan to work as laborers. The number of economic migrants who moved to Manchuria was particularly high. The political repression and economic depression they experienced were the main reasons for their migration to neighboring territories.

Chapter 3 highlights the difficult situation faced by Korean industrial workers during Japanese colonialism. Most industries were established in North Korea, and when the country was divided in 1945, both North and South Korea had to face challenges as the economies of both regions were interconnected in manufacturing and agriculture. The Japanese owned most of the industries since they had more capital and paid lower interest rates on loans. They also monopolized Korea's natural resources and paid their workers more than the Korean workers who had to work longer hours. The Korean workers suffered from unhygienic working conditions but had no other choice than to take the job. Despite the challenges, some Korean entrepreneurs built companies with their hard-earned capital. One such company was An Hui-je's Paekan Trading in Pusan, which contributed substantial money to the Korean independence movement, Korean educational promotion, and cooperative movement. The knitwear and rubber factories were funded by Korean capital invested by struggling small merchants who were able to build their factories through determination, frugality, honest dealing, hard work, and enterprising spirit. The rubber factories produced rubber shoes, traditional Korean footwear that the Japanese could not produce.

Chapter 4 is about the different movements in Korea. The first was by the traditional leaders, and the second was by the organized movement of students and the people. The latter movement was more effective. The first social resistance organization was Poanhoe (1904), when, even before annexation, Japan tried to seize Korea's uncultivated land. Another organization, Kongjiho, was started in 1904. When these attempts failed, the same social organizations tried to recover Korea's sovereignty through native industrial and educational development to self-strengthen the society. In 1906, dissolved by the Resident-General after annexation, the movements reappeared as social and cultural programs.

The chapter also gives a vivid description of religion, which affected education and indirectly helped in the process of Korean independence. Christianity and the Protestants influenced politics and education in Korea and also campaigned about sobriety, anti-smoking, equality of sexes, strict monogamy, ethics, and simplicity of popular ceremonies. The Korean intellectuals and businessmen welcomed Protestantism, leading to economic development in some provinces. Religious movements also instilled national consciousness. Confucius leaders wanted to reform Confucianism to adapt to the changing conditions. A reform movement within Buddhism started and had strong nationalistic ideals. The G-G supported Buddhism and Confucianism to counterbalance the religious movements. The state attempted to develop Shintoism but failed to succeed. There was an effort to rediscover old Korean textbooks and standardize the Korean language and spelling. Ancient Korean texts were reprinted, the history of the nation-building of other countries was a model to the Koreans, and they read biographies of heroic figures.

The Korean nationalists who fled to Manchuria and the Russian Maritime Territories started their movement for the independence of Korea. While inside Korea, the nationalists had contracts with patriotic elements abroad. Organizations aimed to restore the country's freedom by force of arms. Widespread disturbances took place all over Korea. March First Movement started with a peaceful declaration of independence. It was crushed ruthlessly by the Japanese military force. The movement needed the support of the Western powers and failed to achieve Its goal.

When the independent farmers became tenant farmers, they faced starvation. There were sporadic revolts by the farmers against the landlords. In the industrial sector, Korean workers were also dissatisfied and began to express their discontent through strikes. The entire Korean population was waiting for an opportune moment to rebel against Japan. This opportunity finally presented itself in 1945, at the end of World War II. With the support of students and political leaders, various tenants, farmers, and labor organizations played a crucial role in Korea's independence movement. With outside Korean organizations in Shanghai, the U.S. mainland, Hawaii, and others, and inside Korea, the farmers, workers, students, and political leaders fought against the Japanese and were able to free Korea from Japanese colonialism.

Chapter 5 discusses Japan's complete economic control over Korea. Due to the Sino-Japanese War, the Great Depression, and World War I, Japan had to develop mines and heavy industries, which led to more economic control over Korea. During the Sino-Japanese War in 1937, Japan developed mines in Korea for gold, silver, and smokeless coal, which Japan needed. The Japanese government, military agencies, and big capitalists explored the Korean mines, and only one mine belonged to a Korean capitalist, as Korean investment was not encouraged. The availability of cheap labor and hydroelectric power attracted Japanese investors, and Japan's big Zaibatsu constructed factories in Korea.

Due to the war, heavy factories were built, and manufacturing expanded. Women and juveniles were working at lower wages. Mine workers had long working hours as the Japanese capitalists took advantage of the Korean working class and burdened them for the war effort. Japan's trade increased tenfold between the opening and annexation of Korea, as Korea already had trade relations with Japan even before the colonial period. The Korean economic growth in the colonial period is termed by many as "export-led growth."

Chapter 6 highlights Japan's control over Korea's finances to develop railways and industries for their own benefit. The government played a significant role in the economy of colonial Korea, propelling modern industry in a centrally controlled system. The largest industrial undertaking was G-G's railway works, which employed around 1,000 laborers in Seoul to build passenger and freight cars and repair locomotives and train cars. The Government-General attracted more industries like the Onoda Cement Factory (OCF) established by Mitsui near P'yongyang in 1920.[1]

So, it was evident that the finance of Korea was controlled by the Japanese, either by the G-G or by the Japanese private companies. Sometimes, Koreans had more factories than the Japanese, but the Japanese invested more capital, resulting in higher production levels in their factories. Often, the Koreans and the Japanese had joint ventures again for the benefit of the Japanese. The loans and deposits were also higher on the Japanese than on the Korean side. One of the reasons the Koreans were suffering was that the loan interest rates for the Koreans were higher than for the Japanese. Even the rate of interest on loans for real estate of the Japanese was lower than that of the Koreans.

Rice exports to Japan increased to a maximum during the colonial period. They increased by 96% between 1929 and 1938. The governor-general did not release any data on rice exports after 1939. It is possible that more rice was exported to Japan than what was reported during those years if the production data were made public. Primary products (raw materials, semi-finished, and finished foodstuffs) amounted to 83.5% of exports. Secondary industrial products comprised 55.7% of the imports, showing the colonial economic relationship between Japan and Korea. The Japanese investment in 1910–1923 was 1,888 million yen, and the outflow of interest and profit from Korea to Japan was 363 million yen (i.e., 18% return on the net investment).

The revenues generated from Korea were used to cover the expenses of the Choson Dynasty, as the Choson government had a monopoly over various services, such as railways, post, telephone, telegraph, and the sale of tobacco, ginseng, salt, and opium. Some of the expenses were incurred for maintaining the Japanese army presence in Korea, which increased after the Sam-Il movement and the Great Depression in the 1930s, the Japanese invasion of Manchuria, and the Sino-Japanese War (SJW). All the banks operating in Korea were owned by Japanese, with only a few owned by Koreans, which also became a source of profit for Japan. In essence, Japan financially exploited Korea in every possible way.

Korea was not only a supplier of food grains but also a market for Japan's expanding industrial goods. The rural labor surplus was exhausted as thousands of them were sent into heavy industries and mines; others went to Japan under compulsion or voluntarily. Korean industries and the labor force were exploited with harshness, and the conditions at home and on the battlefield deteriorated. Many died of diseases, accidents, allied bombing, or were brutally murdered.

Only one Korean was appointed to the Japan Parliament's Upper House (JPUH), and only one to the Lower House as well. The Japanese also attempted to revise the Korean historical narrative. During World War II, Korean patriots fought against the Western powers in Asia. In 1942, Japan's Home Ministry took over Korea as an integral part of the Japanese Empire. The Japanese Prime

Minister was responsible for appointing the Governor-General of Korea.

Conscription was applied to Korean workers, who were to fight and work for construction and transport. Young Korean women, some hardly more than a child, were forced to serve as prostitutes for the Japanese troops. Rumors were there that the Japanese used to extract oil from Korean teenage girls' bodies as there was a shortage of oil for the war machinery. The Koreans were being prepared to repel an invasion by the US forces in the South and the Soviet troops in the North. Korea finally gained independence in 1948 after it was evacuated by the US Army-run government in the South, and the USSR's government in the North after occupying them in 1945. Two countries emerged from a united Korea: The Republic of Korea in the South, and The Democratic People's Republic of Korea in the North.

ACRONYMS

◆

AKP	Association of Korean People
APM	American Presbyterian Mission
ATB	Agricultural Technological Bureau
AWM	Association for Women Education
BC	Bank of Choson
CCR	Choson Company Regulations
CD	Choson Dynasty
CG-G	Choson Government-General
CL	Corporation Law
CR	Company Regulations
CCP	Choson Communist Party
CG	Capital Gazette
CHPC	Choson Hydro-electric Power Company
CI	Communist International

CLU	Communist Labor Union
CNFC	Choson Nitrogenous Company
CP	Communist Party
CPC	Choson Petroleum
CRM	Company Chosen Riken Metal
CT	Choson Tobacco
CWI	Cold War Imperialism
DI	Declaration of Independence
ESMA	Ex-Service Men's Association
FFP	Fire-Field People
FBK	First Bank Korea
FQR	Feminist Question Research Society
G-G	Governor-General
GKRA	Government of Korean Restoration Army
IKRP	Increased Korean Rice Production
IC	Independent Club
IP	Imperial Post
ISC	International Socialist Congress (Stockholm)

JEC	Japanese Episcopal Church
JPUH	Japan's Parliament's Upper House
KPS	Korean Preservation Society
KA	Korean Association
KDN	Korea Daily News
KG	Korean Govt.
KIG	Korean Independence Group
KLMAA	Korean Labour Mutual Aid Association
KLMRA	Korean Labour Mutual Relief Association
KNA	Korean National Association (Hawaii)
KPA	Korean Peasant Association
KSS	Korean Self-strengthening Society
KYIC	Korean Youth Independence Corps
KYIG	Korean Youth Independence Group
LHR	Lower House of Representatives
LKLF	League of Korean Labourers and Farmers
LN	League of Nations

MAF	Ministry of Agriculture and Forestry
MAS	Mutual Assistance Society
MFM	March First Movement
MM	Mitsubishi Mining
NKYA	New Korean Youth Association
NPA	New People's Association
NVHFIC	Nippon VHF Industrial Company
ODC	Oriental Development Company
OWTC	Oral and Written Tenant Contracts
OCMC	Oriental Consolidation Mining Company
OFHC	One Hundred Five Cases
PM	Prime Minister
PGRK	Provisional Government of the Republic of Korea
RDC	Rapidly Development Choson
RPIP	Rice Production Increase Plan
RRM	Rural Revival Movement
RA	Righteous Army
RA	Restoration Army

R-G	Resident-General
R-JW	Russo-Japanese War
RND	Redemption of National Debt
RPU	Red Peasant Unions
SSCG	Society for Study of Constitutional Government
S-JW	Sino-Sino-Japanese War
SP	Spring Poverty
SPC	Socialist Party Congress
SYMCA	Seoul's Young Men's Christians Association
TMS	Taehan Maeil Sinbo
TFMAS	Tenant-Farmers Mutual Aid Society
TOC	Texas Oil Company
USMEM	US Methodist Episcopal Mission
USSR	Union of Soviet Socialist Russia
WCSN	World Conference of Small Nations
WTA	Woman Traders Association
YMCA	Young Men's Christian Association

PREFACE

......◆......

Korea was historically called a "hermit kingdom." It was a small, reclusive country in the Far East about which little was known. Its history was marked by periods of significant intellectual and cultural achievement and a sense of national identity fostered by a common language, ethnic homogeneity, and historical unity. Korea opened to the modern world by signing the Kanghwa Treaty with Japan in 1876. Though more unified than many of today's newer nations, Korea was unprepared when thrust into the world by outside events. Chief among those external events were the imperial aspirations of Western countries and their aroused interest in the Far East and the Meiji restoration in Japan.

Korea's backwardness as late as the third quarter of the nineteenth century, or the period immediately before the opening of the country to the West, is documented in letters of French missionaries to Charles Dallet and in the work of Homer B. Hulbert, one of the first American missionaries to Korea (he stayed there from 1886–1907).[2] Both Dallet's missionaries and Hulbert described a highly centralized form of government during the period before the opening of Korea that became less viable as weak kings and regents allowed power to slip away from the center. Civil and military administrations were in the hands of the yangban, or nobles (similar to the Chinese mandarins). They were divided into four hereditary factions devoted mainly to each other's downfall.

During this period, power in the palace was divided among different groups, including the eunuchs who had the king's trust and could conspire with the concubines. These eunuchs often sold government positions and engaged in "tax farming," where they would collect taxes for the government and keep a portion of the profits. While there was a chance for individuals to advance based on merit through a public examination system similar to that of the Chinese, higher government positions were typically reserved for nobles. The most prestigious position, that of Prime Minister, was usually only attainable by a wealthy noble who could successfully bribe the eunuchs and concubines. This often resulted in the king needing help to address the issues facing his people effectively.

The government implemented a policy that excluded certain groups, which had a negative impact on the economy. Communication was difficult due to the mountainous terrain and lack of navigable streams. The government needed to improve road infrastructure. Coastal vessels were not suitable for long-distance travel. The government prohibited sea trade, denied foreigners entry into Korea, and tightly controlled its borders, resulting in no trading with other countries.

The Catholic missionaries were interested in finding ways to enter Korea and had to conceal themselves once there. As narrated by Dallet, the difficulties faced by the people indicate that the government's isolation policy was strictly implemented. The government also discouraged internal commerce. The only legal tender was a denomination coin produced by private foundries on the king's order. There was no gold/silver coinage; the coins were often debased by those who obtained minting privileges; low denominations made transport a real problem. The system's inadequacies were also prevalent in the swap, especially in the northern provinces.

During the early days, industrial-commercial developments were not common. Since people used to manufacture everyday necessities at home, there was little specialization and no factory operations. When the services of specialized artisans were required, they would come to the house, as they did not have workshops. Potters and ironsmiths required unique materials or heavy equipment, which had to be transported from place to place as their raw material supply dwindled. In the early Yi Dynasty (1392–1410), several specialized artisans worked for the court. Later on, metropolitan merchants lent funds to artisans as a wage-labor or putting-out system. This may be regarded as the origins of an incipient manufacturing stage, if not the beginning of a modern factory system. During those times, there were fairs, but business was not conducted at the fair. Instead, it was handled by peddlers, and there were some stores as well.

Korea's political and economic underdevelopment was a result of its isolation. However, with Korea's opening up to Japan, the end of Korea's isolation was inevitable. This led to a transformation of Korea's political and economic institutions, which were influenced by foreign powers. This was a necessary pre-condition for Korea's later economic development. Despite the partition of Korea into North and South in 1945, the country's historical background as a single country and its high ethnic, linguistic, and cultural homogeneity have aided development in both regions. The homogeneous language, culture, and historical background have fostered development in both regions.

Between 1876 and 1910, a power struggle among China, Japan, and Russia determined Korea's fate while domestic factions competed for control. Korea was often called "a shrimp among whales" during this time. After Japan's defeat, Korea became divided, falling victim to the new Cold War. The North became a Soviet pawn, while the South was under US military government from 1945–48. An independent Korean government emerged during the first national election, and the Republic of Korea was established in the South. In the North, the People's Republic of Korea became a Communist country under the influence of Russia. The Korean War began in June 1950 between North and South Korea, resulting in battles that raged throughout most of the peninsula until the front stabilized around the 38th parallel in 1951. A truce was finally signed in July 1953.

The Opening of Korea

(1870–1910)

◆

From the eleventh century onwards, Korea faced a series of invasions from various forces, including Manchuria, Mongols, and the Japanese. In the thirteenth century, the Mongols under Genghis Khan conquered Korea, while in the fourteenth and fifteenth centuries, the Wako (Japanese marauders) raided the coastline. At the end of the sixteenth century, the Japanese under Hideyoshi attacked the country, causing devastation. In the early seventeenth century, the Manchus conquered Korea after overthrowing the Ming Dynasty in China. These defeats highlighted Korea's weakness and led the government to close the frontiers and withdraw as much as possible from outside contact. Scholars' contributions were the only things sent to Peking and Japan during the Tokugawa period, and any attempts to violate Korea's seclusion policy or introduce foreign ideas were forcefully discouraged. Consequently, Korea became known as the "hermit kingdom."[2]

French priests trying to enter Korea were executed, and many Christian converts were massacred. An American ship, the General

Sherman, was burnt down, and the crews were killed near P'yongyang in 1866. An American fleet sent in 1871 to obtain a treaty with Korea failed after a battle with the Koreans at the mouth of the Han River. In 1875, Japan sent a gunboat to the same place and was fired upon by the Koreans. Japan then dispatched a fleet, and Korea was forced to sign a treaty of commerce with Japan (February 1876). Although formerly a vassal of China, Korea was recognized as an independent nation. Similar treaties were signed separately with the United States, England, and Germany. So, in the 1880s, Korea was no longer a hermit kingdom.

During the Choson Dynasty, corruption, internal conflicts among the ruling factions, and exploitation of the poor peasants were rampant. Meanwhile, Western capitalist nations began to express interest in trading with Korea. Visits by foreign vessels started to occur, such as Lord Amherst's request for trade in 1832, French warships' several visits in 1846 and 1847 to protest the executions of missionaries such as Imbert, Maubant, and Chastan, and five Russian merchants requesting permission to trade near the Tumen River in 1864. Later, a Prussian named E. Oppert also wanted to trade in 1866. In the same year, a French fleet under Admiral Roze assaulted Kanghwa Island, and five warships led by Admiral J. Rogers arrived at the same island to request trade in 1871.

Japan was the first East Asian country to overthrow its ancient feudalistic regime to achieve capitalism. Japan also wanted to have trade with Korea and made some unsuccessful attempts to gain it. Japan did not retreat and, using military strength, forced Korea to make a treaty of "friendship," which was signed at Kanghwa Island in 1876 under the guns of some Japanese warships. Kuroda

Kiyotaka and Inouye Kauru led the Japanese. The most important terms of the treaty were:

1. Japan confirmed Korea to be an independent and sovereign state.
2. Opening the port of Pusan to Japan that Korea agreed to.
3. Korea also agreed to open two more ports within 20 months after the treaty's signing.
4. Japan agreed not to interfere with the Korean government's trade regulations.
5. Both nations agreed to exempt customs duties for exports and imports and to collect only port duties.[3]

The following table shows that all ports along the Korean coast were opened by 1910:

Table I:
Opening of Korean Ports in Chronological Order

Port	Date
Pusan	October 1870
Wonsan	April 1880
Inch'on	January 1883
Yanghwajin	August 1883

Port	Date
Kyonghung	1888
Chinnamp'o	1897
Kunsan	May-1897
Mokp'o	October-1897
P'yongyang	1898
Masan	1899
Songjin	June-1899
Yongamp'o	1906
Ch'ongjin	April-1908
Shinuiju	1910

Source: Choson Boeki Kyokai (ed.): Choson Boeki Shi (*The History of Trade in Korea*), Seoul, pp. 40–41.

The treaty's signing was followed by the opening of Wonsan in 1880 and Inch'on in 1883. This allowed Japanese goods to flow in without any customs obstacles. The Korean government also signed treaties with other foreign countries:

- Treaty of Friendship and Commerce with the U.S. in May 1882.

- Treaty of Trade with Ch'ing in September 1882.

- Amendment to the Treaty of Friendship with Japan in July 1883.

- Treaty of Friendship and Commerce with Great Britain in November 1883.

- Treaty of Friendship and Commerce with Germany in November 1883.

- Treaty of Friendship and Commerce with Russia in July 1884.

- Treaty of Friendship and Commerce with Italy in June 1884.

- Treaty of Friendship and Commerce with France in June 1886.

For several years following the signing of the Kanghwa treaty, Korea became an exclusive market for Japanese commodities. An army revolt (1882) strengthened China's position in Korea. So, Japan and China began to compete for supremacy for trade in the country.

The Treaty of Friendship and Commerce between Korea and the United States was not negotiated directly between the two nations, but instead through the famous Chinese diplomat Li Hung-Chang. Li sought to gain the friendship and support of the United States in China's rivalry against Russia and Japan for dominance in Korea. Four months after the Korean-American treaty was signed, Li negotiated with representatives of the Korean government and finalized the Sino-Korean trade treaty, which essentially amounted to modern-day diplomatic subjugation of Korea to China. This gave China the legal grounds to interfere in Korea's internal affairs. A Korean minister named Yuan Shi Kai later recommended P.G. von Mollendorff as an advisor to the Korean customs office to control it.[4]

In 1884, the Min faction attempted to invite Russia to intervene in Korea to prevent either Japan or China from gaining control over the country. Karl Weber, a Russian diplomat to Korea, and Paul Georg von Mollendorff, a customs specialist in Korea, held secret negotiations. In 1886, Weber met with Korean politicians Min Yong-Hwan, Min Ung-shik, Kim Ka-jin, and Kim Hak-wu to discuss the plan further. However, the plot was exposed when Min Yong-ik, a leader of the Min faction, leaked the information to Chinese Minister Yuan. Instead of exploiting foreign conflicts, Korean leaders' internal struggles made them vulnerable to a better-prepared Japanese invasion.[5]

Korea's primary relationship with the outside world for centuries was with China. As a dependent country (Shu-pang), Korea was in a Confucian relationship, much like a younger brother to an elder brother, in which the younger brother owed allegiance to the older in return for protection. Chinese domination continued until 1894 when the Tonghak (or "Eastern learning") Rebellion broke out. Dissatisfied nobles and Confucianists who wanted to drive out foreigners, especially the Japanese, led the movements. The leaders took command of a peasant rebellion that threatened King Gojong. He called for China's help, and when China sent troops, the Japanese took advantage and sent their troops, too. Though the

King's forces were able to put down the rebellion, the Chinese and the Japanese refused to leave first. The Japanese seized the palace, reinstated the King's father (the regent Taewon's gun), and sank the Kowshing, a British steamer that was bringing Chinese reinforcements. After that, the Sino-Japanese War broke out, and China was defeated, which ended Korea's Shu-pang relationship with China.[7]

Japan's capitalism was developed under the landowners, bureaucrats, and feudal lords who ruthlessly suppressed the peasants and civil rights leaders. Japan's prosperity was achieved by exploiting peasant laborers, especially women and children. Its domestic market was too narrow for the expanding array of goods, so the Japanese leaders tried to seek foreign markets in Korea and China. After the progressives' short coup d'état in 1884, Japan regained its political influence in Korea and began competing with China.

Table II:
Volume of Korean Trade

(In Thousand yen*)

During	Imports					Exports		
	From Japan	%	From China	%	Total	%		Grand Total
From July–	88	38.1	141	61.9	229	100.0	119	348

During	Imports						Exports	Grand Total
	From Japan	%	From China	%	Total	%		
June 30, 1877–78								
From July–Dec 31, 1878	29	20.6	113	79.4	142	100.0	155	297
1879	56	9.8	511	90.2	567	100.0	677	1,244
1880	116	11.9	862	88.1	978	100.0	1,374	2,352
1881	202	10.4	1,743	86.6	1,945	100.0	1,883	3,828
From Jan–June 30, 1882	47	6.4	695	93.6	742	100.0	897	1,639
	538	11.7	4,065	88.3	4,603	100.0	5,105	9,708

Source: Choson Boeki Shi, 1943, Seoul, pp. 42–43.

*Yen: The basic unit of Japanese currency, which was applied in Korea from the annexation in 1910 to the end of Japanese rule in 1945.

In trade in Korea, China was far behind and tried it's best to bridge the gap with Japan. Table III shows that in 1885 China's share in Korea's exports was only 19% against 81% by Japan.

Table III:
Exports to Korea by China and Japan

During	By China	By Japan	% China	% Japan
1885	$313,343	$1,377,392	19%	81%
1886	455,015	2,604,353	17%	83%
1887	743,661	2,080,787	26%	74%
1888	860,328	2,196,715	28%	72%
1889	1,101,585	2,229,118	32%	68%
1890	1,660,075	3,086,897	32%	68%
1891	2,148,294	3,226,468	40%	60%
1892	2,055,555	2,555,675	45%	55%

Source: Chon Sok-Tam et al., Ilche-ha ui Choson Kyongje-Sa (*The Korean Economic History under the Japanese Rule*), p. 18, 1947, Seoul.

In 1892, China's share of trade had increased to 45%, just before the Sino-Japanese War broke out. This was because China typically acted as a trans-shipment hub for foreign goods, particularly those of Britain and Japan, while also selling its own products from its rapidly expanding industries. Japan wanted to eliminate Chinese influence to monopolize the Korean market.[8]

During the Sino-Japanese War (S-JW) from 1894 to 1895, Korea's Foreign Minister, Kim Yun-Shik, and the Japanese Minister to Korea, Otori Keisuke, signed a provisional agreement. Under this agreement, Japan got control of the Korean telegraph and railways, while Korea promised to open more ports to Japan. However, after the war, the Korean Government (KG) became even more powerless and lost control over national decisions. They could not take advantage of the conflicts between Japan and Russia, which led to heated competition among foreign powers for privileges in Korea. The following table shows how intense the competition was.[9]

Table IV:
Concessions Granted to Foreign Capitalists

During	Concessions	Nationality
1896	Construction of the railway between Seoul-Inch'on	America
1896	Exploration of mines at Kyongwon and Chongsong in Hamgyong-do	Russian

During	Concessions	Nationality
1896	Exploration of the gold mine at Wonson, P'yongan-Pukto	America
1896	Construction of the railway between Seoul and Shinuiju	French
1896	Felling rights along the Yalu basin and on Ulleungdo Island	Russian
1897	Exploration of the gold mine at Kumsong, Kangwon-do	German
1898	Construction of the tramway in Seoul	America
1898	Construction of the railway between Seoul and Pusan	Japanese
1900	Exploration of the gold mine at Usan, P'Yongan-Namdo	Britain
1900	Exploration of the gold mine at Chiksan, Ch'ongch'on-Namdo	Japanese

In the late nineteenth century, Japan reformed the Korean government, reducing the monarchy's power and appointing ministers who favored Japan. These moves occurred before the Treaty of Shimonoseki was signed in 1895 to end the war with China. The Japanese also changed Korean fashion, requiring cutting top knots, and adopting Western hairstyles and clothing. By early 1896, the Korean king was practically a captive in his palace. However, he managed to escape to the Russian embassy and receive the necessary concessions. He was also allowed to train the Korean Army. At this point, Russia replaced China and became Japan's main rival in Korea.

Japan had the most significant impact on the Korean market. Japanese merchants traded not only at the authorized ports and cities but also in local towns and villages through various promotional organizations. There were approximately 25,000 Japanese merchants, and their shipping accounted for almost 90% of all goods that entered Korean ports. Japanese products were cheap and could attract Korean consumers better than other options. Table V shows that Japan's trade with Korea significantly increased despite the war with China, rising from 50.2% of Korea's total imports in 1893 to 72.2% in 1895.[10]

Table V:
Principal Exports to Korea by Percentage

During	Japan	China	Russia	Others	Total
1893	50.2	49.1	0.7	----	100.0

During	Japan	China	Russia	Others	Total
1894	62.5	35.1	2.1	----	100.0
1895	72.2	26.2	1.6	----	100.0
1896	65.8	33.0	1.2	----	100.0
1897	63.9	35.1	1.0	----	100.0
1898	57.4	41.7	0.9	----	100.0
1899	65.1	33.9	1.0	----	100.0
1900	75.3	23.6	I.I	----	100.0
1901	61.6	38.2	0.2	----	100.0
1902	64.2	35.7	0.1	----	100.0
1903	63.4	29.4	0.7	6.5	100.0
1904	70.9	18.9	0.3	9.9	100.0
1905	73.7	18.6	0.3	7.4	100.0
1906	77.3	13.8	0.2	8.7	100.0
1907	66.0	10.8	----	23.2	100.0
1908	58.6	11.9	0.1	39.4	100.0

During	Japan	China	Russia	Others	Total
1909	59.6	12.2	0.1	28.1	100.0
1910	63.7	9.7	----	26.6	100.0

Source: Choson Boeki Kyokai ed. Choson Boeki Shi, pp. 49–50.

The Western powers and Japan had started a race to acquire concessions and privileges in the Far East, which included Korea. The rivalry between Japan and Russia was more significant, but they reached a deal in the Nishi-Rosen Agreement of 1898 to acknowledge each other's interests and Korea's sovereignty. Korea enjoyed independence for the next six years, but this period was not peaceful in Korean history. In 1896, the king's progressive advisors were removed, and the government became more conservative, returning to a Confucian-style administration. Absolute power prevailed, and Horace Allen described the court as a "corrupt cabal."[11]

In 1900, the Boxer Rebellion in China caused external events to intrude into Korea. Western and Japanese forces entered Beijing, while Russian troops occupied Manchuria. This geographical tension led observers in Seoul to predict that Japan would soon take over Korea but avoid the cost of annexation. As noted by Horace Allen, "content herself with securing an agreement whereby she might maintain a sufficient force in the country to preserve order, which would give her the power of a dictator with the happy illusion of independence still maintained."[12]

To make any move, Japan had to consider Russia's interests. By the time the Trans-Siberian Railway was almost complete to the last 6,000 miles, Japan still had no foothold on the continent, and Korea was vulnerable to military attacks. In 1903, Japan proposed a compromise to Russia, suggesting that they could pursue their ambitions in Manchuria if Russia gave up their claims in Korea. Unfortunately, Russia rejected this proposal, leading to the Russo-Japanese War (R-JW) (Feb. 1904–Sept. 1905). Internal unrest brought about the Korean War in 1894. A decade later, no external agitation was necessary.

Russian forces were holding back from the Korean capital, and Japan had the opportunity to intimidate the Korean government into signing two agreements. The first agreement, signed in February of 1904, removed all limitations on Japanese action in Korea. The second agreement, signed in August of the same year, allowed Japan to place informal advisors in the Korean government to control finance and diplomacy. Japan sent an American employee, Durham Stevens, to Seoul to appear more diplomatic. A Japanese police advisor was sent to Korea in 1905, and the Korean army was reduced to 8,000. Japan took control of the postal services and punished Korea's attempt to elicit Russian aid for economic reasons. Japan used the necessities of the war to acquire power over Korea's significant institutions, albeit informally. Due to this, it took a lot of work for Korean officials to implement passive resistance effectively.[13]

Japan's military strategists emphasized attempts to control the Korean monarch to defuse the possibility of Korean resistance, as in 1894. Gojong was treated better in public than he had been ten years prior. As a result, he generally complied with Japanese demands. Due to its large military, Gojong believed that Russia would emerge victorious in the war. However, the war changed Korean society, with some supporting and others opposing cooperation with Japan.

Japan was concerned about Russia's interests and ambitions in Korea, which threatened Japan's monopoly of influence in the region. Japan signed a non-aggression treaty with Britain in 1902 to strengthen its position. However, Russia allied with France to counter Japan's alliance with Britain, which increased tensions in Korea and Manchuria. Negotiations between the two countries broke down, leading Japan to sever diplomatic relations with Russia in February 1904. Shortly after that, Japan declared war on Russia and attacked Russian ships in Port Arthur and Chemulp.[14]

Japan attempted to control Korea even before declaring war by capturing Seoul and surrounding the palace. A protocol was signed, and Korea agreed to adopt Japanese advice to improve the government with no treaties contrary to the protocol. The Korean independence and territorial integrity were to be protected by Japan in return. The emperor's absolute power was renounced, and the Finance-Foreign Affairs departments were to have Japanese advisors with veto power. Japan took over police functions, and Korean legations abroad were recalled, requiring Korea to give indemnity for Japanese killed by them in the previous decade. Before the Japanese occupation (1910), Korea was forced to sign Korean-Japanese pacts (1904), and during the period, Korean exports were mainly directed to Japan.

Table VI:
Position of Farm Products in Total Export.

During	Total exports	Farm products	Percentage
1893	1,698	1,502	88
1894	2,311	2,119	91
1895	2,481	2,315	93
1896	4,532	4,532	95
1897	8,973	8,712	97
1898	5,709	5,428	95
1899	4,997	4,508	90
1900	9.439	8,696	92
1901	8,461	7,687	90
1902	8,317	7,848	94

Source: Ibid, pp. 58–59.

In the wake of the Korea-Japan pact, Megata Shotaro, a former chief of the Taxation Bureau in Japan's Finance Ministry, was appointed as Korea's financial advisor. His primary objective was to facilitate Japan's eventual takeover of Korea. Megata interfered with financial and internal politics to achieve this goal. Following Japan's victory over Russia, the United States, Britain, Japan, and Russia signed the Treaty of Portsmouth in September 1905, which recognized Japan's paramount political, military, and economic interests in Korea. From then on, Japan made several attempts to control Korean affairs, especially foreign ones.

Table VII:
Export of Korean Gold to Japan and China

(In thousand yen)

During	To Japan Amount	%	To China Amount	%	Total Amount	%
1893	425	46.3	494	53.7	919	100.0
1894	639	68.4	295	31.6	934	100.0
1895	953	77.8	400	22.2	1,353	100.0
1896	803	57.7	587	42.3	1,390	100.0
1897	947	46.6	1,087	53.4	2,034	100.0
1898	1,193	50.2	1,183	49.8	2,374	100.0
1899	2,094	69.9	884	30.1	2,933	100.0

	To Japan		To China		Total	
During	Amount	%	Amount	%	Amount	%
1900	3,065	84.4	568	15.5	3,633	100.0
1901	4,857	97.3	136	2.7	4,993	100.0
1902	5,004	98.8	60	1.2	5,064	100.0

Source: Ibid, p. 46.

Japan sought to establish a protectorate over Korea by winning recognition from Russia, Britain, and America for its paramount interests in the peninsula. To achieve this, Japan created a front organization called the Ilchinhoe, led by Song Pyong-jun and Yi Yong-gu, and propagated the need for a protectorate treaty. The aim was to make the impression that the treaty was not Japan's demand but a response to the Korean people's wish. However, the Ilchinhoe was formed by an interpreter for Japan's headquarters in Seoul, Song Pyong-jun, and a Tonghak apostate, Yi Yong-gu, with financial support from Japan and under the direction of Japan's advisors. Despite the presence of Japan's occupation forces, a Society for the Study of Constitutional Government, led by Yi Chun Yang Han-muk, took a stand against the Ilchinhoe and condemned its betrayal of the nation.

Japan's policy towards Korea had already been decided, so the wishes of the Korean officials did not matter. In 1905, Japan sent Ito Hirobumi and Hayashi Gonsuke to negotiate a treaty. However, they threatened the Korean emperor and his ministers to accept Japan's draft treaty instead of negotiating. When the Korean officials refused, especially Prime Minister Han Kyu-sol, for his violent opposition, Japanese gendarmes forcefully removed him from the palace. The Japanese soldiers then brought the Ministry of Foreign Affairs seal from the Foreign Ministry Office. They affixed it to the treaty, which was validated despite the illegality of the proceedings. The Koreans refer to the treaty as the "Protectorate Treaty," but it was just the Treaty of 1905.[15]

The Treaty of 1905, signed at bayonet point, began Japan's absolute subjugation of Korea. The treaty granted Japan complete authority over Korea's foreign affairs and prohibited Korea from entering any international treaties except through Japan's government. Additionally, the treaty established a Japanese Resident-General (R-G) directly under the emperor of Korea to manage the country's foreign relations. Essentially, Japan stripped Korea of its power to conduct foreign relations with other countries.

Japan's next move was to eliminate Korea's status as an independent country in the international community. Marquis Ito (Ito Hirobumi), the first Japanese Resident-General of Korea in 1906, oversaw the power transfer to Japan for the "protectorate rule." This move effectively destroyed Korea's claim as an independent nation. In 1909, Japan abandoned Korea's claim to the Chientao (Korean: Kando) region of southeast Manchuria in exchange for China's permission to construct a railway line between An-tung and Mukden (now Tan-tung and Shenyang) in Manchuria. This step granted Japan's complete control over Korea's foreign affairs. Another arbitrary Japanese action regarding Korean territory was the forced seizure of Tokto Island, an administrative dependency of Ulleungdo during the Russo-

Japanese War. Although the treaty's wording limited the Resident-General's authority "primarily" to diplomatic matters, the whole Korean internal administration was under his control. As a result, Korea was deprived of its sovereignty to its entirety.[16]

The treaty caused great anger and opposition among the Korean people. The Korean press played a leading role in rousing public opinion against the treaty despite strict Japanese censorship. The outrage quickly reached a boiling point; countless oral protests and memorials occurred, and businesses closed their doors. Min Yong-hwan, the military aide-de-camp to the emperor, left a testamentary letter to the nation and took his own life. Many other outraged officials, including Cho Pyong-se, Hong Man-sik, and Song Pyong-son, followed Min Yong-hwan's example.

During the Japanese occupation of Korea, guerrilla groups known as Righteous Armies (RA) emerged throughout the country to resist Japanese rule. Min Chong-sik took control of Hongsong in Ch'ongch'on province and the surrounding area, while Ch'oe Ik-Hyon and Im Pyong-ch'an led a rebellion in Sunch'ang, Challa province, and Sin Tol-sok rebelled in Kyongsang province. However, these acts of defiance failed to bring about any change in Japan's policy towards Korea. Despite efforts to extinguish Korean independence, Japan was waiting for the right time to present a positive image to the international community.[17]

The Treaty of 1905 was not signed by the Korean emperor, despite Gojong's wishes. A royal letter was published in the Taehan Maeil Sinbo newspaper, stating that the emperor had not consented. In response to Japan's violation of Korean sovereignty and the exclusion of Korea from the Hague Peace Conference in 1907, opposition and the need for joint protection from powers arose. A Korean delegate tried to attend the conference to protest against Japan's actions but was denied permission to attend. The Korean envoys asserted that the treaty was invalid without the emperor's seal. One of the delegates, Yi Wi-jong, spoke out against Japanese aggression and sought support for restoring Korean sovereignty at an international meeting of journalists in The Hague, but this effort also failed. Sadly, one of the three envoys, Yi Chun, died at The Hague due to the overwhelming grief.

The secret mission was unsuccessful but received worldwide attention and caused an international uproar. In retaliation, Japan demanded that the emperor abdicate his throne. Under pressure, the emperor stepped down and was succeeded by his son, the crown prince, who was known to be mentally weak. In July 1907, the crown prince was crowned emperor and given the title of Yunghai, which means "Abundant Prosperity." News of the abdication spread, leading to massive protests and demonstrations. The mob even destroyed the building of the newspaper and Ilchinhoe and attacked the Japanese everywhere.

After violence broke out in Korea, Japan responded with military force and imposed stricter rules on Korea. A new agreement granted the Japanese Resident-General formal interference in Korea's internal administration. This meant that legislative enactments and major administrative measures required his prior consent. High officials' appointments and dismissals were also to be done with his approval. Moreover, his approval was necessary for the employment of foreign advisers. The agreement mandated the appointment of Japanese subjects recommended by the Resident-General to critical positions. Japan abandoned its previous method of using departmental advisers and opted for government by vice-ministers. As a result, several Japanese bureaucrats were appointed in each ministry as second-in-command or in other strategic posts.

Following the new agreement in August 1907, the remaining Korean army was reduced to a few soldiers. There were only 3,600 men in two infantry guard regiments and 400 men in mounted guards, artillery, and transport units in Seoul. Outside the capital, there were 4,800 infantry in eight local garrisons. This small group was barely 8,800 in total. Japan used a financial pretext to dissolve the Korean army, claiming that it was a temporary measure until a conscription system could be introduced. Korea, lacking in self-defense, became a mere puppet. The commander of the First Infantry Guards regiment, Pak Song-han, killed himself when the army was dissolved. The officers and army men, supported by the Second Infantry Guards regiment, took up arms against the Japanese military in Seoul's streets. When they ran out of ammunition, they retreated to join the guerilla forces in the countryside. The provincial garrison troops also joined them. Table VIII displays the principal imports from Korea by different countries until Japan's annexation of Korea.

Table VIII:
Principal Imports From Korea by Percentage

During	Japan	China	Russia	Others	Total
1893	90.9	7.9	1.2	---	100.0

During	Japan	China	Russia	Others	Total
1894	88.8	7.0	4.2	---	100.0
1895	95,3	3.7	1.0	---	100.0
1896	93.0	5.6	1.4	---	100.0
1897	90.2	1.8	2.6	---	100.0
1898	79.2	19.8	1.0	---	100.0
1899	84.2	13.7	2.1	---	100.0
1900	76.6	20.9	2.6	---	100.0
1901	87.5	9.5	3.0	---	100.0
1902	78.8	16.4	2.8	---	100.0
1903	80.2	16.3	3.5	---	100.0
1904	82.2	17.8	---	---	100.0
1905	78.1	21.8	0.1	---	100.0
1906	85.1	8.6	6.1	0.2	100.0
1907	76.7	19.3	4.0	---	100.0
1908	77.8	15.9	5.4	0.9	100.0

During	Japan	China	Russia	Others	Total
1909	74.4	19.7	4.8	1.1	100.0
1910	77.2	15.2	5.8	1.8	100.0

Source: Ibid, pp. 51–52.

During Japan's takeover of Korea, their repression sparked anti-Japanese riots. A Korean insurgency followed, requiring increased police forces to maintain order.[19] Japan emerged victorious in the war against Russia between 1904 and 1905, thereby cementing its supremacy in Korea. The Portsmouth Treaty was signed between Japan and Russia, wherein Russia acknowledged Japan's political, economic, and military dominance over Korea. Japan's acquisition of southern Manchuria made Korea a crucial rail corridor to the north, and Koreans' primary desire was to be governed with ease and at a low cost. Despite leaving the symbols of Korean independence, such as the monarchy, the cabinet, and local government, in place, the protectorate's nature was similar to that of France's control over Indo-China. Ito and his officials continued to assert informal control over Korea, similar to Lord Cromer's control over Egypt. Japanese representatives were confident that the benefits of justice and efficiency would eventually lead to the Koreans accepting the protectorate.

Ito soon realized that satisfying the Koreans required rapid, visible benefits through railroads, hospitals, schools, and agricultural expansions. As money was the key for all these developments, a 10-million-yen loan was secured in Tokyo for major projects like roads, waterworks, and improved medical facilities in Seoul. Ito's hopes were neither aided by the exploitative actions of postbellum Japanese carpetbaggers, by the insulting behavior of Japanese civilians kicking and cuffing Koreans in the streets, nor by Japanese administrative insensitivity (i.e., naming the Korean railways as 'up' or 'down' line according to their path to Tokyo).[20]

The issue of Japanese emigration to California was posing a challenge for Prime Minister Katsura Taro of Japan. The matter demanded his prompt attention and resolution. He promised to limit the migrant flow, allowing better access to the Asian continent, particularly Manchuria and Korea. Back at home, retrenchment and debt repayment policies were implemented to restore economic stability. Military costs were lowered in Korea, and policies were implemented to promote socio-economic stability. In April 1909, a decision was made to annex Korea once Russian approval had been gained. Ito was sent to Harbin to meet with the Russian foreign minister, but upon arrival, he was assassinated by a Korean freedom fighter named An Chung-gun. Although his name has been revered as that of a Korean hero, the murder served no purpose as the annexation had already been decided upon. In Seoul, the Ilchinhoe attempted to prevent any retaliation for Ito's murder by suggesting a voluntary union between Korea and Japan.[21]

For several months, the political climate in Korea was tense. Following the assassination of Ito, Tokyo informed its British ally that the annexation of Korea would remain unchanged. However, the United States' efforts to restore Chinese control over Manchurian railways in late 1909 significantly improved Russo-Japanese relations. Though it was reluctant, Russia ultimately accepted Japan's annexation of Korea. The British minister in Tokyo was deeply concerned about the annexation, viewing it as a breach of trust on Japan's part. Despite this, no significant world power was moved to defend Korean interests. After the assassination of Ito in Harbin, General Terauchi (Terauchi Masatake), a prominent member of Japan's military faction, was appointed as Resident-General. Upon his arrival in Seoul, the Korean emperor renounced his sovereignty, and a treaty of annexation was signed on August 22, 1910. This marked the end of Korean identity until 1945 when a divided Korea emerged following Japan's defeat in World War II. The annexation treaty was signed, ending the Korean monarchy, renaming Korea as Choson, and reducing it to a subordinate part of the Japanese empire.

Japan's annexation of Korea severely damaged its reputation in East Asia. The Chinese media warned of Japan's possible designs on Manchuria, and even Japanese intellectuals admitted the failure of their good intentions amidst all the Machiavellianism. The 35 years of Japanese rule in Korea were marked by a mix of social chaos and expanding horizons. While some individuals experienced more wealth, others suffered impoverishment, and violence and despair grew. The traditional state and monarchy were abolished, and after a few years, a new Korea slowly emerged.

The question arises as to why Japan wanted to occupy Korea. There are two possible answers to this question. The first answer is that it was for strategic reasons. The second answer, which has wide support among Japanese historians, is that it was for economic factors. This includes the search for new markets, the need to protect commercial interests, and the desire to develop

Korea as a colony.[22] Motivation remains an unanswered and complex question. It is crucial to understand motivation as it drives individual and organizational performance. Continued research is necessary to uncover insights and knowledge to make a meaningful impact.

Korea found itself in a challenging situation as a result of being caught in the midst of power struggles among different nations. Unfortunately, a small number of Koreans prioritized their personal interests over the country's independence. This led to an almost sell-off of Korea to the Japanese, who occupied the country from 1910 to 1945 and took advantage of its resources. This resulted in great suffering for the Korean people, including farmers who experienced "Spring Poverty" for up to six months a year to supply Japan's people with food. The industries established in Korea were primarily designed to meet the needs of Japan, rather than the Koreans. Korea's minerals were taken away, leaving Koreans with only coarser rice to eat while the better quality rice was exported to Japan. Minerals necessary for Japan's war materials were the only ones mined.

CHAPTER 1:

Korea Becomes a Japanese Colony

Japan had a plan to annex Korea for a long time, and they waited for the right opportunity to put this plan into action. General Terauchi Masatake was appointed as the new Resident-General (R-G) and given the task of bringing about the annexation. Upon arriving in Korea, he expanded the Japanese gendarmerie force and gave them the power of the police. He also ordered the publication of several Korean newspapers to prevent the public from finding out what was happening. Together with the Korean Prime Minister (P.M.) Yi Wan-yang, General Terauchi formulated the terms of the annexation treaty, which the P.M. signed in August 1910.

In 1907, Gojong was forced to give up his throne to his son. This decision angered the people, who burned down the P.M.'s house. The P.M. was also attacked by an activist named Yi Chae-myong in an assassination attempt. Despite all this, the P.M. remained focused on drafting the annexation agreement, which he hoped would preserve the position of the royal household and his fellow traitors. Unfortunately, this only solidified his legacy as a traitor to his country. The treaty was ultimately signed, and as a result, the Japanese disbanded patriotic organizations and arrested leading dissidents. Sunjong-the, the last emperor, was also forced to surrender his throne and country.

The Korean nation was forcefully annexed by Japan against the will of the Korean people, due to the actions of a group of traitors.[23] Japan claimed that the annexation was for the good of both nations and to ensure peace in Asia, but in reality, it was for the benefit of the Japanese at the expense of the Korean people. This annexation paved the way for Japan's invasion of China and disrupted the peace in Asia. Japan established its rule in Korea through a governor-general (G-G) appointed from the ranks of active generals or admirals. The governor-general was given all the executive, legislative, and judicial powers. The first governor-general, Terauchi Masatake, prioritized law and order, employing a gendarmerie (military) police system. In 1911, 7,749 gendarmeries and 6,222 regular police were deployed nationwide, and half were Korean. The Japanese gendarmerie's commanding officer served as the police director in Seoul, while the gendarmerie commanders controlled the provinces.

Any small action or statement of aggression by an individual from Korea was met with punitive measures. In 1912, more than 50,000 people were detained, and the number grew to over 140,000 in 1918, with Koreans being arrested on various charges. Following an unsuccessful assassination attempt on Terauchi's life by An Myong-gun in December 1910, over 600 influential Koreans were arbitrarily apprehended, including well-known figures like Yun Ch'i-ho, Yang Ki-t'ak, Yi Sung-hun, and other prominent members of the New People's Association (Sinminhoe), the most influential nationalist organization in Korea at the time. From the group of detainees, 105 individuals were later formally accused, and this event gained notoriety as the "Case of the One Hundred-Five". The accused were faced with criminal charges and subjected to brutal acts of torture.[24]

During the time of Japan's governor-general, those who did not comply with the rules were arrested. The judgments were given without any proper judicial process, and the punishment included flogging and/or fines. All newspapers that spread nationalist ideas were shut down to prevent any negative public opinion. Japanese officials and schoolteachers were required to wear uniforms and carry swords, and all political activities by Koreans were banned. The Japanese government used the Peace Preservation Law (PPL) of 1907 to prohibit political meetings and public gatherings, and many other regulations were introduced to limit the freedom of expression of Koreans.[25]

During Japan's colonial rule of Korea, the governor-general (G-G) established a Central Council comprising Koreans. However, this council was not a means for the Koreans to express their political participation, as it was merely a consultative body designed to provide information to the G-G. The president of the Central Council was a Japanese administrative superintendent who was the second-highest official in the governor-general's office. The councilors were appointed by Japan, and instead of discussing important political or economic issues, they were tasked with studying traditional Korean customs and practices. The council's vice-president was Yi Wan-yong, and other councilors who collaborated with Japan in exploiting Korea were also appointed.

Japan claimed to encourage Korean participation in politics but viewed any political concerns by Koreans as subversive or seditious.

Intensification of the Resistance of the Righteous Armies

The resistance against Japanese aggression in Korea took on many forms. One of these was the royal house's struggle to restore its disintegrating sovereign power. Another was the mission to The Hague, which some yangban officers participated in. From the beginning, the Korean king and his ministers relied on foreign powers. However, in the end, Korea had to settle for other aggressive policies as outside support was not guaranteed. Russia was defeated in the Russo-Japanese War (R-JW), leaving Korea with no way to cope with Japan's mounting pressure. Only a few officers resisted Japan individually and did not think of resisting with the people. Gojong and his government feared the people more than they feared Japan, which is why they suppressed the Independence Club (IC). The Protectorate and the Annexation Treaties were also done secretly without the knowledge of the people. When the traitorous, pro-Japanese elements in the cabinet prepared to go for the R-G, it was not possible for the emperor to resist, and the efforts of a few officers to thwart Japan's aggression were unsuccessful.

In the past, some Confucian scholars in Japan opposed the country's rule by persuading the emperor to resist Japanese influence. They assembled outside the palace and presented petitions to the emperor, but the emperor and government could not act on these requests due to the Japanese's control. As a result, some of these scholars resorted to suicide out of despair. Others formed the "Righteous Armies" and engaged in armed struggle against Japan.

The "Righteous Armies," initially organized by literati leaders, consisted mainly of peasants. The combat effectiveness of these guerrillas was greatly enhanced when soldiers from the disbanded Korean army joined the peasant fighters. These soldiers had previously fought with the Japanese troops in Seoul's streets. When their ammunition ran out, they retreated to the countryside to join the RA. In central Korea, the provincial garrison in Wongju, under Min Kung-ho, defeated the Japanese at Wongju, Ch'ungju, Yoju, Ch'ongch'on, and other places. Yu Myong-gyu moved to Hwanghae province with the Kanghwa garrison after defeating the Japanese to join the Righteous Armies. Ho Wi, resigning from a high post, took command of a group of like-minded literati and disbanded soldiers in action in Chongsong and other counties in the Imjin River region. Others were active in different areas, including Yi Kang-nyon and Sin Tol-sok. Sin Tol-sok, a commoner, commanded a large RA, which was noteworthy.[26]

The RA activities started after the assassination of Queen Min in 1895. They emerged from their hatred against the Japanese, but initially lacked military discipline and weapons. However, when disbanded troops joined them, they gained military organization and weapons. Min Kung-ho had several thousand men under his command, while Ho Wi and Yi Kang-nyon led over a thousand soldiers each. Other RA groups had a strength of only a few hundred or even just a few men. Most of these guerrillas based themselves in mountainous areas, from where they launched attacks on Japanese armies and destroyed railways and telegraph facilities. These guerrilla fighters could compensate for their lack of soldiers and arms as the local people supported them, and they knew the areas well.

The RAs were very active in Kyongsang, Kangwon, Kyonggi, and Hwanghae provinces, but their operations included the whole Korean peninsula. There were hardly any areas where the guerrillas were not operating. In Kanda in S. Manchuria, the guerrillas even crossed the Tumen River to attack the Japanese armies in North Korea. Yi In-yong and Ho Yi brought together about 10,000 guerrillas from Korea (1907) to attack the R-G's headquarters and the advance team even went within eight miles of Seoul's East Gate, showing the vigorousness of RA's struggle against the Japanese armies.

Guerrilla activities were at their highest in 1908 but eventually declined. After Japan's annexation of Korea, the operation scene shifted to Manchuria and the Russian Maritime Territory (RMT). The guerrillas became independent fighters and continued fighting. Over 17,600 guerrillas lost their lives in the struggle, including Min Kung-ho, Ho Wi, Yi Kang-nyon, and other commanders. The table below, from official Japanese statistics, shows the dimensions of the operations of the RA. However, the scale of operations must have been much larger than shown in the following table.

Table I:
Scale of Operations of Korea's 'Righteous Armies'

Year	Guerrillas Under Righteous Armies	Number of Clashes with Japanese Forces
1907	44,116	323
1908	69,832	1,451
1909	25,763	898
1910	1,891	147
Total		2,819

Source: Ki-baik Lee, op. cit., p. 317.

Japan desired complete power over Korea right from the start. Initially, Japan claimed that the strict policies were to prevent foreign investment in Korea. However, Japan itself was a foreign country. Japan had invested a lot of effort into developing transportation and communication systems. Even before the Japanese annexation, Korea's first telegraph lines were set up in 1885, connecting Seoul and Inch'on to Uiju at the Yalu River mouth. The line was then extended to Manchuria to facilitate communication between China and Korea, and it was solely under China's control. In 1888, the Seoul-Pusan telegraph line was constructed and linked to Japan by an undersea cable. While the

Korean government initially operated it, it came under Japanese control during the Russo-Japanese War. The postal service had collapsed in 1884 following a failed coup. However, a postal bureau was established in 1895 to handle mail exchanges with foreign countries beginning in 1900.

During the period of the R-JW, the Japanese took control of the postal service from the R-G and handed it over to the G-G. The railways were also constructed to support Japan's aggressive policy. The Japanese saw Inch'on as an entry point to the capital and received permission from the Korean government to build the Inch'on-Seoul rail line. Although an American company took over the construction in 1896, it was later returned to Japan amid Japanese opposition and was completed in 1900. The Seoul-Pusan and Seoul-Uiju lines were essential for the Japanese in prosecuting the R-JW in Korea. Japan built these lines urgently, administered by the railroad bureau of the R-G, then later by the G-G. An American and Korean joint venture capitalized on the electric line, and the R-G did not take over the streetcar and electric lighting facilities. However, they were brought under the G-G after the annexation.

Thus, the modern transportation and communication systems were established for Japan's advantage, not Korea's. The railroad was constructed using Korean laborers forced to work on Korean soil and employed at low wages. The Koreans hardly benefited from the rails, as the Japanese mainly utilized them. These modern facilities impacted the Koreans more negatively than positively because these commodities were primarily used to keep Korea under Japan's control.

During this period, Japan implemented the education system to control social order, discipline, and economic efficiency in Korea. In 1911, an educational ordinance was established that separated the Korean and Japanese school systems (following the example of Taiwan). The Korean school system included common and higher common schools, equivalent to primary and junior high schools in Japan. The higher common schools offered four years of education for boys and three years for girls. Additionally, there were specialized schools for law, medicine, industry, and agriculture, which offered four years of training. However, the 1911 Ordinance removed the ethical foundation of pre-annexation education in the 1890s. Instead, colonial education aimed to instill loyalty to the Japanese emperor. As an official publication put it in the 1930s, "The important point for education in Korea is to acquire the knowledge of the national language [Japanese], to absorb the spirit of true love for honest toil, to strengthen an inclination for thrift and industry."[27]

During the colonial period, the leaders of Korea aimed to move away from the individualism prevalent in the Chinese and Japanese political youth movements. The governor-general (G-G) refrained from interfering with the traditional village Seodang, providing primary education to around 280,000 children since 1923. The Seodang taught Confucian ethics and provided intellectual continuity with the past. However, it was urged to include Japanese language and mathematics in 1918, which was not followed until the late 1920s. The Seodang remained popular during the Pacific War, with around 3,000 still operating. However, over time, Koreans gradually accepted Japanese education as the only path to employment, and attendance at traditional schools declined.[28]

By 1910, Western missionaries had established 800 schools in Korea, with around 41,000 to 50,000 students. These establishments were almost double the number of Korean government-run schools. However, General Ito, who was in charge then, refused to grant licenses to private schools to prevent the growth of missionary schools. Instead, he focused on building government-run schools. Following the Sam-Il uprising, Admiral Saito launched an expansion plan to improve education. By 1928, there was a typical school in every township in the south and half of the townships in the north. In 1922, the Korean boys' and girls' ordinary and higher common schools were placed at the same level as Japanese elementary and secondary schools. Religious teaching in private (missionary) schools was also abolished.

The Japanese placed more importance on primary and practical education rather than on advanced studies. Their schools focused on teaching language, morals, mathematics, and basic science. They provided funds for industrial, technical, agricultural, and commercial schools. In Korean schools, the Japanese language was prioritized at all levels as it was considered crucial for assimilating the Korean people, even after the educational revision in 1922.[29]

The first primary history book was Fusto Gakko Kokushi (2 vols. 1923–24), identical to the one used in Japan, with a few Korean materials added to satisfy the critics. It focused on historical biographies, especially of Japanese emperors and heroes like Oda Nobunaga and Motoori Norinaga. The book portrayed Hideyoshi as a great man who rose from low status, pacified the nation through wisdom and courage, respected the imperial power, set the people at ease, and demonstrated the nation's might overseas by raising an expeditionary force. Similarly, Korean figures were mainly portrayed as wise kings or priests/scholars, with the theme of virtuous rule and reversing the history of confrontation established by Sin Chae-ho. The book created a myth that Korea was almost always dependent on some external force from ancient days, such as Paekche and Shilla.

The Japanese who settled in Korea during colonial times experienced a freedom they were deprived of in their own country. This progressive mindset influenced the colonial policies, and the textbooks developed for use in Korea, particularly in natural sciences, were regarded as far superior in stimulating a child's imagination than those used in Japan. Korean children were encouraged to explore the world around them, from garden plants to the life cycle of insects, while in Japan, children approached science through a list of symbolic flowers such as camellia and cherry blossoms. This approach to education in Korea helped shape the children's minds and improve their analytical power, which, in turn, could be used to challenge the colonial rulers.

Child labor was prevalent in rural areas of Korea due to economic hardships and customs. Children as young as ten years in the north and eight years in the south were made to start working on farms. Education was not accessible to most Korean children during the colonial period, and it was only in the late 1920s that it became available to some. The Japanese government's monopoly on cigarette production resulted in the employment of children in the capital. While education was not compulsory as it was in Japan, local police encouraged children to learn Japanese and mathematics to enhance their prospects of securing industrial employment. Historically, the Japanese and the Koreans showed little interest in educating girls, especially in rural areas. The number of girls receiving primary education was only one-third of the number of boys (306,000 girls compared to 912,000 boys), and even Seoul University did not accept female students at first in 1920. Despite this negative attitude towards women's education, a few women still aspired to modern careers. In 1939, almost 9,535 girls attended high schools, whereas 17,343 boys were enrolled. Girls also participated in colleges or teachers' seminaries, but the number was relatively low at 1,131 compared to 5,182 boys.[32] The Korean girls gained self-confidence and physical awareness through sports, which Western women had recently achieved.

Table II:
Statistics of Student Enrollment 1910–37

School	1910	1919	1930	1937
Common	20.1	89.3	450.5	901.2
Higher common*	0.8	3.2	11.1	15.6
Girls' higher schools	0.4	0.7	4.4	7.1
Teachers' seminaries	---	---	1.3	3.8
Industrial schools	1.0	2.8	12.1	20.3

School	1910	1919	1930	1937
Elementary industrial	0.1	1.7	3.2	6.3
Colleges	0.4	0.9	2.5	4.0
University Prep. Courses	---	---	0.3	0.4
University	---	---	0.6	0.5
Non-standardized schools	71.8	39.2	47.5	142.6**

Source: Grajdanzev, 1944, p. 261.

Notes: *School for Koreans and Japanese

**Includes 60,077 students of the short-course elementary schools. Figures in 1,000 students.

In the late 1920s, the increased awareness helped boost women's confidence to get involved in politics, and Korean high school girls actively participated in protests. In May 1927, about 400 students from Sunmyung Girls' High School protested to demand better treatment and employment opportunities for Korean teachers. After an incident of the Japanese at Kwangju assaulting a girl student, the girl students of nine schools in Seoul, including Ehwa and Sunmyung, joined in mass protests from 1929–30. Another incident was when Korean schoolchildren protested to retain their favorite Japanese teacher.

In Korea, abolishing differences between the two races allowed Korean students to enter post-elementary schools previously reserved for the Japanese. However, many Koreans could not access these schools due to their lack of proficiency in speaking Japanese. As of 1937, only 2,050 Koreans were enrolled in Japanese primary schools, while just 1,040 (580 girls and 460 boys) were studying in Japanese middle and girls' schools.[34] During the 1930s and 1940s, Korean schools were often considered of lower quality, leading many Koreans, especially the wealthier ones, to study in Japan. In 1935, 12,633 Korean students were studying in Japan, with 234 of them attending the prestigious imperial universities and 897 in private universities. By 1940, this number had more than doubled.

There is evidence through testimony that Koreans were accepted by their Japanese classmates and teachers into the elitist student community. This acceptance was likely a result of the Japanese fluency as a prerequisite for admission. Japanese universities, particularly in Tokyo, discussed radical ideologies more than in Korea or the West. The Koreans who studied at these Japanese universities later became involved in tenant, labor, and nationalist movements. They learned from young Japanese who conflicted with their prevailing ethics of "character" and capitalism and followed the ideologies of the Chinese radicals and nationalists from the 1900s. As such, modern Japan played a paradoxical role as both the liberator and oppressor of East Asia.

In 1922, Korean mainstream nationalists aimed to establish a People's University in Seoul to educate the country's future leaders. However, the G-G had strict policies regarding higher education that benefited Japanese colonialism. Western missionaries established the existing colleges in Korea a generation earlier. Encouraged by the new liberalism of the Saito years, moderate nationalists planned to establish a People's University in 1923. The plan included four colleges of law, literature, economics, and science, with industry, medicine, and agriculture to follow. Despite sporadic fundraising, public enthusiasm waned due to official hindrance, and more specifically, the G-G's announcement in 1926 that Keijo (Seoul) Imperial University would open its doors.

In May 1924, a two-year preparatory school was established at Seoul University to give students access to foreign languages, like German and English. It had faculties of science and literature comparable in standard with Japanese universities in Japan. The preparatory school had a capacity for only 150 students, and mainly Japanese students occupied it. The same was true at Keijo Imperial University, where the Japanese predominated. In 1930, the number of Japanese students was greater than that of Korean students, possibly due to an informal quota system. There were 359 Japanese students and 260 Korean students. Apart from a brief period of Korean staff recruitment in 1930, all teachers were Japanese.

In 1941, the departments of medicine and law, literature, and later, a faculty of science and technology were established in Korea to meet the demands of the war. These departments gained an excellent reputation, and their research publications contributed significantly to understanding Korean society and culture. However, it was challenging for Korean graduates to secure better jobs, as such jobs were typically reserved for the Japanese. Additionally, Koreans were often paid lower salaries for the same work as their Japanese counterparts. Even neutral people were not shielded from politicized job allocation. It's important to note that in 1944 only a few young people had an education. In Gyeonggi-do province, about 43.5% of men aged between 20–30 had at least a primary education; in South Pyongan, it was 34.2%. Another form of education was offered to Koreans through industrial employment.

This chapter covered Japan's annexation of Korea, protests against Japanese rule, and guerrilla activities in Korea. It also discussed how Japan developed transportation and communication systems for its benefit and controlled education in Korea. The Japanese required Koreans to learn the Japanese language and attend separate schools. Ironically, Koreans learned more progressive ideas in Japan than in Korea. The text also mentioned the lack of education for girls, especially in rural areas, during the colonial period.

In the upcoming chapter, we will explore the initial consequences of Japan's economic control over Korea. To promote this dominance, the Japanese conducted a land survey, which resulted in a land grab by Japanese individuals and companies. The resistance of the RA and the sacrifices made by patriotic individuals ultimately proved unsuccessful. Following the annexation, Japan exploited Korea in all areas of life, including the grains and minerals sectors. The Koreans had to wait until 1945 and for an additional three years before gaining independence and becoming a developed country, eventually joining the G8 nations.

CHAPTER 2:

The Colonial Period (1906–1918)

Japan's Preparation for Economic Domination

······◈······

Before 1910, Korea's economy transitioned from a closed economy to a colonial one. Japan began penetrating Korea's economy by establishing a banking system, railroad, and the Oriental Development Company (ODC). After gaining supreme power in Korea, Japan began exploiting the country's resources. They first focused on developing agriculture and conducted a nationwide land survey. Japan then persuaded the Korean government to invite Japanese surveyors and select Koreans for training to establish private landownership. Several laws were created to ensure that only the Japanese could own land and other real estate, allowing them to sell, purchase, mortgage, and exchange land and houses in Korea.

In 1910, before the formal annexation, a "Land Survey Bureau" (LSB) was created and later termed "the Provisional Land Survey Bureau" (PLSB) of the governor-general. In 1912, the "Land Survey Law" and the "Real Estate Certificate Law" were made to ensure legal guarantees for private landownership by land-house ownership certificates. The adopted Civic Code (CC) was modified according to the Japanese CC. The land survey confirmed the "report system" whereby many Japanese living in Korea could claim land owned by Korean peasants.

Most Korean farmers were illiterate and needed help understanding the complex rules for registering ownership, the methods of completing the detailed forms, and the deadline for registration. The "Land Survey Bureau" (LSB) created a foreign approach, and the doubling of landlord numbers from 1914–19 (1.8 to 3.4% of total farmers) implies that the survey did benefit the landlords, not the farmers. The survey also examined land prices to establish a better land taxation system. Another purpose was to have a topographical map of Korea. The regulations on cash payment of the land tax pushed the former yangban to make their land more productive and engage in the cash economy.

The Japanese land reform had defects but did force the pace of modernization in the Korean agriculture industry. It deprived Koreans of their landownership and helped establish a modernized agriculture system.[37]

Table I:
Increase in the Acreage of The Oriental Development Company

(In chŏngbo)

During	Dry Land	Rice Paddies	Others	Total
1910	2,300.6	8,643.8	91.1	11,035.5
1911	6,502.3	18,763.4	1,554.1	26,819.8
1915	18,753.7	46,642.1	4,748.2	70,144.0
1920	19,405.1	51,149.7	6,743.0	77,297.8
1925	19,078.6	50,992.7	15,718.8	85,790.1
1929	17,459.1	48,226.0	30,594.6	96,279.7
1930	16,944.4	46,682.5	41,709.1	105,336.0
1931	16,887.8	46,584.8	60,062.8	123,565.4

Source: Choson Government-General (ed.): Choson Sotokufu Tokei Nempo (*The Statistical Year Book of the Chosen Government-General*), March 1933.

The survey project lasted for more than eight years and the cost was more than 2,410,000 yen and employed more than 3,400 personnel.[38] It affected Korean farm communities as:

(1) The ruling feudalists who had the right to collect land taxes from the peasants were raised to the status of landowners. The peasants who used to cultivate land became mere tenant farmers. The former land rulers had only 3.4% of all the farmland, households came to possess 50.3% of the land[39], and the land rulers transformed into landowners. Meanwhile, the tenants lived on 39.5% of the land. The figure would increase to more than 60% if the number included petty farmers as partial owners.[40]

Table II:
Movement of Acreage Per Household

(In chŏngbo)

During	Rice Field	Dry Land	Total
1918	0.58	1.05	1.63
1919	0.57	1.04	1.61
1920	0.56	1.02	1.58

During	Rice Field	Dry Land	Total
1921	0.56	1.02	1.58
1922	0.56	1.02	1.58
1923	0.57	1.02	1.59
1924	0.57	1.02	1.59
1925	0.57	1.02	1.58
1926	0.57	1.01	1.58
1927	0.57	1.00	1.57
1928	0.57	0.99	1.56
1929	0.57	0.98	1.55
1930	0.56	0.96	1.52
1931	0.56	0.96	1.52
1932	0.56	0.94	1.50
1933	0.55	0.91	1.46
1934	0.55	0.92	1.47
1935	0.55	0.90	1.45

During	Rice Field	Dry Land	Total
1936	0.55	0.90	1.45
1937	0.56	0.89	1.45

Source: Himeno Mineru (ed.): Choson Keizai Zuhyo (*The Statistical Charts of Korean Economy*), 1940 Seoul, p. 169.

(2) The land possessed by Japanese companies and landowners increased for the land survey. Japan nationalized most of the public land and auctioned off the real estate in the possession of the Choson Dynasty to the highest bidders from Japan. The ODC in 1910 possessed 11,035 chŏngbo[41]; its possession was increased to 77,297 chŏngbo in 1920. Table I shows the increase in acreage of the ODC, and it was not the only Japanese landowner with 58% of the forest land in Japanese residents' hands, too.

(3) As a result of the survey, Korean tenant-peasants' conditions did not improve but worsened. They now lived at the mercy of the Japanese landowners, who gave ground rent from 50–70% of the harvest. The tenants also had to pay an additional tribute twice yearly and were often forced to do labor without pay. The industries were underdeveloped to absorb the idle peasants, making the tenant farmers' lives difficult. Table II shows that the average acreage per household was only 1.61 chŏngbo (1919), which needed to be more to support a family.[42] Tables III and IV indicate the reduction of tenant-peasants during the period.

Table III:
Percentage of Independent and Tenant Farmers

(In thousand household)

During	Independent	Partial Owner	Tenant
1913–17	55,521.8%	99,138.8%	100,839.4%
1918–22	52,920.4%	101,539.0%	109,840.6%
1923–27	52,920.2%	92,035.1%	117,244.7%
1928–32	49,718.4%	85,331.4%	136,050.2%
1933–37	54,719.2%	73,225.6%	157,755.2%
1939	53,919.0%	71,925.3%	158,355.7%

Source: Suzuki Takeo, Choson no Keizai (*The Korean Economy*), Tokyo, p. 246.

Table IV:
Acreage by Ownership

(In chŏngbo)

Year	Rice Field Independent	Rice Field Tenant	Dry Land Independent	Dry Land Tenant	Rice Field & Dry Land Total
1918	546,140	998,289	1,606,363	1,191,296	4,342,091
1922	551,522	993,601	1,582,710	1,189,484	4,317,318
1926	549,679	1,024,476	1,607,214	1,197,585	4,378,956
1930	549,833	1,093,920	1,435,777	1,386,606	4,446,137
1934	540,041	1,152,691	1,387,915	1,424,832	4,505,480
1937	556,567	1,179,801	1,359,399	1,410,476	4,506,244

Percentage of Acreage by Ownership

Year	Rice Field Independent	Rice Field Tenant	Dry Land Independent	Dry Land Tenant	Rice Field & Dry

					Land Total
1918	12.6	23	37	27.4	100
1922	12.8	23	36.6	27.6	100
1926	12.6	23.4	36.7	27.3	100
1930	12.3	24.5	32.2	31	100
1934	12	25.6	30.8	31.6	100
1937	12.3	26.2	30.2	31.3	100

Source: Choson Keizai Zuhyo, p. 163.

Between 1920 and 1925, more than 530,000 Korean peasants left their homes and villages to travel to Manchuria[43], Mongolia, or Siberia. Additionally, between 1916 and 1925, over 130,000 people migrated to Japan, as per the tables below. In 1931, there was a shift in the Korean industry as Japan took over Manchuria by force. Therefore, there was a growing need for the Japanese army that allowed for better communication links between Korea and its northern neighbor, giving Korean industries more significant access to Manchuria. In 1935, the South Manchurian Railway Company developed Najin on Korea's upper northeast coast as a major port and rail link to Manchuria. The production of opium increased during this time, rising from 57,870 pounds (26,200 kg) to 82,670 pounds (37,500 kg) annually, as the G-G had a monopoly on it. International organizations aimed to reduce drug use in

Korea, and the G-G promised to decrease opium production. The Japanese-controlled Manchukuo government was allowed to purchase 71% of Korean opium.[44]

Kirin in Manchuria served as a sanctuary for Korean refugees, and in the 1920s and 1930s, many working-class migrants arrived. Although different sources recorded different figures, the population in Manchuria rose from approximately 459,000 to over 876,000 between 1920 and 1936. This number increased even further under government-assisted migration from 1935 onward, which gave Japan more control over Manchuria and helped relieve southern Korea's overpopulation. As a result, the total Korean population in Manchuria climbed to 1.45 million by 1940. Between 1920 and 1940, labor migration to Japan increased from about 30,000 to 1.26 million. Political suppression and economic depression were the primary reasons for the Korean population's mass migration to Manchuria and neighboring countries. Before the 1920s, most Koreans migrating to Manchuria were farmers and were received kindlier by the local people than their compatriots in Japan. However, the situation deteriorated and was politicized in 1920 when Japanese forces attacked Korean guerrilla bases in Manchuria.

Table V:
Increase of Korean Residents in Japan

Year	No. of Koreans
1915	4,000

1920	30,000
1925	130,000

Source: Ibid, p. 53.

The number of Koreans who migrated to Japan and Manchuria increased every year. However, the lives of the Korean migrants were rarely less harsh than what they had left behind. The friction between these migrants and the Indigenous population led to unfortunate outbreaks of violence, such as the Wanpaoshan Incident in Manchuria, which was a clash between Chinese and Korean farmers over the use of water resources. Japan twisted such events to justify its aggression against China. The Japanese army relocated ordinary Korean settlers to strategic areas, isolating the guerrilla bands. The merits and demerits of this policy are visible in the later experience of the U.S. in Vietnam. Although the guerrillas were nullified as a threat and were disbanded by 1938, anti-Japanese sentiment increased as Korean farmers were uprooted or impeded from developing crops.[46]

Table VI:
Increase of Korean Residents in Manchuria

Year	No. of Koreans
1920	459,427

Year	No. of Koreans
1921	488,656
1922	516,865
1923	528,027
1924	531,973
1926	542,185
1927	558,280
1928	577,052
1929	597,677
1930	607,119

Source: Ibid, p. 58.

In 1933, as a resistance movement among Korean farmers gained momentum due to their desperate situation, Japan launched the "Rural Revival Movement" (RRM). The RRM was a self-help program to revitalize the rural economy by eliminating the chronic "spring poverty" problem and relieving the farmers' debt. The program encouraged farmers to lead a "rational life" and develop a secondary income source from their farms. However, expecting significant results from tenants living on small plots of land could have been more realistic. The Japanese government implemented the RRM to defuse the growing resistance among Korean farmers.

To summarize, this chapter focused on the land survey conducted by the Japanese G-G, which devastated Korean peasants. The land rulers, primarily Japanese, owned only 3.4% of the land before the survey but became owners of 50.3% of the land following it. After 1906, many Japanese companies and landed gentry purchased land in Korea, becoming the new landowners. This led to the displacement of peasants who had traditionally cultivated their forefathers' land as hereditary owners and were now reduced to tenant farmers. The ODC became one of the largest landowners, and the number of Japanese companies and landowners in Korea proliferated. During the colonial period, the royal lands of the Choson Dynasty were auctioned off to the highest Japanese bidders, while the condition of Korean peasants worsened. As a result, migration to other countries, such as Japan, Manchuria, and RMT, increased rapidly, and resistance movements grew among farmers. In response, the RRM was introduced to eliminate these movements. The land grabbing and peasant torture continued during this period.

The survey system caused many Korean farmers to lose their hereditary land and become landless. They were hastily removed from the land without proper notice or understanding of the system. Japanese capitalists, private companies, and the Japanese R-Gs were permitted to grab land. The ruling feudalists, who used to collect taxes, also became landowners, while the hereditary cultivators became tenant farmers. As a result of the survey, Japanese companies and landowners drastically increased their landownership. The nationalization of public land led to the former

Korean royal household's real estate going to Japan's highest bidders. Additionally, the Japanese owned 58% of forest land in Korea. The economic condition of Korean farmers became so dire that they began to migrate to Manchuria, RMT, and even Japan, where they were forced to work as laborers.

CHAPTER 3:

Japanese Economic Aggression

⋯⋯◈⋯⋯

When Japan opened its ports and began trading with Korea, Japanese traders acquired land from Korean peasants using various means. This practice intensified when prominent Japanese financiers invested in Korean farmland. In 1904, Japan attempted to forcibly acquire large tracts of uncultivated Korean land, which sparked strong opposition from the Korean population. The Agricultural and Mining Company, established by Korean businessmen with the assistance of powerful officials, argued that Koreans, not the Japanese, should cultivate new lands. The Korea Preservation Society (Poanhoe) launched a campaign against the Japanese demands through public lectures. Eventually, Japan withdrew its proposal to take over the uncultivated Korean lands.

To establish the R-G, Japan passed a "Law for the Development of Uncultivated State Lands." This law was successful in achieving its intended purpose. Before this, Japanese entrepreneurs competed with each other to establish companies that could acquire uncultivated lands and paddy fields that the Korean government reserved for supporting the army, government agencies, post stations, and other commodities. In 1904, several Japanese companies were established, including Korea Enterprises,

Sanin Agricultural Products, and the Korea Agricultural Company, Ltd. These companies started to gather lands initially in the granary region of the three southern provinces and later the whole country, and their acquisition kept growing.

In addition to land grabbing, the Japanese implemented economic tactics in Korea, such as establishing a banking system, railroads, and the ODC (the primary tool for agricultural reform). The first modern banking system was introduced by establishing Japan's Dai-Ichi Ginko Branch Office at Pusan in 1878. In 1890 and 1892, two more Japanese banks, Dai Juhachi Ginko (the 18th) and Dai Gojuhachi Ginko (the 58th), respectively, set up their branches in Korea to facilitate currency exchange for Japanese citizens.[47]

In Korea, prior to the establishment of city banks, pawn shops and usurious money lenders were the primary sources for borrowing money. The Koreans created three city banks, namely Taehan Ch'onil in 1899, Hansong Bank in 1903, and Han Il Bank in 1906, but these banks primarily offered loans on real estate mortgages. In 1904, the Joint Warehousing Company of Hansong was formed to allow merchants to borrow money against their merchandise. The Agricultural and Industrial Banks were established in 1906, while the Local Credit Associations came into being in 1907. In 1910, the Japanese government created The Bank of Choson to extend its economic influence to Manchuria and North China.

In 1918, the Agricultural and Industrial Banks were merged to form a single entity known as the Industrial Bank. Also referred to as The ODC (1908), its primary objective was to assist Japanese landowners and companies in expanding their land holdings. The Local Credit Associations catered only to wealthy landowners, making profits through lending money at high interest rates and acting as sales agents for farm produce and fertilizers.

In its first eighteen months of operation, it acquired about 30,000 chŏngbo (73,500 acres) of land, leading to a significant increase in Japanese immigrant farmers. Some of the Japanese farmers first came as owner-cultivators, then became landlords by increasing their landholdings. The Japanese land expropriation continued on the pretext of lands for railways or military installations. State-owned land was taken without compensation, and the Korean government had to purchase private lands by getting loans from Japan and then giving them to the Japanese.[48]

Table I:
Stocks of The Oriental Development Company Held by Region

Region	Number of stocks	Ratio Against 1,000 Stocks
Tokyo	390,861	83.77
Kyoto	517,296	110.87
Osaka	2,220,423	475.92
Nagoya	285,573	61.21
Korea	88,545	18.98

Region	Number of stocks	Ratio Against 1,000 Stocks
Others	1,162,921	249.25
Total	4,665,621	1,000.00

Source: Toyo Takushoku Kabuski Kaisha 20 Nenshi (*Twenty Years History of the Oriental Development Company*), 1928, Tokyo, pp. 131–32.

Following the annexation, Korea was turned into a colony, and the Japanese government accelerated the seizure of Korean land through a land survey. As a result, those who failed to register their lands had them confiscated by the governor-general (G-G). Additionally, lands previously allocated to state instrumentalities, such as the Department of the Royal Household, various government offices, and post stations, became the property of the G-G. This was because the Japanese considered ownership rights to privately held land vested in the landlord and state land in the government agency. Consequently, the G-G became the largest landowner in Korea. Moreover, the G-G acquired all former state-owned forest lands through another forest land law. According to statistics for 1930, the G-G held a combined total of 880,000 chŏngbo of agricultural and forest land, representing 40% of Korea's total land area.

To cover the increased expenditures, the Japanese government had to reorganize the taxation system, primarily by expanding the sources of revenue. In 1909, a house tax, a beverage tax, and a tobacco tax were introduced, followed by a registration tax in 1910. The land tax was increased by 40% in 1914, and the Choson G-G

(CG-G) decided that all land taxes should be collected from landowners only. The landowners then collected additional taxes from the tenants. This policy aimed to avoid direct conflict with Korean tenant farmers who would otherwise have to pay separate ground rent and land taxes.⁵⁰

The G-G took over a portion of the land, later sold to Japanese companies, companies under Japanese management, or Japanese immigrants. The ODC had an area of nearly 110,000 chŏngbo (269,000 acres) by 1930. The rent received from tenants in just one year from these landholdings reached 500,000 sŏk (about 2.5 million bushels, or 3% of the country's total harvest) of rice, and twice the number of other grains. The cadastral survey played a significant role in allowing the government and Japanese companies and individuals to become big landowners.

The Agricultural Policies Under the Government-General

The overwhelming importance of agriculture is evident in the first Korean census under Japan, which showed that in 1910, 84% of all Korean households were engaged in agriculture and forestry. Agriculture in Korea dominated more than Japan during its transition to modern economic growth.⁵¹ The agricultural productivity in Korea was low compared to that of Japan and other sectors.⁵²

After completing the survey, the Japanese colonialists began implementing the Rice Production Increase Plan (RPIP) since agriculture was very important. It had two objectives:

1. Cover the shortage of rice.
2. Overcome the economic depression in Japan.

In Japan, the yearly rice consumption was around 65 million sŏk, more than the country's production of approximately 58 million sŏk.[53] So, there was a shortage of 7 million sŏk each year; hence, rice had to be imported from other countries, including Formosa, presently known as Taiwan. Japanese policymakers encouraged investors to invest in rice production in Korea to overcome this issue.

Japan launched the RPIP in 1920 with two immediate measures. The first measure was to enlarge and improve acreage through irrigation, reclamation, and land transformation. The second was to increase cultivation by improving farm skills, the quality of seeds, compost application, and tools. The Japanese planners had intended to enlarge the acreage by 800,000 chŏngbo within 30 years and raise the total production by 9.2 million sŏk by taking uncultivated or wild lands. However, the plan did not work well. The first attempt was to mobilize private capital by promising 20–30% returns for the initiators. Only some capitalists responded to the program as they saw more profit in cultivated lands with 50–70% tenant rates than in uncultivated or wild lands, which would take many years before yielding fruitful results.

By 1925, nearly 76,000 of the planned 165,000 chŏngbo of new land was added to the existing acreage.[54] The irrigation plan could have gone better, and only 66 irrigation associations could benefit from 78,220 chŏngbo of rice paddies. To improve seeds and farming technology, the demonstration farms at Suwon, Gyeonggi-do were expanded and enhanced, and the construction of seedbeds throughout the country was encouraged. As a result, more than 1 million chŏngbo of rice paddies were planted with improved seeds by 1926. Additionally, chemical fertilizers were used, but they failed to improve the rice crop yield.

Table II:
Measures of Agricultural Production 1910–12 to 1934–36

Market Value Production Indices Rice Current Prices (1929–31=100)

**Export Annual (million yen) Total Indices

Average Crops Other Total Output Rice (1929-31=100)

1910–12	288	30	318	65.7	67,44.0***
1914–16	356	54	410	83.7	82,121.6
1919–21	1,034	102	1,136	84.5	85,937.7
1924–26	987	147	759	89.3	88,876.3
1929–31	618	141	1,759	100.0	1,000,100.0
1934–36	901	179	1,080	104.9	1,108,118.6

| 1939–41* | 1,537 | 330 | 1,867 | 125.3 | 142.8---- |

Sources: (1)-(3), Suh Sang-chul, *Growth and Structural Changes in the Korean Economy Since 1910*, Appendix table A-1; (4)-(5), Ibid, table III-3; (6), B.F. Johnson, *Japanese Food Management in World War II*, p. 264.

*Production indices exclude the year 1939, in which the rice crop was exceptionally poor.
**Includes both agriculture and forestry output.
***Covers only 1911 and 1912.

Japan historically considered Korea to be an agricultural resource. In 1912, the G-G established special offices for soil improvement and the Agricultural Technical Bureau (ATB) for each province to enhance animal husbandry, silk, cotton, and rice production. The agricultural research station at Suwon, the center of agrarian research in the South, developed solutions for diseases affecting cotton, rice, and fruit production. Japan's rapid urbanization, along with the economic boom of 1914–18 and the unrest of the 1918 rice riots, prompted a strong campaign to increase Korean rice exports to Japan. The G-G announced three long-term plans to boost rice production by opening wastelands, expanding the use of natural fertilizers, improving seed quality, and introducing advanced farm machinery. Transport facilities were in place to carry the grains to ports, and more accessible credit was provided for rice polishing and rice wine.

The primary objective was to provide food to Japanese consumers. However, this caused Korea to become excessively reliant on a single crop for a single metropolitan market, turning it into a colony heavily dependent on archetypes, with trends fluctuating accordingly. While Taiwan had diversified its agriculture with sugar cane, tea, and livestock, and Japan had derived supplementary income from sericulture, Korean farmers were almost entirely dependent on rice cultivation. The government-supported over-specialization policy kept rural incomes substantially lower than in Taiwan. With more producers competing for the same market in Korea, the owner-tenant system in Taiwan increased in the 1920s, while in Korea, the reserve was still present. The vulnerability of single-crop production was demonstrated in 1934 when farmers in Japan, reeling from the Great Depression, lodged complaints that resulted in the temporary abandonment of Korean rice expansion, causing hardship for Korean farmers.

In the 1920s, the G-G's project to expand cultivated land did not succeed as planned. The increased acreage was less than half of planned production, and between 1915 and 1939, the amount of land under cultivation only increased by 5%. It was easier and safer for farmers to profit from established tenant land. Although the G-G provided subsidies for new land development, the congested south, with fierce competition among tenants, made it difficult to achieve success. High rent meant landlords would take any increase in productivity, giving farmers no incentive to grow additional crops. However, the yield per hectare increased by one-quarter due to improved seeds and chemical fertilizers from 1930, and rice exports increased eight-fold. Most exported rice was rented from absentee landlords (who controlled over 60% of Korean arable land by 1930) and then exported through the Japanese to the home island. Exported rice far exceeded the increase in output, and rising imports of coarser Manchurian grains failed to stop a qualitative decline in the local Korean diet.

Using 1915 as an index of 100, the level had fallen to 90 in 1939, with an even harsher dip to 82 in the depression years of 1930–34. Basic figures for rice production, export, and consumption by Koreans for the period up to 1926 are shown in Table III.

Table III:
Rice Production, Export, and Consumption by Koreans to 1926

During	Production	Index	Exports	Index	Consumption
1912–16	12,302	100	1056	100	0.7188
1917–21	14,101	110	2196	208	0.6860
1922–26	14,501	118	4342	411	0.5871
1927–31	15,798	128	6607	626	---
1932–35	17,002	138	8757	829	*0.444

Source: Choi, 1971, p, 216. Figures for production and export are in 1,000 sŏk, and consumption is per person in Korea.

*Figure for 1930–34.

Between 1935 and 1939, consumption in Korea bounced back to 0.641 sŏk per capita due to record harvests in 1937 and 1938. However, the catastrophic drought of 1938 was blamed on insufficient irrigation, leading to a 40% crop decline in 1939. The subsequent war years were characterized by failing confidence among farmers and economic disruption.

In the 1920s, rural Koreans could organize themselves in the relatively political freedom of the Saito years and adapt to the changing agricultural situation. However, the problem of tenant farmers remained as many people without land could only retain their leases by paying exorbitant rents or doing additional services for landlords. Rent ranged from half to three-quarters of the crops, meaning farmers could not save enough to become owner-tenants. Instead, the number of tenants increased, with nearly 6.7 million, or 45% of farm households, being tenants by 1928. Another third were owner-tenants, working in plots of just over a hectare for tenant-farmers, and two hectares of owned and rented land for owner-tenants. The number of landlord-tenant disputes varied from place to place, with about 88% happening in the southern provinces in 1925 (especially South Cholla, South Kyongsang, and South Ch'ongch'on), while none happened in North Hamgyong and only four in South Hamgyong.[55] The disputes were mainly for the cancellation of tenant rights and not for lower rents. These were common with the absentee landlords who lived in the village or nearby market towns.

Song Pyong-jun headed the Tenant Farmers Mutual Aid Association (TFMAA) in Seoul, which had branches all over Korea. These were generally localized, and the broader organization was weak, and it declined after Song's death in 1925.[56]

The Korean Labor Mutual Aid Association (KLMAA) of 1922 saw more radical farmer and tenant branches. Over a thousand people attended the country-level tenant conference of the Chinju branch. The conferences were for debate and public meetings. The landholders, threatened by the tenant societies, were forced to organize their societies for self-defense. Some of them did not follow the democratic methods, as the U.S. Consul-General noted that "the Mutual Love Society of Pak (Chungum) and his followers were "two-fisted" fellows who believed in strong-arm methods, and for its actions, the party might more properly be called the Militant Love Society."[57]

The tenant groups initially included wealthy independent farmers. However, as tenant protests grew, the wealthy independent farmers withdrew as the nature of the groups became apparent.[58] Although the tenant bodies lacked articulation and cooperation, they successfully presented their group demands and forced the landlords to counter with their own organizations. In 1924, intense disagreements led to police intervention in South Cholla. As a result, 344 leaders of tenant societies were arrested. The political activism of the tenant-farmers was primarily driven by young intellectuals who had returned from studying in Japan. These intellectuals were more interested in journalism in the capital than in the village. The farmers wanted reform instead of revolution and responded coolly to activist students. As one college graduate of the 1930s recalled later, "As time passed, we had to acknowledge the crude fact that farmers and the countryside were not a repository of national spirit and conscience... as long as their lives were not threatened and the social order maintained, they seemed rather indifferent to the nature of their lordship."[59]

As agricultural conditions deteriorated, tenant associations transitioned into peasant unions. They focused on educating peasants by providing night schools, lecture tours, and creating consumer unions. In 1925, they launched a freedom of speech campaign. Between 1926 and 1928, many unions experienced rapid growth, but the Korean farming groups made little progress. As a result, the G-G established a committee to investigate tenancy issues and created regulations to safeguard tenants' rights. The official survey conducted during this time revealed that the annual income of a farmer who had a subsidiary receipt from sericulture, making sandals, straw bags, and ropes, was only $140 USD. Shockingly, 95% of all tenants experienced either a full or partial deficit at the end of the year. Many people had to pay interest rates ranging from 12–48% per year, including half a million individuals identified as "fire-field" squatters. These squatters would burn forest land in the mountains to survive on very little. Additionally, almost half of all farmers had to endure what was known as "spring poverty" every year. During this time, they would have to eat grass and tree bark to survive because they had spent all their money on rent and debt repayment and had nothing to buy food.[60]

During the world depression, the Japanese and Korean governments recognized the problems faced by tenants in their countries. In 1927, the Japanese government attempted to address these issues by buying land from wealthier landlords and redistributing it among the tenants. Similarly, in Korea, starting in 1932, the G-G Ugaki ordered that tenant disputes be handled individually by a County Tenancy Mediation Committee. Official control over farm management was initiated to prevent the exploitation of Korean tenants, and a minimum of three-year contracts were guaranteed for land. A rural regeneration plan was introduced to alleviate the peasants' poverty further and promote self-reliance, but it was unsuccessful. To help with this, typical Korean school graduates were selected for a one-year training program as village advisors on household budgeting and farm management.[61]

Ugaki had plans to broaden the agricultural program in South P'Yongan and South Hamgyong by introducing wool and cotton production, which the Japanese military found attractive. However, the tenant leaders pushing for change were forced to leave the fertile south and start anew in the mountainous northeast. Despite facing challenges, including government policies and a split within the tenant movement, the radical group called the New Red Peasant Unions (RPU) managed to gain support in the Hamgyong area. They could do so by taking advantage of their distance from Seoul, proximity to communist influence across the border in Manchuria and Siberia, and the protective cover of the mountainous terrain. The RPU was the most militant among the peasant movements and offered a revolutionary challenge to Japan's authority through various means, such as theater, political publications, night schools, and a semi-militaristic organization. However, their effectiveness was short-lived. Japanese repression of even moderate groups increased following the Manchurian incident, and many RPU members were arrested from the start of 1932.[62]

Korean agriculture mainly focused on crops, particularly food grains and rice, as opposed to livestock, fertilizers, and silk products. Crops accounted for 91% of net agricultural product in 1910–12 and 81% in 1934–36. Rice production consistently accounted for more than half the value of the main crops throughout the colonial period, and it increased significantly in the 1930s. The table presents data on agricultural output, rice production growth, and the rising proportion of rice exports. One might wonder how this increase in rice exports was possible, given that the cultivated area (paddy and dry fields, respectively) doubled between 1910–38 and 1910–19.

During this period, the Japanese conducted a comprehensive cadastral survey to improve the tax base and establish ownership rights. According to Grajdanzev, the increase in agricultural production might be mainly due to a statistical phenomenon, showing better coverage of cultivated land on which the farmers had failed to pay taxes. There could be various other reasons for the rise in production, such as land improvement through irrigation construction and drainage facilities or better material inputs, such as superior seeds, greater use of fertilizers, increased use of machinery, draft animals, farm implements, etc. Another possibility was more double cropping of land or more labor-intensive methods of cultivation. Shifts in the land-tenure system cost-price relationship, providing more significant incentives for production increase, might also be a reason. Finally, the effects of changes in Japanese policy that encouraged Korean agriculture could also have contributed to the increase in production.[63]

During the early colonial period, the ODC played a significant role in irrigation and agricultural finance. In 1920 and 1926, the organization took charge of the first and second RPIP. After the 1918 riot in Japan caused by a rice shortage, the G-G devised plans to increase rice production by implementing better irrigation systems, reclaiming land, and using improved seeds and compost materials. While government and private efforts to boost rice output succeeded, the increase was minimal (refer to Table II).

The tables below depict the inefficacy of the plan implemented during 1912–1926 in boosting rice production. Despite the effort to increase rice production, it failed miserably, leading to a significant rise in the export of Korean rice to Japan. To facilitate the export of rice, Koreans had to decrease their consumption. Another plan, The Second RPIP, was initiated in 1926 to enlarge the acreage by 350,000 chŏngbo within 10–12 years and increase the production by 4.72 million sŏk. The second plan saw somewhat greater success, but it was canceled by the Japanese government in 1934. During 1926–1934, nearly 142,095 chŏngbo was reclaimed, and the yield increased by 1,173,000 sŏk. To provide water for 15,346 chŏngbo, 123 new irrigation associations were established.[64]

The government had implemented irrigation projects to increase the yield of rice. However, due to the high cost of these projects, the irrigation associations faced a severe financial crisis. Consequently, the water charges imposed on land within the irrigation districts were substantially increased. This increase caused the price of newly irrigated land to decrease in many cases instead of rising as expected. The new irrigation facilities, which were supposed to benefit the farmers, drove many of them into poverty. As a result, opposition movements against the irrigation association emerged throughout Korea.[65]

The second plan's suspension was due to the worldwide depression, including Japan. During the economic crisis, Japanese farmers threatened to boycott Korean rice as domestic rice prices slumped. To overcome the farm crisis, the Japanese government first restricted Korean rice imports and ordered the colonial government to stop the production plan altogether. In the late 1930s, there was an attempt to increase Korean rice production (IKRP) after facing renewed rice shortages after the war with China. However, the increase was to be achieved mainly by methods other than increased irrigation or land improvement.

Unfortunately, improvement and reclamation attempts did not succeed. It is argued that the return rates on the cultivated land were so high that landlords were unwilling to invest in land improvement. This failure had an adverse effect on land utilization as it depended on irrigation. By 1938, the utilization rate had reached 1.34 to 1.35, with a second crop being gathered on a third of the cultivated land. Grajdanzev felt that the utilization rate could have been expanded with more attractive rice cost-price relations.

Table IV:

Production, Exportation, and Consumption of Korean Rice Production

During	(thousand sŏk)	Index	(thousand sŏk)	Index	Per Person in Korea
1912–16	12,302	100	1,056	100	0.7188
1917–21	14,101	110	2,196	208	0.6860
1922–26	14,501	118	4,342	411	0.5871

Source: Bureau of Agricultural Forestry, Choson Government-General (ed.): Choson no Nogyo (*Agriculture in Korea*), 1936, pp. 36–39.

Table V:
Production and Exportation of Korean Rice

(In thousand sŏk)

During	Production	Index	Export	Index
1911–16	12,303	100	1,056	100
1916–20	14,101	115	2,196	208
1921–25	14,501	118	4,342	411
1927–31	15,798	128	6,607	626
1931–35	17,002	138	8,757	829
1936	19,410	159	7,161	678
1937	26,796	218	10,702	1,013
1938	24,138	196	6,051	573
1939	14,355	116	---	---

Source: Toyo Keizai Sinposha (ed): Choson Sangyo Nenpo (*The Industrial Annual Book of Korea*), 1943, Tokyo, p. 53; see also Hochin Choi op. cit., p. 216.

Agricultural production almost doubled in 1910–12 and 1939–41 (Table II). As already stated, the expansion of the agricultural area, increased utilization, and different improvements (irrigation, seeds, fertilization) were not enough for the growth. Draft animal usage doubled, labor inputs were 50% higher, and there was a rise in mechanization. Ban estimated, as the cultivated area was relatively fixed, that the land productivity increased substantially due to capital and inputs. He concluded that although Korean agriculture might have been subject to diminishing returns, output could have been expanded with more inputs of labor and capital.[67]

Table VI:
Supply and Demand of Principal Farm Products

(In thousand sŏk)

During	Production	Exports	Export to Japan	Carried over to next year	Domestic consumption
1912–1916	12,421	253	1,056	---	11,112
1923–1927	15,336	20	4,916	---	10,400
1933–1937	18,424	83	8,575	478	9,288

1. Rice

2. Millet

1912–1916	4,199	0	0	0	4,199
1923–1927	6,771	---	---	---	6,771
1933–1937	6,011	---	---	---	6,011

3. Barley & Rye

1912–1916	6,560	---	2	---	6,557
1923–1927	7,365	56	2	---	7,419
1933–1937	9,176	284	29	---	9,432

4. Wheat

1912–1916	1,620	139	29	---	1,730
1923–1927	2,034	306	57	---	2,284
1933–1937	1,786	556	117	---	2,222

Source: Choson Keizai Zuhyo, p. 204.

Change in Landowners/Tip and Land Tenure System

Between 1910 and 1918, Japanese officials conducted a comprehensive survey of agricultural land in the country. This survey allowed the government to change the landownership and land tenure systems. As a result, land that belonged to royal households and was unused was sold to Japanese land companies and landlords. Meanwhile, peasants who had previously farmed the land under hereditary arrangements with the owners were stripped of their rights and became tenant-farmers. Due to these changes, agricultural output in the country increased significantly, particularly in rice production, which saw rapid export growth. The survey required a full-time workforce of over 3,000 people to complete.

The concentration of landownership in Korea is demonstrated in the changing distribution of ownership. The proportion of pure tenants (not proprietors or part-owners) increased from 39% in 1913–17 to 56% by 1938. Japanese landlords owned significant holdings (over 100 chŏngbo=2.45 acres). The proportion of Japanese ownership was 54% in 1921 and increased to 62% in 1935. However, the official data did not include some Japanese-owned farms under Korean charters. If the government properties under Japanese control were included, it could be shown that the Japanese controlled half of the land in Korea.[68]

The land survey at the time created an even wider gap between petty farmers and landowners, as indicated in the following tables. Between 1914 and 1930, landowners increased from 1.8% to 3.6%, independent farmers decreased from 22% to 17.6%, and partial landowners from 41.1% to 31%. The number of tenant-farmers increased from 35.1% to 46.5%. Although the land survey introduced modern landownership, it did not improve agricultural management. The agricultural production mode remained almost the same during the semi-feudalistic production system. To understand farm management under Japanese colonial rule in Korea, we need to examine the relationship between landowners and tenant-farmers. Tenant-farmers had to pay tenant rents mostly in kind (89.1%), and only 10.9% were allowed to pay in cash, primarily by proxy.[69] The Japanese capitalists preferred collecting rent in kind to maximize their profits through high tenant rent rates.

Table VII:
The Number of Farm Households by Landownership

1914–1915

Landowners	46,754 (1.8%)	97.105 (3.6%)
Independent	569,517 (22.0)	533.188 (19.6)
Partial owners	1,065,705 (41.1)	994,976 (36.6)
Tenant	911,261 (35.1)	1,091,680 (40.2)
Burnt-field cultivators		
Total (100)	2,592,237 (100.0)	2,716,949 (100.0)

1926–1930

Landowners	104,614 (3.8%)	104,004 (3.6%)
Independent	525,747 (19,1)	504,009 (17.6)
Partial owners	895,721 (22.5)	890,291 (31.0)
Tenant	1,193,099 (43.3)	1,334,139 (46.5)
Burnt-field cultivators	34,315 (1.30)	37,514 (1.3)
Total (100)	2,752,497 (100.0)	2,869,957 (100.0)

Source: The Choson Government-General, *The Statistical Year Book*, March, 1936, Seoul.

Table VIII:
Annual Changes in Number of Owners and Tenant

Year	Owner	Part owner	Tenant	No. of	Landlord	Upland Employee	Farms Operator
1914	220	411	351	1,000	18		
1919	197	393	376	1,000	34		
1920	195	374	398	1,000	33		
1921	196	366	405	1,000	36		

Year	Owner	Part owner	Tenant	No. of	Landlord	Upland Employee	Farms Operator
1922	197	358	402	1.000	37		
1923	195	352	416	1,000	37		
1924	195	345	422	1,000	38		
1925	199	332	431	1,000	38		
1926	191	325	433	1,000	38		
1927	187	327	438	1,000	38	10	
1928	183	319	449	1,000	37	12	
1929	180	315	456	1,000	37	12	
1930	176	310	465	1,000	36	13	
1931	170	296	484	1,000	36	14	
1932	162	253	528	1,000	36	21	
1933	181	241	519	1,000	-	28	31

Source: *Agriculture in Korea*, 1936, pp. 73–74, Seoul.

There were three methods used to determine the rent rates for tenant farmers. The first method was called Chipcho. It involved landowners' representatives estimating the value of the crops in the presence of the tenants in the field. The rent was split between the landowners and tenants. However, the cost of seeds and fertilizer was charged to the tenants. The rent rate varied from 50% to 80% of the produced crop. The second method was T'ajo. It involved dividing the crop at a predetermined rate, usually 50/50, upon the completion of thrashing in the presence of both the tenants and the landowners' representatives. The tenants were responsible for paying the land taxes, transportation, fertilizer, and irrigation charges. The rent rate varied from 30% to 79%. The last method was called Chongjo. It involved tenants paying the rent in advance, regardless of the crop yield. The tenants were also responsible for the cost of seeds and fertilizers. The rent rate varied from 20% to 90%.[70]

It is no surprise that life was extremely difficult for Korean farmers, often forcing them to flee their land. The number of "fire-field people"—those who cleared vegetation in uninhabited upland areas and then cultivated small patches of the bare ground before continuing the process—almost tripled from 245,626 in 1916 to 697,088 in 1927. By 1936, this lowest stratum of the Korean farming population was officially recorded at over 1.5 million.

Table IX:
Comparison of Tenant Rates (unit: %)

	Chongjo system			T'ajo system			Chipcho system		
	High	Av	Low	High	Av	Low	High	Av	Low

Rice paddies	74	46	30	65	53	37	65	52	50
Dry land	67	43	32	57	52	32	61	47	30

Source: Bureau of Agriculture and Forestry, Choson Government-General (ed.) *Choson ni okeru Kosaku ni kansuru Sanko Jiko Tekiyo* (*Reference Materials for the Tenancy in Korea*), 1932.

It is important to note that two types of tenant contracts were deployed in different parts of the country. In the north, tenants had oral contracts that lasted for a few years. In the south, written contracts were used with much shorter terms, sometimes only lasting one year. This disparity made southern tenants feel more vulnerable and often led to disputes with their landlords, who were seen as greedy. The tenants were at the mercy of the landlords and were forced to pay more than just the rent. Agents appointed by the landowners to supervise their land and rent it to tenant-farmers would take advantage of the tenants. They would collect additional rent, tributes of various kinds, and charge commissions for renewing the contract, among other irregularities.

Land rent was collected in kind; it was usually taken as a proportion of the annual output, which was often half of the crop. However, the rent could be as high as 90% in some cases. In 1932, the Japanese investigated the distribution of output. They found that the average amount of rice available per family member was 11.4 koku (1 koku is equivalent to 5.12 US bushels) for landlords' families. In contrast, it was only 0.4 koku per member for tenants' families.⁷¹ This system of land taxes, along with an uneven distribution of output, allowed for the exportation of Korean rice to Japan, accounting for over half of the Japanese government's revenue before 1920. It resulted in the decline of Korea's average per capita consumption of rice and food grains.⁷²

Poor farm families were reduced to eating wild grass in the spring months before the harvest: "The phrase 'starvation export' was quite commonly applied by Japanese food officials."⁷³ According to a study, the annual per capita rice consumption in Japan is over 1.0 sŏk, whereas in Korea, it has steadily declined to less than half of that. A question raised by Ki-baik Lee is what the Koreans could eat to fill their half-empty stomachs. Various less palatable grains, such as millet, kaoliang, soybeans, etc., were brought in from Manchuria to address this issue. These grains were used to replace Korean rice and feed the Japanese. As we can see, the imports of Manchurian millet, which were only 15,000 sŏk in 1912, increased to more than 100 times that amount, 1,720,000 sŏk, in 1930.

It is interesting to compare the agricultural development of Korea and Formosa (now Taiwan) under Japanese colonial rule. In both cases, the colonial policy aimed to increase agricultural output and send the surplus back to mainland Japan. Between 1910 and 1935, rice production in Korea increased by 2% annually, while Formosa saw a slightly higher increase of around 3%. To encourage land improvement, the government provided subsidies for irrigation and sent agricultural technicians to improve farming practices. Schools were established to train farmers. As in Korea, less desirable food (such as potatoes) was substituted, which may have led to a decline in per capita food consumption. However, "technical progress in Formosa was much more impressive," one reason for this could be the different methods used to expropriate the agricultural surplus.[75]

In Korea, the government used land taxes, high rents, and allowed Japanese people to own land to increase rice exports to Japan. In Formosa, the government imposed taxes and allowed large Japanese food processors to monopolize the market. How land was owned and managed was also different between the two places. In Formosa, absentee owners had to relinquish their hereditary rights in exchange for interest-bearing bonds. In contrast, resident owners had guaranteed rights to their land, and rents were fixed at lower levels.[77] So, the incentives to increase production were much more significant in Formosa.

Manufacturing

Before the Japanese annexation, there was some manufacturing activity in Korea. The Americans had started an electrical power station and a gold mine, while the Russians had established a metal factory. The Korean government had also set up modern cocooneries and industrial training centers. However, the Corporation Law (CL) or Choson Company Regulations (CCR) delayed the development of the modern manufacturing sector in Korea. This law gave the G-G the power to approve the establishment of new firms, which could limit investment in the non-agricultural sector, restrict the outflow of capital from Japan, and impede the growth of Korean enterprises. Despite this, the Japanese founded soy manufacturing, rice refining, electric power, and lumber mills before 1910.[78]

At the beginning of the colonial era, the total manufacturing output was low. Fewer than 1% of households engaged in manufacturing activities in 1910–1912, whereas 11% of Japanese households were involved in manufacturing. The share of manufacturing in total commodity products was less than 7% (Table X).

Table X:
Output Growth, Population Increase, and Industrial Structure
(1910–12 to 1939–41)

A. Output and population indices (1929–31=100)
(net commodity product in 1929–31 market prices)

Period	Agriculture	Forestry, fishing, and mining	Manu-facturing	Total	Population***
1910–12	67.3	33.7	17.4	54.2**	66.0
1914–16	86.5	45.9	31.5	69.6	---
1919–21	86.6	46.2	59.7	76.9	84.5

1924–26	91.2	69.0	97.5	89.6	---
1929–31	100.0	100.0	100.0	100.0	100.0
1934–36	98.7	161.5	194.2	127.1	---
1939–41	117.3*	227.6	255.5	165.5	115.2
				(155.5)	

*Excludes 1939, an exceptionally poor rice year. The index for total output in parentheses includes 1939.
**Only 1911 and 1912.
***Based on Oct. 1 census counts in 1920, 1930, and 1940.

B. Industrial Structure (percent share of net commodity product)****

Period	Agriculture	Forestry	Fishing	Mining	Manufacturing	Total
1910–12	84.6	5.3	1.9	1.5	6.7	100.0
1919–21	78.6	2.7	3.0	1.4	14.3	100.0
1929–31	63.1	6.6	5.8	2.2	22.3	100.0
1939–41	49.6	7.2	6.3	7.9	29.0	100.0

****Based on current values.

Sources: Suh Sang-Chui, *Growth and Structural Changes in the Korean Economy Since 1910*, Tables B–5 and L 1–4; Statistical Append 9x, table A-I.

The number of companies and amount of paid-in capital mushroomed when the Corporation Law was abolished in 1920. The amount of paid-in-capital rose 3.5 times, and the number of companies quadrupled in 1921–30.

In 1920, manufacturing was dominated mainly by handicrafts and cottage industries, except for rice mills and imports that fulfilled the demand for other manufactured goods. According to a rough estimate by Suh, handicraft establishments produced about half of the total manufactured goods in the early 1920s. However, by 1935–38, this figure had declined to approximately a quarter of the total output. This conclusion is supported by the factory output structure of light industries, which includes food, textiles, ceramics, printing, lumber, and other products. Food and textiles accounted for less than half of the total factory output. These new products must have competed with handicraft industries.

Despite being inhibited by the CL or CCR in the early years, the manufacturing sector's output witnessed significant growth rates. This growth was due to Japan's decision to replace imports from other regions with those from the Yen Block. Although it began from a small base at the time of annexation, the net commodity product of manufacturing almost doubled between 1929–31 and 1934–36 and rose by 30% between 1934–36 and 1939–41.[79]

During the period under consideration, the share of the manufacturing sector in the total product increased to 29%, as indicated in Table X. This growth was accompanied by changes in the structure, location, and ownership of the industry, as well as in the composition of exports and imports. The handicraft industry experienced a rapid decline in the 1930s, while the share of light industry decreased from three-quarters of factory production in 1930 to less than half in 1940. The growth was mainly driven by the production of chemicals, fertilizers, and possibly war goods in heavy industries (by 1940, chemicals accounted for over a third of factory output). Since no direct information is available on capital formation, it can be inferred that the share of producers' goods quadrupled from 4% in the early 1920s to 16% in the late 1930s out of the total finished goods. That is if commodity products for domestic use are broken down into materials for finished goods and the latter again into producer and consumer goods.

Obtaining accurate information on ownership and capitalization can be challenging, as data is only available for corporations. The available data only shows paid-in capital, which sometimes excludes large debts. Additionally, the data does not include establishments with less than five workers, although their output is still included in the gross production value. In 1938, Japanese-owned establishments produced 75% of the gross output value, and Japanese firms owned 60% of all firms, with 90% of paid-in capital. This data indicates the dominance of the Japanese in Korea's industry but may only be partially accurate. Even before the 1930s, Japanese and mixed Japanese-Korean firms held the majority of ownership and paid-in capital. In the 1930s, large Japanese financial-industrial firms (Zaibatsu) such as Mitsui, Mitsubishi, Yasuda, and Sumitomo became interested in Korea. They began building large complexes and some younger companies like the Noguchi.[80] During the late 1930s, Choi and Suh provided data indicating that less than 7% of textile, metal, machine tools, ceramics, and chemical firms accounted for a large portion of employment and output.[81] In 1939, 12% of all factories produced over 60% of products. The rapid growth of manufacturing led to increased output demands from large Japanese-controlled firms.

During the 1930s and 1940s, most industries were established in North Korea, which accounted for less than 40% of the country's total manufactured products in 1934. However, by 1940, this figure had increased to 50%. The rapid growth of all sectors, except mining, was observed in North Korea, leading to a rise in population. During Japanese colonialism, the northern region of Korea was recognized for its advantages of cheap labor, strategic location, and abundant supply. The economic conditions of the North and South were complementary to each other, not only in manufacturing but also in agriculture. In the South, three-quarters of the cultivated area was dedicated to rice and summer grains (barley and wheat), while in the North, 60% of the area was used to grow beans, and 80% for cereals (millet, sorghum, corn, buckwheat). In 1939–40, the South produced five times the value of textiles than the North, machine tool output was 2.5 times as high, printing volume was over six times greater, and manufactured food about 1.8 times greater. On the other hand, the North dominated the South in metals (8:1), ceramics (2.5:1), and chemicals (5:1).[82]

Table X indicates that the growth rate of commodity products from 1910–12 to 1939–41 was 4% on average or 2% per capita. Despite the reduction in services, the growth was still impressive, even by today's standards. Agricultural output per capita did not increase, and the domestic rice supply was limited due to exports (refer to Table II). Although most Koreans did not benefit from this growth during the colonial period, it is evident when we look at the trade statistics of that era. Grajdanzev discovered that the imports mainly comprised high-value products such as sake, beer, canned goods, wool, and silk tissues. On the other hand, the exports mainly comprised low-value, mass-consumption items such as rice, cotton, and hemp tissues. He concluded that consumer goods imports were mainly for the Japanese residing in Korea and wealthy Koreans.[83] During the 1930s, the per capita consumption of domestic consumer goods increased considerably in Korea. However, there was a decline in the consumption of rice and grain. This divergence between domestic production and consumption and differences in the income elasticity of demand for exports and imports suggests that the average Koreans were not benefiting from the expansion of industrialization and trade.

Before the 1930s, Korea had only a few large industries, mainly related to spinning and light manufacturing. Table XI shows that most factories were small. From 1911 to 1932, the number of factories increased by more than 17 times (from 252 to 4,643), and the output almost increased 16 times (from 19,639,000 yen to 323,271,000 yen). The number of employees also increased 17 times (from 14,575 to 110,650).

Table XI:
Movement of Factories by Employment and Production

(In thousand yen)

Number of Index (100 in 1911)

During	Factories	Workers	Production	Factories	Workers	Production
1911	252	14,575	19,639	100	100	100
1916	1,075	28,646	59,026	427	197	301
1921	2,384	49,302	166,414	946	338	847
1926	4,293	83,450	365,849	1,704	573	1,862
1930	4,261	101,943	263,275	1,691	699	1,340
1932	4,643	110,650	323,271	1,842	759	1,646
1934	5,126	138,809	486,522	2,034	952	2,477
1936	5,927	188,250	720,319	2,351	1,291	3,667
1937	6,298	207,002	967,364	2,499	1,420	4,926

Source: Choson Keizai Zuhyo, p. 269.

Table XII:
No. of Factories by Industry and Employment

(As of the end of June 1931)

No. of Factories	No. of Employees						
	10–30	30–50	50–100	100–300	300–500	Over 500	Total
Total	780	187	131	61	22	18	1,199
Textile	53	34	21	12	11	9	140
Metals	47	9	4	---	---	1	61
Machine & tool	43	6	8	5	---	1	63
Pottery	62	17	10	3	1	1	94
Chemicals	43	11	18	11	3	2	88
Sawing, wood, & cork	41	10	17	3	---	2	73
Printing & bindery	84	10	12	4	1	---	111

	No. of Employees						
Foodstuff	340	83	32	17	5	2	479
Gas & electricity	9	3	2	---	---	---	14
Others	58	4	7	6	1	---	76

Percentage

Total	65.1	15.6	10.9	5.1	1.8	1.5	100.0
Textile	37.8	24.3	15.0	8.6	7.9	6.4	100.0
Metals	77.0	14.8	6.6	---	---	1.6	100.0
Machine & tool	68.3	9.5	12.7	7.9	---	1.6	100.0
Pottery	65.9	18.1	10.6	3.2	1.1	1.1	100.0
Chemicals	48.9	12.5	20.4	12.5	3.4	2.3	100.0
Sawing, wood, & cork	56.2	13.7	23.3	4.1	---	2.7	100.0

Printing & bindery	75.7	9.0	10.8	3.6	0.9	---	100.0
Foodstuff	71.0	17.3	6.7	3.6	1.0	0.4	100.0
Gas & electricity	64.3	21.4	14.3	---	---	---	100.0
Others	76.3	5.3	9.2	7.9	1.3	---	100.0

Source: Ibid, p. 286.

Table XIII:

Owners and Employees of Factories With More Than 1,000 Workers

(As of the end of June 1991)

Factory	Owner	Employees
Seoul Factory, Bureau of Railways	Bureau of Railway Choson Government-General	1,314
Tobacco Factory	Bureau of Monopoly Choson Government-General	1,203
Choson Textile Co., Ltd.	Mabuchi	1,913

Mitsubishi Seitetsusho	Mitsubishi Seitetsu Co., Ltd.	1,288
Choson Chizuso Hiryo Co., Ltd.	Noguchi	4,246

Source: Bureau of Education, Choson Government-General (ed.); Kojyo Oyobo Kosan ni okeru Rodosha Jyokyo Chosa (*The Survey Report on the Factory and Mine Laborers*), 1933, Seoul.

The Japanese capitalists also dominated small and medium factories and large industries. Table XIV compares the companies' ownership in Korea by nationality. In 1938, the Japanese capitalists owned 3,136 companies, or 57.7% of the total, versus the Koreans who had 2,278 firms, or 42.1% under their possession. It should be noted that most Korean firms were smaller in scale and in capital than those owned by the Japanese, so their share in the holding of companies was meager.

Table XIV:
Company Ownership by Nationality

(As of the end of 1938)
(In thousand yen)

Industry	No. of Companies			Paid-in Capital		
	Korean	Japanese	Total	Korean	Japanese	Total
Banking	98	77	175	10,233	76,705	86,938

Industry	No. of Companies			Paid-in Capital		
Commerce	846	1,050	1,896	23,395	65,754	98,149
Manufacture	740	804	1,544	30,198	214,705	244,903
Electricity	---	16	16	---	213,065	213,065
Agriculture/ forestry	86	179	265	13,451	51,563	65,014
Fishery	27	69	96	915	13,686	14,601
Mining	29	121	150	12,449	171,120	183,569
Transport & warehouse	258	274	532	7,400	90,901	98,301
Miscellaneous	194	545	739	24,619	61,234	85,853
Total	2,278	3,136	5,414	122,660	958,622	1,081,282

Percentage of Ownership by Nationality

Banking	56.0	44.0	100.0	11.8	88.2	100.0
Commerce	44.6	55.4	"	26.2	73.8	"
Manufacture	47.9	52.1	"	12.3	87.7	"

Electricity	---	100.0	"	---	100.0	"
Agriculture/ forestry	32.5	67.5	"	20.7	79.2	"
Fishery	28.1	71.9	"	6.3	93.7	"
Mining	19.3	80.7	"	6.8	93.2	"
Transport & warehouse	48.5	51.5	"	7.5	92.5	"
Miscellaneous	26.3	73.7	"	28.7	71.3	"
Total	42.1	57.9	"	11.3	88.7	"

Source: Choson Keizai Zuhyo, p. 315.

After establishing the Company Regulations (CR) in 1920, there was a rapid increase in the number of companies. In 1910, there were only 152 companies with a capital of 16 million yen or more. However, by 1920, the total paid-in capital increased to 180 million yen, with 544 companies. Furthermore, by 1930, there were 2,035 companies with 359 million yen of paid-in capital.[84] During the early 1900s, Koreans were permitted to participate in business. By 1911, there were 27 Korean companies with a total paid-in capital of 2,742,000 yen. Over time, the number of Korean companies increased to 39 in 1918 with a total paid-in capital of 7,316,000 yen, and by 1938, there were 2,278 Korean companies with a total paid-in capital of 122,660,000 yen. Table XV shows the number of industrial companies and their paid-in capital by nationality.

It is important to note that very little capital was invested in Korean-owned industries. Korea owned only 36 (17% of the total) companies that were involved in mining and manufacturing, with a capital of 3,075,000 yen or 9% in 1923. The issue was that most of the national capital was invested in commerce and usury. Korean entrepreneurs had to compromise with Japanese capitalists, who adopted appeasement policies after the Independence Movement in 1919. To expand industries, the number of working-class people increased to 203,590 in 1931. This increase led to Koreans becoming class-conscious and formulating an aggressive force in the anti-Japanese struggle.

Table XV:
No. of Industrial Companies by Nationality and Capital

(As of the end of 1933)

Capital	No. of Companies			Paid Capital		
	Korean	Japanese	Total	Korean	Japanese	Total
50,000 yen or less	297	507	804	3,206	5,960	9.166

Capital	No. of Companies			Paid Capital		
50,000 to 100,000	27	82	110	1,561	5,035	6,646
100,000 to 300,000	15	51	66	2,161	7,892	10,053
300,000 to 500,000	1	11	12	425	3,983	4,408
500,000 to 1 million	13	12	15	1,750	7,562	9,312
over 1 million	---	11	12	---	90,267	100,266
Total	343	674	1,019	9,102	120,699	139,851

Percentage

50,000 yen or less	36.9	63.1	100.0	35.0	65.0	100.0
50,000 to 100,000	24.5	74.5	100.0	23.5	75.8	100.0

100,000 to 300,000	22,7	77.3	100.0	21.5	78.5	100.0
300,000 to 500,000	8.3	91.7	100.0	9.6	90.4	100.0
500,000 to 1 million	20.0	80.0	100.0	18.8	81.2	100.0
over 1 million	---	91.7	100.0	---	90.0	100.0
Total	33.7	66.1	100.0	6.6	86.3	100.0

Source: Choson Keizai Zuhyo, p. 329; see also table 31, Hochin Choi, p. 239.

Japan's Monopolization of Korea's Natural Resources

Japan was interested in Korea's natural resources, not just its land. However, the Japanese colonialists only focused on mining gold, silver, and smokeless coal, and disregarded other minerals. Japan needed gold to adopt the gold standard and relied on Korea for a steady supply. They obtained Korean gold through predatory means, crucial in Japan's decision to adopt the gold standard. After annexation, the Japanese Zaibatsu conglomerates surveyed the mineral deposits and exploited them, causing a significant increase in mining output. Gold, silver, iron, lead, tungsten, and coal production increased by 5 to 6 times in some cases or even several thousand times in others. Japan's mining expansion was particularly noticeable during World War I, as they were a vital supplier of raw materials to the Allies. Table XVI demonstrates the incredible growth of mineral output in Korea, especially towards the war's end, from mines owned by the Japanese and others.

Table XVI:
Mining Output by Nationality of Mine Owners

Year	Koreans	Japanese	Others	Total
1909	325,979	1,297,074	2,964,562	4,587,615
1910	331,248	1,968,034	3,768,670	6,067,952
1911	296,019	1,401,569	4,488,370	6,185,958
1912	181,769	1,683,931	4,949,418	6,815,118
1913	276,359	1,934,072	5,987,095	8,197,526
1914	313,335	1,783,577	6,425,506	8,522,418
1915	384,010	2,820,682	7,311,274	10,515,966
1916	1,042,284	3,622,695	9,413,209	14,078,188

Year	Koreans	Japanese	Others	Total
1917	857,839	7,625,982	8,584,281	17,058,102
1918	299,110	24,673,745	5,865,219	30,838,074

Source: Ki-baik Lee, p. 320.

Japan needed gold and silver for payment of foreign obligations, and smokeless coal was used to fuel the ships of the Japanese navy. Table XVII shows the mines that attracted the Japanese.

Table XVII:
Classification of No. of Mines*, Percent of No. of Workers, and Percent of All Mine Workers

Gold and silver	151	70.9%	15,509	51.5%
Iron	9	4.2	4,452	14.8
Coal	34	15.9	9,273	30.8
Graphite	10	4.7	358	1.2
Molybdenum	1	0.5	43	0.1
Copper	1	0.5	12	0.1

Mica	1	0.5	35	0.1
Silica stone	1	0.5	45	0.1
Barite	1	0.5	86	0.3
Kaolin	2	0.9	111	0.4
Aluminum	2	0.9	169	0.6
Total	213	100.0%	30,093	100.0%

Source: Bureau of Education, Choson Government-General (ed.): Kojyo oyobi Kosan ni okeru Rodosha Jyokyo Chosa (*The Survey Report on the Factory and Mine Laborers*), 1833, p. 13, Seoul.

*Mines with permanent employment of 10 or more.

Table XVIII:
Owners and Employees of Mines With More Than 1,000 Workers

(As of the end of June 1931)

Mine (Owner)	No. of Workers
Chaeryeong Iron (Mitsubishi)	1,015

Pongsong Coal Mine (Omori)	1,127
P'yongyang Coal Mine (Navy)	1,599
Kyodong Gold Mine (Pang Ung-mo)	1, 113
Wonsan Gold Mine (Oriental Joint Mining Co.)	1,409

Source: Ibid, p. 12.

Table XIX:
No. of Mines by Employment

(As of the end of June 1931)

Employment	No. of Mines	Percentage	No. of Workers	Percentage
10–29	62	29.1%	1,117	3.7%
30–49	47	22.1	1,778	5.9
50–99	35	16.4	2,446	8.1
100–299	42	19.7	7,001	23.3
300–499	12	5.6	4,792	15.9
500–999	10	4.7	6,696	22.3

Employment	No. of Mines	Percentage	No. of Workers	Percentage
1,000 and over	5	2.4	6,263	20.8
Total	213	100.0%	30,093	100.0%

Source: Ibid, pp. 20–21.

Capitalists, the military, and government agencies controlled the mineral resources in Korea. By 1925, 29 mines with a capital of over 100,000 yen were present in Korea. Among them were nine gold and silver mines, seven iron mines, twelve coal mines, and one copper mine. Except for one Korean national gold mine, the military, government agencies, or prominent businessmen affiliated with the Japanese government controlled all other gold mines. All mining activities were in the hands of the Japanese. Japanese capital amounted to 94.8% of the total coal mining investment in 1945. The Japanese investment in other mining industries was even higher, at 96%. Thus, development occurred not with Korean but with Japanese capital. Japan referred to the growth of mining and industries as a Rapidly Developing Choson (RDC), but the Japanese, not Koreans, achieved it. Korea's industrial economy was constructed for Japanese goals, causing Koreans to suffer and sacrifice.

Despite challenging conditions, there was still some growth in native capital investment in Korea. Kim Song-su's Seoul Textile Company was established in 1919 with Korean capital, mainly by large landowners in Cholla Province. The company produced durable and heavy clothing that was popular among Koreans, especially in the northwest region of P'Yongan Province, with strong nationalist sentiments. The company also had a policy of only hiring Koreans, which it maintained throughout its history. Kim Song-su provided education with Korean content at his middle school and Bosung College (now Korea University). He was also one of the founders of the Tonga Ilbo newspaper in 1920 and remained a vital supporter of this nationalistic voice for Korean public opinion.[85]

An Hui-je's Paekan Trading Company was a well-known general trading company established in Pusan by landowners in Kyongsang province. It supported the Korean independence movement and was crucial in developing Korean education and the cooperative movement. The knitwear and rubber factories in P'yongyang were remarkable for Korean capital investment. The knitted factory flourished after 1920 and mainly produced Western-style socks and stockings. Although the owners were struggling small merchants at the beginning, they were able to build their factories through hard work and determination.

The rubber factories primarily manufactured rubber shoes and gained popularity when they created a style modeled after traditional Korean footwear. The owners of the knitwear and rubber factories were known for their honest business practices, hardworking nature, and entrepreneurial spirit, and they were also followers of Christianity. These industries grew into significant Korean business networks where the Japanese could not compete.[86]

During a time of desperation, Korean farmers initiated a Rural Revival Movement in 1933 to revitalize the rural economy and resist the chronic "spring poverty" and the burden of debt faced by farmers. The movement aimed to encourage the farmers to live a "rational life" and develop alternative income sources. However, it was challenging to achieve the desired result as the rural population struggled to make a living as tenants on small plots of land.

Japan also encouraged reforestation to protect Korea's forestry resources, but in reality, the amount of timber taken by Japan was more than the amount replaced by new planting. Japan promoted reforestation around the cities, but the large trees on remote mountain slopes were cut down. This trend became prominent after 1920. Japan also took measures to protect the Korean fishing industry. The illegal incorporation of Dokdo Island into Japan caused consideration, and Japanese fishermen were encouraged to migrate to Korea after the annexation. The Japanese fishing boats and equipment were far superior to the Koreans, resulting in a more significant share of the fishing industry for the Japanese, as shown in the following table.

Table XX:

The Fishing Industry by Nationality of Operator

Year	Korean Operators			Japanese Operators		
	Vessels No. of Crew	Value of Catch	(Yen)	Vessels No. of Crew	Value of Catch	(Yen)
1912	10,502	160,809	5,989,375	5,653	22,488	6,629,981
1913	18,570	114,160	5,055,051	12,059	49,646	6,001,232
1914	22,158	177,791	5,615,459	11,135	48,451	6,449,226
1915	30,187	261,213	6,365,669	11,995	54,772	6,869,272
1916	34,627	216,295	7,960,982	10,621	63,186	7,994,940
1917	45,892	247,139	9,760,592	11,897	70,184	11,152,700
1918	39,000	272,077	14,670,068	14,118	74,349	18,193,334

Source: Ki-baik Lee, op. cit., p. 320.

With the backing of the G-G, the Japanese companies exploited Korea's natural resources. The G-G was, by far, the largest Japanese entrepreneurial enterprise in Korea. It took control of railways, harbors, communications, and airports and monopolized products like ginseng, salt, tobacco, and opium, and the profits from these were enormous. The G-G and the Japanese businessmen almost monopolized Korea's natural resources and reaped enormous profits.

During the development of the mining and manufacturing sectors, the number of Korean wage laborers increased significantly yearly. In 1931, there were 106,781 factory workers and 35,895 mine laborers. However, in 1937, when hostilities between China and Japan erupted, the number of workers rose to 207,000 and 162,000, respectively. During the first year of the Pacific War (1942), the number dramatically increased to 520,000 factory workers and 224,000 mine laborers. By 1944, when the war was at its peak, there were 600,000 laborers in factories and 350,000 in mines. If workers in construction, transport, and other sectors of the economy were added, the total number of Korean wage laborers in 1944 would be over 2 million. It is worth mentioning that the wage-labor force constituted a significant portion of the total Korean population if the family members were taken together.

Table XXI:
Composition of Korean Wage-Labor Force by Industry

Industry	No. of Laborers	Percentage	Date of Report
Manufacturing	591,494	27.9	1945.1
Mining	346,424	16.3	1944.9

Industry	No. of Laborers	Percentage	Date of Report
Construction	437,752	20.6	1944
Forestry	205,911	9.7	1944.10
Marine Products	211,520	10.0	1944
Transportation	198,896	9.4	1944
Agriculture	130,377	6.1	1943
Total	2,122,374	100.0	

Source: Ki-baik Lee, p. 358.

These laborers in Korea were required to work long hours, with 47% of factory workers and 34% of mine workers working 12 hours or more a day. Despite such arduous labor, these workers were not rewarded with generous wages. For example, in 1929, Japanese adult male laborers in Korea were paid 2 yen and 32 sen per day, while Korean laborers received less than half of that, only one yen. Similarly, Japanese juvenile male laborers were paid 71 sen, whereas Koreans received only 44 sen. The pay gap was even wider for female workers, with Japanese adult women earning 1 yen 1 sen, and Korean women earning 59 sen only. Japanese juvenile female workers were paid 61 sen, while Korean girls earned just 32 sen per day. These meager wages made it difficult for Korean families to maintain a minimum standard of living, let alone provide education for their children.[87]

Table XXII:
Daily Wages of Factory Workers by Nationality in 1929

Koreans				Japanese			
Male		Female		Male		Female	
Adults	Juvenile	Adults	Juvenile	Adults	Juvenile	Adults	Juvenile
1.00 yen	0.44 yen	0.59 yen	0.32 yen	2.32 yen	0.71 yen	1.01 yen	0.61 yen

Source: Kojyo oyobi Kosan ni okeru Rodosha Jyokyo Chosa, p.88; see Ki-baik Lee, op. cit., p.359.

During this time in Korea, workers were plagued by poor working conditions that led to industrial diseases and accidents, making their lives miserable and uncomfortable. Despite the harsh conditions, jobs were difficult to find, and Koreans had to take whatever was offered, leading to high unemployment rates. Statistics from 1931 show that unemployment among Koreans was 15% compared to the rate of 6.7% in Japan during the same year. As a result, labor was a significant issue in Korean society at the time.

This chapter discussed how the Japanese government, traders, and landowners seized more land from Korean peasants, and Japanese investors started to invest in Korean farmland. The ODC took the lead in this land grabbing, and the G-G's agricultural policy increased rice production for Japan's benefit, leaving Korean farmers to starve for nearly half the year. The focus was on crop production, with little attention paid to livestock, fertilizer, and silk production. The Japanese landlords benefitted from the land survey, and the irrigation project left many Korean peasants destitute.

Japanese controlled larger companies in the manufacturing sector, making them the primary beneficiaries. Korean workers received less pay and had to work longer hours in unhygienic conditions, making it difficult for them to support their families and educate their children. However, through hard work and personal capital, some Korean entrepreneurs managed to build their own companies. These companies contributed to the Korean independence movement, the development of Korean education, and the Korean cooperative movement. The Japanese companies could not compete with the Korean rubber factories' traditional Korean rubber footwear, such as rubber shoes.

Japanese colonialism widened the gap between farmers and landlords. Many independent farmers became tenant-farmers. Manufacturing was necessary, and most industries were in North Korea. After the country was divided, both North and South Korea faced economic problems. The Japanese owned most industries and monopolized Korea's natural resources. Japanese workers received higher wages and worked fewer hours than Koreans.

CHAPTER 4:

Development of the Nationalist Movement

◆

The Choson Dynasty, the last feudalistic society in Korea, ended in 1910 due to the Japanese annexation. After the annexation, the land and financial situation of Korea deteriorated rapidly due to Japanese exploitation. Koreans engaged in vigorous resistance movements for the next decade to restore their independence. The resistance can be divided into two periods—the first from 1905–19 and the second from 1919–30.

During the first period of resistance, spontaneous outbursts of national feeling were guided by old traditional leaders; and the second period had organized movements of students and masses of the people, which were more effective as they were better organized and had more enduring resistance. Some of the resistance movements are discussed in Chapter 1.

The national resistance movements reflected the stratification of Korean society, the change in the structure of Japanese capitalism, and the unbalanced development of productive capacities in Japan and Korea. On the one hand, the change in international relations resulting from the uneven development of capitalist countries also played a role.[88]

Activities of Political and Social Organization

During the early 1900s in Korea, various political and social organizations were established to raise awareness amongst the city's educated population. Their goal was to find a solution to the political and social problems that Korea was facing, and they believed that the Korean people had the power to make a change. These organizations worked towards enlightening the people as a whole. The first such organization was the Korea Preservation Society (Poanhoe—KPS), which was founded in 1904 under the leadership of Song Su-man and others. Their objective was to oppose the Japanese attempt to seize Korea's uncultivated land by giving public lectures and issuing statements. Later, the KPS broadened its goals under the leadership of Yi Sang-sol but was eventually dissolved under Japanese pressure.

The political and national movement during this time was not only against Japanese aggression but also for internal political reform. One example is the Kongjinhoe, established in 1904 by former Independent Club (IC) members. It worked with the Society for the Study of Constitutional Government (SSCG). It advocated that both the monarch and the government should abide by the nation's laws and that the people should enjoy the rights guaranteed by the law. These organizations gave rise to spokesmen for the people.

Independent political organizations that operated publicly in Seoul were prohibited due to the Korean government and Japan's disapproval. As a result, several cultural and social organizations emerged to reclaim Korean sovereignty by promoting native industry and educating the masses. One of these organizations was the Korea Self-Strengthening Society, which succeeded the SSCG. Although R-G dissolved it, it was later reinstated as the Korea Association (KA) to continue the social and cultural programs.

An organization called the Association for Redemption of the National Debt (RND) was established to repay the large sums of money borrowed by the Korean government from Japan, which threatened Korea's independence. Sang-don and Kim Kwang-je came up with the idea that the people of Korea could collectively work towards repaying the nation's debt. Various media outlets, including the Korea Daily News (KDN), the Capital Gazette (CG), and the Independence, were collecting pledges to help pay off the debt. Ordinary citizens also participated in a no-smoking campaign, while women and girls sold hairpins and rings to raise funds. However, the editor of Taehan Maeil Sinbo (TMS) was falsely accused of corruption by the R-G and was arrested, which caused the momentum towards repaying the foreign debt to be lost and thwarted.

With public activity heavily restricted, Koreans began to form secret organizations. In 1907, press members, military personnel, and businessmen came together under An Ch'ang-ho, Yi Tong-hwi, Yi Kap, Yang Ki-t'ak, and Yi Sung-hun to form the New People's Association (NPA), which became a strong organization. The NPA openly promoted Korean industries, established a ceramic factory, and promoted education by opening schools and book stalls for public awareness. Additionally, the organization prepared armed operations to promote Korean independence. However, the One Hundred-Five Cases (OHFC) in 1911 brought the organization's work to a standstill as legal action was taken against its directors.

Development of the Korean Press

It was crucial for businessmen and intellectuals to publish newspapers to raise political and social awareness. The first newspaper, Hansong sunbo, was a government publication that informed the public of current events in Korea and abroad. Unfortunately, it was discontinued after only one year. The Independence, founded in 1896, was the first modern newspaper. It was initially published three times a week but later became a daily. The newspaper wrote only in Korean Hangul and provided unbiased news to the public. It also advocated preserving the nation's independence and expanding people's rights. The Independence was an outlet for the new intellectuals within the IC who had exposure to Western culture. The Capital Gazette (CG) was another IC organ that served as a medium of Confucian reform elements. However, it played a significant role in resisting Japanese aggression. In the same year, 1898, Imperial Post (IP) was founded. It was a vernacular newspaper aimed at readership from the middle and lower classes and women. Therefore, it focused more on social issues.

In 1905, after Japanese censorship led to a loss of freedom for newspapers in Korea, English journalist Ernest T. Bethell and

Yang Ki-t'ak founded the Korea Daily News. This newspaper could remain free of Japanese censorship as an Englishman controlled it, and England was an ally of Japan. The newspaper continued to criticize Japanese aggression and was written in Chinese-Korean script. Later, a pure Hangul edition was published to reach a broader public, and an English version was also added for foreign readers. However, Japanese authorities harassed Bethell and forced him to sever his connection with the newspaper. Despite this, the newspaper continued to publish as before, significantly contributing to raising political consciousness among the people.

After the annexation of Korea in 1910, the Korean press faced severe censorship. Even the Korea Daily News was converted into a mouthpiece for the government. It was renamed Daily News, and some Korean papers published abroad were banned. As a result, the people had no press to speak for them.

Population, Labor Force, and Education

During the Japanese annexation, the population count showed 13.3 million people in Korea, including 172,000 Japanese. By 1944, the population had increased by 95% to reach 25.9 million, with 780,000 foreigners, mostly Japanese. Unfortunately, the vital statistics are unreliable. However, Choe provides data on crude death rates between 18 and 22 per 1,000 and estimated crude birth rates between 42% and 48% per 1,000.[89] This data suggests high fertility and lower mortality, possibly due to early economic development.

Between 1925 and 1945, the mortality rate in both urban and rural areas of Korea decreased due to better social order, public health initiatives, and campaigns against tuberculosis and smallpox. In addition, a seaport quarantine was established to prevent the spread of infectious diseases, and larger families were rewarded. The fertility rate decreased because of restrictions on child marriage, more women entering the workforce, and improved medical care that reduced child mortality rates and extended adult life expectancy. As a result, the average life expectancy for men increased from 37.9 to 42 years and women from 37.2 to 44.8 years.

Colonization had a significant impact on the distribution of the Korean population. Many men were either forced or chose to move to Japan or Manchuria, resulting in a significant emigration of the population during the 1930s. By 1940, there were 1.2 million Koreans in Japan and 1.5 million in Manchuria. Additionally, there was internal migration from other areas of Korea to expand heavy industries in the north starting in the 1930s.

In Korea, Japan and China were the two primary contacts in human and economic activity, and other foreign residency was minimal. The 51,323 non-Japanese foreigners in 1927 included 50,056 Chinese, 743 Americans, and 228 Brits.[90] Western tourists occasionally visited Korea from Japan, but it was a luxury that only a few people could afford. As per historian Hochin Choi, there were 39,000 Korean residents living in Japan in 1920 until the massive labor exodus to Japan after 1931. The interaction between Japanese and Koreans was mainly limited to Korea. Both groups had different ways of thinking and living. However, due to geographical and cultural proximity, the Japanese had a much more visible presence in Korea than British imperialism in Egypt and

India. Nevertheless, the Japanese remained a small minority of the overall Korean population, comprising 1.28% (171,543) in 1910, 2.48% (501,867) in 1930, and 2.91% (707,337) in 1940.[91]

During the war, the Japanese entered the northern provinces of Hamgyong and P'Yongan and constituted 10% and 4.5%, respectively, of the total population in 1942. In Kyonggi and South Kyongsang (the sites of Seoul and Pusan), there was an area of Japanese concentration, which accounted for 40% of the population. The age of the Koreans and the Japanese in Korea was similar, with 40% of all Japanese and half of all Koreans under 19 years old. Adult Japanese were bureaucrats, soldiers of the two army divisions, sailors of the two naval bases, and police of the G-G. These Japanese brought railway lines to Korea to link with Manchuria, expanding them from 481 kilometers (km) in 1907 to 3,737 km 30 years later. Passenger and freight cars increased four times between 1906 and 1926. In late 1928, autobus service around the Seoul railway was introduced, and thrice-weekly air services between Japan, Korea, and Manchuria commenced in 1929, with airports at Seoul, P'yongyang, and Ulsan.

Railways and airplanes in Korea followed strict schedules, just like in Japan, where most of the Japanese population lived in urban areas. The Japanese were known for their adherence to precision standards, which later scholars greatly appreciated as it accumulated a vast and comprehensive record of the societies under their control. These standards provided a more reliable statistical basis to interpret Korea's recent history. On the other hand, the Koreans were mainly farmers who were less concerned with precise timing and were unfamiliar with the strictness of office and army life. They lived in a society with minor physical and social mobility. Due to their different cultural backgrounds, the Japanese ideology of imperialism was not readily accepted by the Koreans. The ideology of Japanese imperialism was weak, and the technological base was Western in origin. Japanese Shintoism was a parochial belief system to generate converts for Japan's "civilized mission." As a result, the authorities, as in Japanese-occupied China, interfered with the minutiae of Korean life and movements. For the first time, Korean farmers were governed by a central administrative system with the power to enforce compliance.

However, the Japanese lacked an understanding of Korean local conditions and even the language despite its basic grammatical similarities. In 1921, the G-G started to pay extra money to officials for showing proficiency in the Korean language by examination. However, only 5,000 successful candidates were recorded. Moreover, intermarriages were very low, at just 2.6 per thousand in 1940.[93] The Koreans had some freedom to conduct their affairs at lower levels due to a lack of understanding by the Japanese.

Given such migration levels, the "only possible conclusion is that the rate of natural increase of the Korean population of pre-war Korea was between two and two and a half percent per year."[94] This was considerably higher than the Japanese rate and was maintained despite an average life expectancy of only three-fourths that of the Japanese because the "family and reproductive patterns of the Korean peasant remained relatively untouched by... the diffusion of... element of Western culture."[95] During the colonial period, although there was an increase in urbanization and changes in labor force distribution, the growth in the rural population was much larger than in the urban population. In 1940, the population of cities with a minimum of 50,000 inhabitants rose to 11.6% of the total population, compared to 4.4% in 1925. Despite this, Korea remained a predominantly rural country at the end of the colonial period. Irene Taeuber, a demographic researcher, stated that the Japanese occupation had prevented the decline in fertility and mortality that typically accompany industrialization and urbanization. She concluded that "the possibility of a demographic crisis is ever-present."[96] However, due to the expanding trade, there were five cities in Korea with populations over 20,000 before the annexation. By 1907, two of the five cities were the present and ancient capitals (Seoul and Pyongyang), while the other three were international ports as shown in the following table.

Table I:
Major Urban Populations, 1907

	Total	Korean	Japanese	Chinese	Western
Seoul	218,225	199,325	16,843	2132	125
Pusan	39,743	23,478	16,040	197	28
Pyongyang	31,757	26,181	4,843	503	49
Inch'on	27,896	14,993	11,467	1,373	63
Kaesong	27,701	26,261	1,309	118	11

Source: Son Chongmok, "Kaehonggi ui tosi ingu kyumo," Hanguk'sa yon'gu, No. 39, December 1932, p. 139–43. See also S. Lone & G. McCormack, p. 37.

Labor force data collected during the colonial period was unclear and non-comparable due to confusion in industrial and occupational category.[97] The term "gainful workers" was used to categorize the entire population (workers and households) by occupation. However, the available estimates do not disclose the number of people employed by the industrial sector. Therefore, the available data is unreliable in describing the labor force structure. However, we know that the rural population increased by almost 10% during the 1930s, while agricultural production rose by 17% (rice 43%), and manufacturing output increased by 260%. This data could suggest an increase in the number of workers in the manufacturing sector.

In addition to information about changes in trade, agriculture, manufacturing, and the labor force that demonstrate the economic growth of Korea during its time as a Japanese colony, there is also data on prices, interest rates, government, education, prisons, and the conditions of laborers and farmers. This data provides insight into the quality of life that Koreans experienced during the colonial period. The data confirms that Koreans were oppressed politically, socially, and economically. The educational system and job distribution between Koreans and Japanese, both of which reflect the colonial situation, deserve particular attention for their adverse impact on Korea's economic future.[98]

In summary, an aspect of Japanese colonialism that had positive effects was the emphasis on the importance of time. The Japanese introduced strict schedules for railways and airplanes and encouraged urban living in Korea. Their work ethic was based on precision, which later scholars appreciated. They meticulously recorded information on the societies they controlled, providing a more accurate statistical base for interpreting Korean history, although some of the records may have been fabricated. In contrast, Koreans were mainly farmers who did not emphasize precise timing or have experience with strict office and army protocols. Their society also had limited physical and social mobility. Due to these differences, it was challenging for the two cultures to understand each other. Additionally, Japanese imperialism lacked a strong ideology and was based on Western technology. Japanese Shintoism was a narrow belief system used to recruit followers for Japan's "civilized mission."[99] During the period of Japanese occupation in Korea, the authorities interfered with the daily lives and movements of Koreans, similar to what happened in Japanese-occupied China. The Korean farmers were governed by a centralized administrative system with the authority to enforce compliance.

The Japanese officials lacked knowledge of Korean local conditions and language despite some grammatical similarities. To address this issue, the G-G introduced a policy to pay extra money to officials who demonstrated proficiency in the Korean language through an examination held in 1921. Only 5,000 candidates passed the test, and the number of intermarriages between Japanese and Koreans was low, with just 2.6 per thousand in 1940.[100] The lack of understanding allowed the Koreans some freedom to conduct their own affairs at lower levels. It also meant that in times of crisis, i.e., the outbreak of the war, the very ignorance of the authorities would bring about a problem for the Japanese to control the Koreans.

The Growing Passion for Education

According to Grajdanzev, the Government-General statistics indicate that the number of registered students in Korea increased from 11,000 in 1910 to over 1.2 million in 1937. However, only one out of three children attended primary school, and the percentage of Koreans in schools decreased as one moved up the educational hierarchy. Eventually, the Japanese outnumbered the Koreans at Keijo Imperial University, considered the "crown of the [educational] edifice."[101]

As discussed in Chapter 2, Japanese became the language used for education in Korea. Korean language lessons were abolished entirely towards the end of the colonial period. Primary and high schools were maintained separately for Korean and Japanese children. However, the expansion of education in Korea was mainly concentrated on primary and technical schools. The curriculum was designed in such a way as to produce loyal subjects for the Japanese empire rather than fostering the development of diverse talent needed for the future of the country. This system did not encourage the training of skilled personnel required to work in government agencies or private enterprises, which is essential for the country's progress.

Despite the challenges, Koreans have always been passionate about education. As early as 1886, the Korean government established a special institute to provide education on Western knowledge. In 1894, a new curriculum was introduced for foreign languages in government schools, including primary, middle, and regular schools. However, since the sons of high-ranking yangban mainly attended these schools to train future officers, they failed to meet the growing demands of education. As a result, numerous private schools were established to meet the educational needs of the younger generation. Many Korean patriots were actively involved in political movements committed to promoting education, thus indirectly laying the foundation for an independent Korea. This became even more important after Korea became a Japanese protectorate in 1905, and open political activities became almost impossible.[102]

During the late nineteenth and early twentieth centuries, various organizations established private schools in Korea. The first private school, the Wonsan Academy of Wonsan, was established in 1883 by the magistrate of the Togwon Council at the request of the Wonsan Traders Associations and other local residents. American missionary organizations also founded several private institutions during this time. One of the earliest women's schools, Ewha, was established in 1886 by US missionaries, and later, many other girls' schools were set up by the Koreans. These schools played an important role in liberating Korean women from their subservient position in the yangban society. By the time Korea ultimately came under Japanese colonial domination, around 3,000 private schools were established (some of the important schools are given in Table II).

Table II:
Private Schools of the Late Yi Period

Year	Name of School	Founder	Location
1883	Wonsan Academy	Chong Hyon-sok	Wonsan, Hamgyong
1886	Paejae Academy	U.S. Methodist (South)	Seoul
	Ewha Girls' School	"	Seoul
	Kyongsin School	U.S. Presbyterians (Northern)	Seoul
1890	Chongsin Girls' School	"	Seoul
1897	Sungsil School	"	P'yongyang, P'yongan
1898	Paehwa Girls' School	U.S. Methodists (South)	Seoul
1903	Sungui Girls' Schools	U.S. Presbyterians (Northern)	P'yongyang, P'yongan
1904	Hasudon Girls' School	U.S. Methodists (South)	Kaesong, Kyonggi

Year	Name of School	Founder	Location
	Young Men's Academy	Chou Tok-ki	Seoul
1905	Osong School	Yi Yong-ik	Seoul
	Yangjong School	Om Chu-ik	Seoul
	Hwimun School	Min Yong-hwi	Seoul
1906	Sinsong (Boys') and Posong Girls' School	U.S. Presbyterians (Northern)	Sonch'on, P'yongan
	Chinmyong Girls' School	Lady Om Poin School Association	Seoul
	Sungmyong Girls' School	Chin Hak-sin	Seoul
	Poin School		

Year	Name of School	Founder	Location
	Yanggyu (Girls) School	Sin Kyu-sik	Seoul
	Chungdong School	Yi Sang-sol	Seoul
	Sojon Lyceum		Seoul
			Kando, Manchuria
1907	Sinhung (Boys') and Kijon Girls' School	U.S. Presbyterians (Southern)	Chonju, Cholla
	Taesong School	An Ch'ang-ho	P'yongyang, P'yongan
	Osan School	Yi Sung-hun	Chongju, P'yongan

Year	Name of School	Founder	Location
	Osong School	North & West Educational Association	Seoul
	Pongmyong School	Yi Pong-nae	Seoul
1908	Kiho School	Kiho Educational Ass'n	Seoul
	Tongdok Girls' School	Yi Chae-guk	Seoul
	Taedong Technical School	Taedong School Association	Seoul
1909	Soui School	Chang Chi-yong	Seoul

Note: Schools listed without indication of sex of student educated boys only.

Source: Ki-baik Lee, op. cit., pp. 333–34.

During that time, private schools were open to the public and were not restricted to the yangban class. The students who attended these schools also came from non-yangban backgrounds. The curriculum included new Western learning and thought, history, geography, politics, law, arithmetic, and algebra. These schools became hotbeds of the nationalist movement, with debates, oratorical contests, and other activities that fueled the patriotic feelings of the students. Some students were already adults, and some higher-level classes even acted as teachers at lower-level schools. Although the conservative Koreans were unsure of these private schools, they flourished.

During the R-G period, a law required private schools to obtain government authorization and use approved textbooks. Consequently, many private schools were forced to shut down. The Japanese authorities only wanted to provide vocational education to the Koreans, with no provision for higher education that might produce criticism of the colonial administration. Japan's primary aim was to teach the Koreans to perform menial tasks for Japanese bureaucrats and technicians. The Korean students' primary education was centered on learning the Japanese language, which was essential for Japanese rule to prevail, and vocational education was viewed as a form of hard labor. Despite Japanese colonial rule, private schools remained vital to Korean education and served as a center for the Korean nationalist movement.[103]

Religious Movements

Christianity, and Protestantism in particular, had a strong influence on the political and educational activities of the Koreans. In 1884, an American Presbyterian Missionary (APM) arrived in Korea, followed by another Presbyterian and one U.S. Methodist Episcopal Missionary (USMEM) the following year. Other Protestant sects also arrived to carry out missionary work in Korea. To spread their faith, they engaged in medical work, made significant contributions to Korean society, promoted Western liberal thought, and helped awaken Korean national consciousness. Notable Korean Protestants such as Chae-p'il and Yi Sang-jae were central figures in this movement.

The Korean and missionary-run Protestant private schools played a significant role in shaping nationalist ideology. In particular, the Seoul Young Men's Christian Association (SYMCA), established in 1903, offered social and political programs that inspired the creation of similar youth organizations. These groups were not only engaged in politics and education but also worked to promote social causes, such as gender equality, strict monogamy, and the simplification of popular ceremonies. Additionally, they campaigned against unhealthy habits like smoking and drinking, as well as superstitious beliefs.[104]

Protestantism was widely embraced by the intellectual and business classes, indirectly contributing to the economic development of P'Yongan province. The religion was welcomed not only for its spiritual beliefs but also for its political, social, educational, and cultural activities. Many Koreans believed that adopting

Christianity would help to make up for the shortcomings of their society, which had led to the loss of Korean national identity.

There were other religious movements as well that aimed to instill a sense of national consciousness. One of these was Tonghak, which eventually merged with the pro-Japanese Ilchinhoe. Tonghak's third patriarch, Son Pyong-hui, led the movement into an active nationalist role under the new name Ch'ondogyo (Religion of the Heavenly Way). This movement included a comprehensive cultural program, including the publication of the nationalist newspaper Independence News (IN).

Another group, known as the followers of Confucianism, upheld conservative values and often opposed modernization. They believed the Japanese should withdraw from Korea and expressed their support for the RA. Additionally, they attempted to reform Confucianism to adapt to the changing circumstances. By participating in the activities of the IC, they became part of the new intellectual class. Within Buddhism, a reform movement called Taejonggyo emerged, which sought to revive the ancient belief in Tan'gun as the divine forefather of the Korean people. It was a conservative and religious movement that had strong nationalist ideals.[105] To counterbalance the influence of Christianity, the government provided official support for the study of Confucianism and Buddhism in Korea. The G-G established a Society for the Protection of Buddhism (Pulgo Onghohoe) under the guidance of Japanese officials and notable Koreans. The Korean Buddhists, who had suffered throughout the Yi Dynasty, cooperated with the G-G's policies and worked to rebuild their religion. The 1,371 existing Buddhist temples were reorganized into 30 districts, each under the leadership of an abbot appointed by the G-G. Buddhist priests went to Japan to study. Korean Buddhists published journals promoting Buddhism and supporting official policies, such as Choson Pulgyo Ch'ongbo (1917–21), edited by Yi Nunghwa, one of the greatest Buddhist scholars of his time.[106]

The Confucians, fearing the spread of Christianity, accepted funding from Japan. As a result, a Confucian institute called Meirin Gakuin was established within the traditional Songgyungwan. The institute offered a one-year course on the Confucian classics, Japanese language, and civics. Shintoism, a blend of animism and ancestor worship, was introduced, and a state shrine called Choson Jingu was opened in Seoul's Namsan (southern mountain) in October 1925. Over 100 smaller shrines called Ginshi were established by the end of 1925. However, controversy arose about whether Shintoism was a religion or a system of ancestor worship and civic ritual, which was unacceptable to many Korean Christians.[107] The Korean newspaper Dong-a Ilbo criticized Shintoism for being superstitious and hindering the moral development of Korean children. In 1935, the Japanese government ordered all schoolchildren to worship at shrines. However, Korean Christians and American missionaries, such as Dr. George McCune, strongly defended religious freedom. Some Koreans, like the Presbyterian Minister P'yongyang and Chu Kick-ol, even sacrificed their lives for their cause.

Despite the Japanese government's efforts to promote Shintoism, Christianity and Buddhism continued to grow in popularity. There were 1,657 Korean Buddhist temples (not under Japanese control) with 7,244 monks and nuns and 194,800 followers. The various churches, including the Japan Episcopal Church (JEC), had

479,000 members. Of these, 287,000 were Presbyterian, and 114,000 were Roman Catholic. In contrast, Shintoism only had 53 shrines or halls, with 613 priests and 21,000 Korean followers. Many of these followers were known as "rice bowl" believers, who only pretended to follow Shintoism to please their Japanese overlords.[108]

During the religious movement, various scholarly organizations emerged in provincial areas of Korea. Some of these organizations were the North and West Educational Association by Yi Kap, the Kyongsang Educational Association by Chang Chi-yon, the Cholla Educational Association by Yi Ch'ae, and the Association for Women's Education by Chin Rak-sin. Most of these organizations published journals, and many educational magazines were also printed, such as the monthly of the IC and the Korea Self-Strengthening Society Monthly. In addition, several commercial publishing companies, including Kwanghak Sop'o, Hoedong, and Sogwan, published books reflecting the new learning.

The grammar of Korea was standardized, which paved the way for studying the Korean language. Two societies, the Society for the Standardization of Korean Writing and the Society for the Standardization of the Korean Script, devoted themselves to studying spelling and writing problems in Hangul. In 1907, the Korean Language Institute was established under the Ministry of Education to standardize Korean language spelling and usage, following Chi Sog-yong's proposal. Sog-yong authored *A Korean Grammar* and *Phonology of Korean* and formed the Korean Language Society (KLS) with his disciples.[109]

The writings of Chang Chi-yon, Pak Un-sik, and others helped to instill a sense of pride and self-respect among the Korean people. Biographies of Ulchi Mundok, Kang Kam-ch'an, Ch'oe Yong, and Yi Un-sin were accounts of the lives of heroes who fought against foreign invaders. Efforts were made to discover old Korean texts and gain new insights into their value. Subsequently, a series of reprints of these texts were made available. Koreans were also interested in the history of other nations' nation-building, such as the creation of the Swiss nation, the history of American independence, the history of Italian independence, and the fall of Vietnam. Similarly, the Korean people eagerly read biographies of heroic world figures, such as George Washington, Emperor Peter the Great, and Joan of Arc.

During this time of nationalist ideals, new novels and songs emerged to inspire the people. These novels were written entirely in Hangul and advocated for the independence of a Korean nation. They urged new education and family values based on gender equality and the need to eliminate superstitions and build an enlightened society. These novels championed the values of the contemporary enlightenment movement. Yi In-jik was a pioneer among the new novelists, with works such as *Tears of Blood*, *Pheasant Mountain*, and *Value of a Demon*, while other novels like *Liberty Bell*, *Color of the Autumn Moon*, and *Proceedings of the Council of Birds and Beasts* appeared at the same time. These constituted the mainstream fiction writing in Korea until the March First Movement (MFM) in 1919.

New songs, sung to Western melodies, were also immensely popular, starting with Protestant hymns. Many ch'angga glorified love for the country, independence, new education, and culture, reflecting the era in which they were created. Students and independence fighters sang these songs to uplift their spirits, and many were infused with intense national feelings. Around this time, Western literature became accessible to Korea, with the Bible being the first work of Christian literature translated into Korean, followed by *Pilgrim's Progress*, *Aesop's Fables*, *Robinson Crusoe*, and *Gulliver's Travels*.[110]

The March First Movement (Sam-Il)

Many Korean nationalist activists fled to other countries for safety when Korea was under Japanese colonial rule, and the independence movement became impossible. They aimed to establish bases in neighboring territories that could serve as a launching pad for military operations to restore Korean independence. The freedom fighters who went to West or North Kando in Manchuria or the Russian Maritime Territory (RMT) mainly engaged in these activities. A base for armed operations was established in West Kando under the leadership of Yi Si-yong, Yi Sang-nyong, and others. In 1911, a Military School of the New Rising was opened to train the freedom fighters. Meanwhile, in the RMT, Yi Sang-sol and Yi Tong-hwi created the Government of the Korean Restoration Army (GKRA), organized a military force, and planned an armed struggle against Japan in 1914.

Many Koreans who sought independence from their colonizer, Japan, had different approaches. Some believed in using military force by training freedom fighters, which was in line with the tradition of the Korean resistance army. Many of these guerrilla fighters later joined the new forces in exile. Meanwhile, some Koreans advocated for diplomatic means to gain independence. One example is the Mutual Assistance Society (MAS), which Sin Kyu-sik established in Shanghai in 1912. The group formed ties with the Chinese Revolutionaries (CR) and maintained a good relationship with China. In Hawaii, Yi Sung-man founded the Korean National Association (KNA) in 1909 and conducted international activities from an American base.

Meanwhile, Pak Yong-man established a military school for Korean youth in the US, demonstrating his belief that a force of arms should back the diplomatic approach. After Japan annexed Korea, Koreans took every opportunity to present their case for independence before international gatherings. For instance, Korean independence activists in exile in China attended the International Socialist Congress (ISC) in Stockholm in 1917 to demand Korea's independence. Furthermore, Korean representatives attended the World Conference of Small Nations (WCSN) in New York in the same year to appeal to the international community to restore Korea's independence.

During a difficult time in Korea's history, nationalists maintained contact with patriotic individuals abroad to continue their struggle for independence. They formed various organizations, including the New People's Association (NPA), led by An Ch'ang-ho, who, along with a group of Korean Christians, followed the traditions of the IC. Living in America, An believed that education and economic development were essential to achieve Korean independence. However, many leaders were arrested and imprisoned in the Case of the One Hundred-Five (COHF) in 1911, leading to the dissolution of the NPA. Nonetheless, the organization's ideals continued and were upheld by its previous members.

During the Japanese colonial rule, various organizations, including the Association of Korean People led by Chang Il-hawn, a Christian group, carried out the patriotic enlightened movement. The ultimate goal of these organizations was to restore Korea's freedom by force of arms. Other organizations also emerged to carry on the tradition of the RA movement. Diplomatic patriots living in foreign countries, independence forces outside Korea, and the energetic work of clandestine organizations and educational bodies within Korea all contributed to the Korean people's will to oppose the Japanese and strengthen the resistance spirit. Widespread protests erupted throughout Korea due to harsh Japanese colonial rule. The nationalistic spirit had spread to all segments of Korean society, and tensions were mounting.

The Outbreak of the March First Movement (MFM)

The doctrine of self-determination of nations made the Korean nationalist movement a nationwide effort to regain Korea's independence. Woodrow Wilson, the American President, introduced the doctrine as part of the post-World War I peace settlement in response to independence movements among the national minorities of Europe. However, the Treaty of Versailles, dominated by the desire for revenge, made it impossible to realize the principle of self-determination. Only a few nations emerged as independent nations, such as Czechoslovakia, Yugoslavia, and Romania within the former Austro-Hungarian Empire, and

Poland, Finland, Estonia, Lithuania, and Latvia under Russian domination.

The Korean people received the principle of self-determination with great enthusiasm. In 1919, Korean patriots in Shanghai established the New Korea Youth Association (NKYA) and sent Kim Kyu-sik as a representative to the Paris conference to appeal for Korean independence. The association also dispatched representatives to various regions, including Korea, Japan, Manchuria, and Siberia, to explore ways for specific independence activities. In February 1919, Korean students in Tokyo formed the Korean Youth Independence Corps (KYIC), and about 600 students gathered at the Kanda YMCA Hall and issued a declaration demanding independence for their country. This declaration emboldened Koreans to openly bring the independence movement forward, leading to nationwide demonstrations within a month.

In Korea, various religious organizations such as Religion of the Heavenly Way (Ch'ondogyo), Christian organizations, Buddhist organizations, and others coordinated the new phase of the movement. The central figures were the thirty-three men who signed the Korean Declaration of Independence (DI) for the entire Korean people. Son Pyong-hui led Ch'ondogyo, Yi Sung-hun led the Christian groups, and Han Yong-un led the Buddhists. On March 1, 1919, those thirty-three representatives of the Korean people met at the T'aehwagwan restaurant, taking advantage of the scheduled date for the funeral rites of the former emperor, Gojong, which would bring people to Seoul from all over the country. They formally promulgated a Declaration of Independence (DI) and proclaimed Korea an independent nation. Students gathered in

Seoul's Pagoda Park to hear the declaration, and they marched peacefully in the streets in a procession, shouting 'Long Live Korean Independence' (Tongnip manse). This march marked the beginning of the March First Movement (MFM), the most significant movement of the Korean people in their entire history. The opening lines of the declaration, translated after the event, read as follows:

> We herewith proclaim the independence of Korea and liberty of the Korean people. We tell it to the world in witness of the equality of all nations, and we pass on to our posterity as our inherent right. We make this proclamation, having back of us 5,000 years of history and 20 million of a united loyal people. We take this step to insure to our children, for all time to come, personal liberty in accord with the awaking consciousness of the new era. This is the clear leading of God, the moving principle of the present age, the whole human race's just claim. It is something that cannot be stamped out, or stifled, or gagged, or suppressed by the means.[111]

The Korean Declaration of Independence expressed the fundamental principles of a people's right to national existence and the equality of all human beings. It did not encourage acts of revenge against Japan's colonial rule. The Korean people were determined to achieve self-determination without resorting to hostility towards others. All Koreans would willingly follow the Declaration's common consensus and the proper procedures in a peaceful and orderly manner for national honor and rectitude.

After the Declaration of Independence, the thirty-three signers immediately informed the Japanese authorities of their actions and were arrested. Their plan was for the independence movement to be led by students and then spread to the entire nation. The student demonstration on the streets, holding the Korean flag and shouting "Long live Korean independence" gave the movement an added fervor. Students, shopkeepers, farmers, laborers, and other citizens joined in, while Koreans employed by the G-G found ways of showing their sympathy. The demonstrations for independence gradually spread to the countryside until the chant of "Tongnip manse" could be heard nationwide. Men and women, old and young, people from every walk of life, all cried out for independence. These demonstrations were of such a vast scale that they surprised the Japanese. More than 2 million Koreans directly participated in over 1,500 separate gatherings in all but 7 of the country's 218 counties.[112] It then quickly spread to Manchuria, the RMT, and to other overseas areas.

Military forces violently suppressed peaceful demonstrations. Japan mobilized not only police forces but also the military and navy. The unarmed demonstrators were met with bullets, and the Japanese put fire to schools, churches, and private houses. The official reports of the Japanese recorded that 46,948 demonstrators were arrested, 7,509 killed, 15,961 injured, and 715 houses were destroyed or burned, along with 47 churches and 2 schools. However, the numbers in all these categories far exceeded those officially reported. In the village of Cheam-ni near Suwon, 29 people were pushed into a church, which was then set on fire to burn them alive. Japan was on the victorious Allied side in World War I, and its international position was strong.

Despite the brutal treatment of unarmed Koreans by the Japanese, the MFM failed to gain support from Western powers and ultimately did not achieve its purpose. Religious and educational organizations led the MFM, but it was not a strong and cohesive movement. Additionally, the independence movement overseas was carried out independently by various Korean activists in exile. Several provisional governments were established inside and outside Korea, including the Provisional Government of the Republic of Korea (PGRK), established in Shanghai in April 1919. The PGRK included already active overseas Koreans and others who had gone into exile after the MFM. Significantly, a democratic government was formed for the first time in Korean history, not to restore the old monarchy but as a republic that manifested in the MFM. This demonstrates that the Korean people had reached a new stage in their political consciousness.[113]

The PGRK, or the Provisional Government of the Republic of Korea, maintained contact with the Korean people through a liaison. Individuals in every province, county, and town received the responsibility of the liaison, which allowed participation from all parts of the country. The Korean public collected funds for the independence movement abroad and sent them through this mechanism. In May 1919, the PGRK dispatched Kim Kyu-sik as an envoy to the Paris Peace Conference (PPC) to plead for the cause of independence. In August 1919, a representative was sent to the International Socialist Party Congress (SPC) in Switzerland. The independence fighters in Manchuria and the RMT regrouped under a single banner with the General Headquarters of the Restoration Army (RA) in An-tung in Manchuria to continue the independence struggle through military means. The PGRK started a newspaper called Independence News, which made the circumstances of the independence movement known to people in Korea and the outside world, keeping the idea of freedom alive in people's minds.

The Korean Economy After the Annexation

Following the annexation of Korea by Japan in 1910, the Japanese took control of the Korean economy, including fertile land, mines, and critical infrastructure such as financial, transportation, and communication systems. This monopolistic control added to the already heavy burden on the Korean people. During the first ten years of Japanese imperialism, Korean tenant-farm households increased from 945,398 in 1915 to 1,003,003 in 1919. The number of independent farm households with tenant farming also increased drastically, from 833,711 in 1913 to 1,045,606 in 1919, an annual increase of 35,000. On the other hand, the number of independent farm households decreased from 586,471 in 1913 to 525,813 in 1919, showing a decline in middle-class farm households. In 1919, the Japanese and Korean landowners, who made up only 3 to 4% of the total farm households, owned more than half of the cultivated land.

Table III:
Number of Factories and Workers by Working Hours

(end of June 1931)

Working Hours	No. of Factories	Percentage	No. of Workers	Percentage
8 hrs. or less	11	0.9%	521	0.8%
8–9 hrs.	56	4.6	7,434	11.4
9–10 hrs.	102	8.5	5,504	8.4
10–11 hrs.	294	24.5	13,266	20.3
11–12 hrs.	234	19.5	7,785	11.9
12 hrs. and over	493	41.1	30,689	46.9
Inconsistent	9	0.9	175	0.3
Total	1,199	100%	65,374	100%

Source: Kojyo oyobi Kosan ni okeru Rodosha Jyokyo Chosa, p. 36.

Table IV:
Number of Mines and Workers by Working Hours

(end of June 1931)

Working Hours	No. of Mines	Percentage	No. of Workers	Percentage
8 hrs. and less	4	1.9%	623	2.1%
8 hrs. and over	21	9.9	5,050	16.8
9 hrs. and over	14	6.6	1,112	3.7
10 hrs. and over	45	21.1	7,325	24.3
11 hrs. and over	56	26.2	5,643	18.8
12 hrs. and over	73	34.3	10,340	34.3
Total	213	100%	30,093	100%

Source: Ibid, p. 40.

During the colonial era, Japanese real estate companies and landowners took advantage of farmers in Korea in several ways.

They charged high rents, shifted the tax burden to farmers, and made usurious loans. Tenant farmers were left to face starvation right after the harvest. In the industrial sector, there were 1,900 factories with 48,705 employees in Korea in 1919. The Japanese possessed most of these factories, and most were small-scale, employing less than 50 workers. These conditions were a direct result of the colonial economic policies implemented by the Japanese.[115]

Table V:
Average Daily Wage of Factory Workers

(In yen)

	Korean	**Japanese**
Male (adults)	0.85	1,87
Female (adults)	0.46	0.85
Male (child)	0.30	0.50
Female (child)	0.29	0.74

Source: Ibid, p. 84.

Table VI:
Average Daily Wage of Mine Workers

(end of June 1931) (In yen)

	Korean	Japanese
Male (adults)	0.54	1.64
Female (adults)	0.29	0.57
Male (child)	0.33	0.40
Female (child)	0.23	---

Source: Ibid, p. 87.

Tables II, III, IV, and V show that the Korean laborers' pay was about half of their counterparts, and their working hours were longer than the Japanese workers (17–18 hours per day).[116] During this time, the Japanese deliberately delayed industrial development in Korea. As a result, the Korean labor movement was not very active. However, as Japanese capital increased in Korea, Korean workers became aware of their position and expressed their dissatisfaction through a growing number of strikes. The following table illustrates a rising trend in the number of strikes and participants, indicating a growing awareness among workers.

Table VII:
The Number of Strikes

Year	No. of Strikes	No. of Participants (A)	No. of Participants (B)	BIA%
1915	9	1,951	828	42
1916	8	458	362	79
1917	8	1,148	1,128	98
1918	50	6,105	4,442	72
1919	84	9,011	8,283	92

Source: Bureau of Internal Affairs, Choson Government-General (ed.): Kaisha oyobi Kojyoni okeru Rodosha no Chosa (*The Survey Report on the Company and Factory Laborers*), 1923.

Japan also held a monopoly in commerce, while Koreans were mainly involved in small-scale retail trade. This stark division resulted in class disparities and widespread poverty. During this period, we observed that the Japanese oppressed the Koreans through a system of civil and military police rule. The Japanese, supported by the military police, resorted to armed repression, torture, and mass killings. Akaishi Genjiro served as the head of the Japanese Military Police and adopted brutal methods comparable to those of imperial Russia. Many patriotic leaders were arrested and unjustly killed while imprisoned on the false pretext of conspiring to assassinate Governor-General Terauchi.

The brutal colonial policies formed the basis of colonial exploitation. The Koreans reacted by organizing voluntary uprisings and waiting for the right time to rebel against the Japanese by closely monitoring the international situation. World War I aimed to redistribute international colonies. By the time Japan and China were drawn into the chaos of the war and the United States joined the conflict, around 1.5 billion people from 30 nations were involved. The war lasted for five years and resulted in the loss of nearly four million lives and $350 billion in property. In November 1918, a peace treaty was signed, and the world was captivated by President Wilson's 14 points, which emphasized the principle of self-determination.

When Yugoslavia, Czechoslovakia, and other countries were becoming independent, Korea was also looking for an opportunity to rise against Japan. Korean residents in the US, exiles in Shanghai, and Korean students in Tokyo mainly led the independence movement. However, the international situation was unfavorable as the victors of World War I were more interested in expanding their colonies than liberating suppressed nations. In this context, the Korean people were further dismayed by the death of "King Gojong" on 22 January 1919. He had been imprisoned by the Japanese authorities and was poisoned to death in a Japanese plot. This tragedy fueled national feelings against Japan, and on 8 February, the Korean Youth Independence Group in Tokyo led the uprising.

After King Gojong's death, Korean exiles connected and got closer together to achieve Korean independence. Those still in Korea also started preparing for the same reason. Yo Un-hyong and Kim Kyu-shik led the independence movement in Shanghai. In Tokyo, Choi Pak-yong and their followers formed the Korean Independence Group (KIG), demanding Korea's independence. In Siberia, Yi Tong-hwi, and the US, An Ch'ang-ho led the independence movement with added vigor. Religious leaders and leading figures in education in Korea laid the foundation for national independence, and students responded to their call, avoiding the Japanese police network.[117]

Following the declaration of the national funeral date for the late king, a massive crowd of hundreds of thousands flocked to Seoul, gathering in front of the king's palace. Marketplaces and schools shut down in response. Led by students, a multitude of people paraded through the streets, unfortunately encountering Japanese police gunfire, which claimed numerous lives. The movement also resonated with rural communities, sparking a widespread response. Despite its peaceful nature, the Sam-Il national movement faced the brutal suppression by Japanese police, resulting in the tragic massacre of many individuals. Japanese soldiers and civilians indiscriminately attacked ordinary Koreans, disregarding age, gender, and even whether they participated in the demonstrations or not. Regarding the social stratification of those arrested, farmers accounted for 56% of the total, students 21%, merchants 14%, and workers 9%.[118]

Therefore, as shown with the percentage above, farmers exhibited the most forceful resistance to Japanese aggression. They launched attacks on numerous police stations and other structures. In South

P'Yongan province, Japanese forces apprehended the Ch'ondogyo villagers of Mangsan, resorting to fatal shootings when confronted with any form of opposition. Elsewhere, farmers were forcibly taken to rural areas and restrained for imminent execution, only to be spared at the last moment, leaving them in a state of constant fear. Young women were unjustly arrested and subjected to public humiliation, being stripped in front of predominantly male audiences at police stations and enduring savage beatings of extreme cruelty.

In Hamhung, a Canadian missionary described (March 4) the Japanese fire brigade assaulting a crowd and noted: "On this same date, at least 7 Korean men and a number of girls were taken to the police station in a pitiful condition from the wounds received... So far as was seen, there was no resistance made by the Koreans; they neither lifted a stick nor hurled a stone to defend themselves nor did they utter a word of abuse against the Japanese."[119]

Western missionaries were not involved in organizing the demonstrations. However, the Japanese press found it hard to believe that the Koreans, who were often depicted as helpless, could organize themselves efficiently and demonstrate passionate commitment. Some journalists suggested that the Americans were involved, claiming that there was funding from the US and that Soviet-armed Korean guerrillas were present on the Manchurian border. Initially, the Western missionaries welcomed the Japanese annexation as a stabilizing force. However, in 1919, they were appalled by the Japanese brutality and began to publicize Japanese atrocities through the Western media. G-G Admiral Saito attempted to mend the relationship by praising the missionary contribution to Korea's enlightenment, but the conflict in aims between the Japanese and the missionaries remained unresolved.

The MFM (Sam-Il) uprising is considered a significant event in Korean nationalism. Historians from North and South Korea focus on the efforts of students, workers, women, and peasants on the streets rather than intellectual leadership. The Sam-Il uprising in the north marked the end of the bourgeois nationalist movement initiated by Kim Okkyun and his associates and the newly formed worker-peasant-led agitation against imperialism and feudalism. P'yongyang scholars gave more credit to the Bolshevik revolution than Wilson's liberalism for the development of Korean political consciousness, and younger historians in the south agreed with this view. Some historians consider the Sam-Il uprising a failure as Korea remained under Japanese rule, and activist youths in the 1920s advocated violent struggle as the only means to liberation.

Despite the failure of the Sam-Il uprising, it showed the world the Koreans' heroic determination. After the uprising, Japan had to abandon its past colonial policies. The "military police" system was replaced with a "civil police" system, and the military rule was transformed into a more civilized one, allowing some freedom of speech and press.

There is a debate about whether Japan had planned to reform Korea or was compelled to do so by the Sam-Il rising. Hara Kei, a party politician and opponent of military control in Japanese colonies, became the new prime minister after the rice riot in Japan in August 1918. The uprising certainly accelerated the change in Japanese policy towards Korea. In 1920, Admiral Saito implemented several changes, such as replacing the gendarmerie with regular police, Japanese teachers and officials abandoning the swords they used to wear as badges of superiority, and freedom for Koreans to publish vernacular newspapers and hold meetings. There would be more consultation with Koreans for reform, less discrimination between Korean and Japanese officials, and promotion of the Korean language among Japanese officials. The government would support industrial development such as rice production, expansion of sanitation, and communications. Education would be expanded and brought in line with the Japanese system while respecting Korean culture, including Korean burial systems and religious freedom.

The wedding of Korea's Crown Prince Yi and Japanese Princess Nashimoto in April 1920 marked the start of the new "cultural rule." On this occasion, several thousand political prisoners were released. Under Admiral Saito, there was an improvement in the salaries of the Korean officials. However, the bonus system given to the Japanese continued the salary disparity. Japan maintained control over economically important regions in Korea. However, compared to earlier periods, more Koreans were given positions in government services. By mid-1931, five out of the thirteen provincial governors were Koreans, and they filled 31 out of the 220 district magistracies. Additionally, on a cultural level, the Koreans enjoyed more freedom when the Hangul Study Society was established in 1921. Native newspapers like Dong-a Ilbo (1920)[120] founded by educator-industrialist, educationist Kim Song-su and others expanded the Hangul use and were permitted to question official policy.

During the colonial era, the administration in Korea was a combination of freedom and force. An ordinary police force replaced the gendarmerie, but their numbers increased rapidly from around 1920. A network of plain-clothes officers and informers supported them. The Japanese government feared that Korea's proximity to Siberia made it vulnerable to communism after recognizing the Soviet Union (Russia). Therefore, the police were given extensive powers to investigate and arrest. The Japanese intelligence was proficient in identifying communist activists who were attempting to infiltrate Manchuria or Siberia. The Japanese army heavily invested in wireless facilities across Korea's northern border to strengthen defense. In the 1920s, most Koreans were farmers, making up 83% of all Korean households. They remained the primary focus of colonial policies.

The Sam-Il Movement, while ultimately unsuccessful, served as a powerful demonstration of the Korean people's determination and bravery to the world. This event led to a demand for independence, political freedom, democracy, and social equality in Korea. However, due to a lack of strong leadership and organization, the movement lacked the necessary fighting spirit to succeed despite being a spontaneous mass movement.[121]

Following the Sam-Il Movement, the Japanese authorities shifted their oppressive policy towards assimilation. However, this policy only served as a temporary appeasement and did not bring about significant changes in practical oppression and colonial exploitation. The Japanese intensified their oppression and exploitation using more sophisticated and modern methods, leading to a decline in people's living standards and increased misery. These circumstances ultimately resulted in the Anti-Colonial Struggle of June 10, 1926.[122] Japan had historically viewed Korea as a primary source of agricultural resources. In 1912, the

G-G established special offices for soil improvement and an Agricultural Technology Bureau (ATB) in each province to improve animal husbandry, silk, cotton, and rice production. The agricultural research station in Suwon was the leading center for agricultural investigation in the south and focused on developing solutions for diseases affecting cotton, rice, and fruit. Japan's rapid urbanization, fueled by the economic boom of 1914–18 and the violent social unrest of the 1918 rice riots, led to a major campaign to increase Korean rice exports to the Japanese market. Starting in 1920, the G-G announced three long-term programs to boost rice production.[123]

There was an expansion in the transportation of grains to ports, and more accessible credit was given for rice polishing and rice wine. To cope with unpredictable rainfall, the number of irrigation projects was increased. However, this primarily benefited wealthier landlords at the expense of poorer farmers. The primary goal was to feed the Japanese market with a single crop, which was rice. However, it was different for their counterparts in Taiwan, where they had other crops like sugar cane, tea, and livestock, or in Japan, where income came from sericulture. Korean farmers heavily depended on rice cultivation, and the government intentionally kept their rural incomes lower than those in Taiwan. The number of owner-tenants in Taiwan increased in the 1920s. However, it was the opposite in Korea, leading to the decline of middle-class independent farmers and making the polarization of rural society more severe. The surplus of farmers resulted in worsening tenant relations and declining agricultural productivity.

The number of factory workers in the mining and industrial sector increased from 41,873 in 1919 to 73,345 in 1926.[124] During that same period, the number of miners increased to about 23,000. However, the Japanese forced them to work long hours in hard labor as mining and textile workers. They had to work more than 12 hours a day and receive only half or two-thirds of the pay of their Japanese counterparts. As a result, protest strikes by laborers, farmers, and students became widespread, which was an expression of an anti-imperialist movement. A group of students led this movement.[125]

Table VIII:
Number of Labor Disputes by Cause and Year

Year	Disputes	Participants*	Wage	Treatment	Others	Successful	Successful	Compromise	Solved
1926	81	5,646	44	6	31	27	24	30	---
1927	94	9,761	68	7	19	32	31	31	---
1928	119	7,212	49	23	47	33	39	47	---
1929	102	7,412	57	10	35	24	44	34	---
1930	160	17,192	89	26	45	41	63	56	---
1931	204	16,854	141	16	48	34	100	71	---
1932	152	14,170	99	14	39	30	69	53	---
1933	176	13,599	118	26	32	37	74	65	---

1934	199	12,941	134	16	49	57	86	56	---
1935	170	12,062	107	25	38	47	72	51	---
1936	138	8,100	86	13	39	34	32	51	21

*The participants were all Koreans.

Source: Suzuki Masafumi: Choson Keizai no Gendankai (*The Current Stage of Korean Economy*), 1938, Tokyo, p. 296; Choson Keizai Zuhyo, p. 303.

Table IX:
Number of Tenant-Contract Disputes

Year	No. of Tenant-Contract Disputes
1920	15
1921	27
1922	24
1923	176
1924	164
1925	204

Year	No. of Tenant-Contract Disputes
1926	198
1927	275
1928	1,590
1929	423
1930	726
1931	667
1932	300
1933	1,975
1934	7,544
1935	25,834

Source: Bureau of Agriculture and Forestry, Choson Government-General (ed.): Choson Kosaku Nenpo Dai I Shu (*The Korean Year Book on Tenancy*) September 1, 1937, p. 11, pp. 33–40.

According to data, labor conflicts and farmers' protests constantly increased after the Sam-Il Movement. Under effective leadership and increased social consciousness, the laborers gained strength. They became more organized and experienced, forming many labor-farmer organizations such as the Korean Labor Mutual Relief

Association (KLMRA) in 1920. In 1924, the League of Korean Laborers and Farmers (LKLF) was established after consolidating 182 existing groups. However, in 1927, it was divided into two separate entities, the Korean Labor League and the Korean Farmers League. Although these organizations were formed to achieve specific goals, they required more effective leadership. On the other hand, students reacted strongly against the Japanese policy of cultural assimilation and played an essential role in the resistance movements after the Sam-Il uprising.

Table X:
Causes of Tenants Disputes

During	Cancel of tenant right	Demand for low tenant rent	Others	Total
1927	219	13	43	275
1928	533	885	172	1,590
1929	330	51	42	423
Subtotal	1,082	949	257	2,288
Per-millage	473	416	111	1,000
1930	489	193	44	726
1931	281	225	161	667

1932	216	56	28	300
Subtotal	986	474	233	1,693
Per-millage	583	279	138	1,000

Source: *The Year Book on Tenancy in Korea*, 1937, Series 1.

Chapter 3 discussed how the agricultural conditions of the 1920s allowed rural Koreans to organize themselves. However, due to the lack of alternative industries, farmers were forced to pay landlords huge rents or provide additional services to retain their leases. Rents were kept high, making it impossible for tenants to become owner-tenants, with well over half or three-quarters of their crops going towards rent. Tenant families had plots of just over one hectare, while owner-tenants had an average of just over two hectares as their owned or rented plots. The rental system varied from region to region, with oral and long-term contracts being the norm in the north, and one-year written contracts in the south. In 1925, there were 610 landlord-tenant disputes, with about 885 in the south, none in North Hamgyong, and only four in South Hamgyong.[126] The disputes were related to the cancellation of tenant's rights rather than lower rent demands.

In the early 1920s, rural groups were established with different political leaders. One such group was the Sojagiri Sangjohoe, or TFMASA in Seoul, led by Song Pyong-jun. The TFMASA aimed to assist tenant farmers in resolving disputes. The farmer and tenant branches of the TFMASA were considered more radical. However, their activities were confined mainly to debates and public meetings. The tenant organization even threatened the established landholders, who were forced to organize self-defense. It is worth mentioning that some of these organizations did not follow democratic methods. According to the U.S. Consul-General, they were "two-fisted" fellows who believed in using strong-arm methods. Therefore, it might be more aptly called the "Militant Love Society."[127]

In 1924, disputes among tenant association leaders in South Cholla turned violent and eventually required police intervention. As a result, 344 leaders were arrested. The political activism among tenant-farmers was mainly led by young intellectuals who had recently returned from studying in Japan. However, over time, they realized their true ambitions were in journalism in the capital rather than slowly building rural organizations.

According to some historians, in 1927, the Japanese government contemplated purchasing land from wealthy landlords and distributing it among local tenants. In 1934, Ugaki implemented legal protection for tenants with a three-year contract under official farm management control to prevent exploitation. He had already launched a rural regeneration scheme in 1932, which had limited success in reducing peasant poverty. Korean school graduates were selected for one year of training as village advisors to guide household budgeting and farm management to help with this project.[128] Ugaki attempted diversification by producing cotton and wool and importing sheep from Australia and Canada.

During the 1930s, due to government policies and pressure from radical organizers, activist tenant leaders were forced to leave the south and move to the northeast, where landlord-tenant relations were better. The radical leaders of the RPU found local support in the Hamgyong area due to its proximity to communist influence across the border in Manchuria and Siberia and the protection offered by the mountainous terrain. The RPU was known for its militancy among peasant organizations and used political publications, theatre, night schools, and a semi-militaristic organization to challenge Japan's authority in a violent and revolutionary way. However, their influence was short-lived as Japanese repression increased after the Manchurian incident, resulting in the arrest of many members in 1932.[129]

The "October Revolution" in Russia greatly impacted laborers and farmers worldwide. In 1919 and 1920, the Communist International (CI) and the Communist Labor Union (CLU) were established, influencing labor movements in Europe and the US and nationalistic movements in Asia and other colonies. This development also affected the labor class in Korea, leading to the formation of the Koryo (Korean) Communist Party (KCP) in Shanghai in 1920, under the leadership of Yi Tong-hwi. Additionally, an anarchist movement emerged among Korean students in Tokyo, promoting absolute freedom for individuals, denying the legitimacy of any political authority, and adopting extreme terrorism. For example, Pak Yol attempted to assassinate the Japanese emperor in 1923. Marxist theoreticians concluded that Korean independence could only be achieved by overthrowing Japanese capitalism. Hence, they established the Choson Communist Party (CCP) in 1925, launching organized anti-Japanese struggles based on fostering labor unrest. The resistance movement of students and farmers mainly formed the national resistance movements. However, the left-wing movement in Korea was weakened due to the formation of numerous groups.

In Korea, democratic nationalists desired to establish their political organization. However, they faced resistance from Koreans who opposed any legal organization that would compromise with Japanese colonial rule. In 1927, nationalist and communist forces collaborated to create Singanhoe, a unified nationalist organization. The Japanese government, still pursuing its "enlightenment" policy, recognized Singanhoe as a legal organization with principles dedicated to promoting political-economic awareness, strengthening solidarity, and rejecting opportunism. The goal of Singanhoe was to actively participate in the Korean fight for independence by dismantling organizations that exploited Koreans (such as the ODC and the Japanese policy of encouraging Korean migration to Manchuria and Japan) and establishing an education system that served the needs of Koreans. This system would teach the national language, allow freedom to study Marxist-Leninist thought, and abolish laws that controlled Koreans.

Despite being under constant Japanese surveillance, Singanhoe established almost 100 branches throughout Korea with a membership of over 30,000. The resistance movements continued to gain momentum, fueled by overseas trends and an increasing national consciousness. In addition, the Kon-u-hoe, an organization composed of females, was formed to fight against Japanese imperialism. There were also centers of armed resistance outside Shanghai and Manchuria. Korean students in Japan played a leading role in the resistance movement and in raising awareness of national consciousness among the people.

Singanhoe supported the Kwangju demonstration in 1929 by organizing mass protest meetings. As a result, many of its members were arrested, and the organization was dissolved at the suggestion of its communist wing. The remaining members went underground.

Following the Sam-Il Movement in August 1920, some independent fighters blew up the Sinuiju Railway Station. In September 1921, Kim Ile-sang attacked the Governor's Office Building and later shot General Tanaka in March 1922. In January 1923, Kim Sang-ok hit the Seoul Chongno police station. In January 1926, Kim Chi-sob bombed the Niju Bridge of the Emperor's Palace in Japan. These incidents demonstrated the Korean people's determination to achieve independence. The armed resistance was mainly led by General Kim Chwa-chin, Ye Ch'ong-ch'on, Hong Pam-To, and others who were very influential in Manchuria. In Japan, the Kanto area was hit by an earthquake that killed many Korean residents.[131]

The Historical Significance of the Yuk-ship Movement

After the Sam-Il Movement, the people of Korea were awaiting another opportunity to rise against Japanese imperialism. On June 10, the date of the national funeral was announced, and many people came to Seoul. On May 28, a youth named Kim Hak-sun stabbed Governor-General Saito in the head when he was about to join a mourning group. As the king's body was carried along the main street, the mourning turned into a mass demonstration demanding independence. This movement was later called the Yuk-ship Movement.

The Yuk-ship Movement holds historical significance due to its improved organizational and managerial leadership. Following the Sam-Il Movement, subsequent movements were led predominantly by farmers, workers, and students. These resistance movements were largely spontaneous and lacked a clear direction. However, the Yuk-ship Movement was better organized and carried out by farmers, workers, and students who worked closely together toward a unified objective. Despite still lacking thorough consciousness, it was a significant movement after the Sam-Il Movement. The primary aim of Yuk-ship was to free Korea from colonial exploitation, which was a prerequisite for ridding Korea of its feudalistic vestiges. Land was considered the fundamental issue that needed resolution, as evidenced by the farmers' demand for "land for farmers."[132]

In this chapter, we discussed the resistance movement in Korea. It was led initially by traditional leaders and later by organized groups of students and citizens. The first social resistance organization was Poanhoe, founded in 1904 when Japan attempted to seize Korea's uncultivated land even before annexation. However, due to Korean pressure, Poanhoe had to be dissolved. Another organization, Kongjiho, was also formed in the same year. When these attempts failed, the same social organizations attempted to recover Korea's sovereignty through native industrial and educational development in 1906 to strengthen society. After annexation, the R-G dissolved this organization, but it reappeared in the form of social and cultural programs.

RNDO was formed to repay the large sum of money the Korean government borrowed from abroad, mostly from Japan. The idea was that all Koreans would unite in their efforts toward this goal. Women and girls even sold their hairpins and rings to contribute, but their enthusiasm waned due to Japan's pressure. Other organizations also existed but were crushed by arrests and legal cases against their leaders. A Korean newspaper, initially published monthly and later weekly, was established by conscientious businessmen and intellectuals. The paper aimed to encourage readership from the middle and lower classes and women to make them more aware of social problems. Even some foreigners attempted to start a newspaper but were forced to abandon it. After the annexation, the Korean Press faced numerous restrictions.

Korea had educational institutions established by the Korean government in 1886 to provide Western knowledge. In 1896, government schools had curriculums for foreign languages. However, those were training centers for officers and attended by the sons of the yangban class, failing to meet the growing demand for education among the people. Private schools were opened to meet the demand, which became the breeding ground for politics and led to the independence of Korea. The missionaries founded girls' schools in 1886, along with other schools, and were followed by the Koreans.

Christianity and the Protestants, in particular, influenced politics and education in Korea. Protestantism was welcomed by Korean intellectuals and businessmen, leading to economic development in some provinces. The religious movement also instilled national consciousness. Confucian leaders, though conservative, wanted to reform Confucianism to adapt to the changing conditions. A reform movement within Buddhism started and had strong nationalistic ideals. The G-G supported Buddhism and Confucian learning to counterbalance the religious movement. A state attempted to develop Shintoism, but it was unsuccessful. There was an effort to rediscover old Korean textbooks and standardize the Korean language and spelling. Old Korean texts were reprinted, and the history of the nation-building of other countries was a model for the Koreans, and they read biographies of heroic figures.

The Korean nationalists fled to Manchuria and RMT when Korea became a Japanese colony and started their movement for Korea's independence. While inside Korea, the nationalists had contracts with patriotic elements abroad. There were organizations to restore the country's freedom by force of arms. Widespread disturbances took place all over Korea. The March First Movement started with the peaceful Declaration of Independence. It was crushed ruthlessly by the Japanese military force, and many were killed, injured, and arrested, and homes, churches, and schools were demolished by fire. The movement failed to have the support of the Western powers and failed to achieve its goal.

The independent farmers became tenant-farmers and faced starvation. There were sporadic revolts by the farmers against the landlords. In the industrial sector, Korean workers had to work longer hours with low wages, and discontent was expressed in increasing strikes. Korea was waiting for the right time to revolt against Japan. Moreover, the opportunity came at the end of World War II in 1945.

It should be noted that the conditions of the farmers and the working class are again discussed in this chapter as they relate to the nationalist movement. Some tenant-farmers and labor organizations like LKLF, TFMASA, KPA-1925, KLMRA, and other organizations like KYIG-Tokyo 1919, KYIC, KIG-Shanghai, and some communist organizations—RPO, CLU, and CCP—emerged. With the support of the students and political leaders, they played an essential part in Korea's independence movement. Though some of them were discontinued, still with outside Korean organizations, PGRK Shanghai, the US, KNA-Hawaii, etc., and the students, army, and political leadership inside Korea, the farmers and workers fought against the Japanese and ultimately became successful in freeing Korea from Japanese colonialism.

CHAPTER 5:

The Economic Domination

(1932–1945)

During the Great Depression of the 1930s, Japan heavily depended on trade with underdeveloped countries in the Far East and Southeast Asia. This period marked the cessation of the lucrative gains for Japanese imperialism, as the depression resulted in a decline in the prices of its key exports such as raw silk, cotton, and yarn. The economic downturn also compelled the Japanese government to abandon the gold standard in 1931 due to the decrease in industrial output.

The decline in prices of agricultural products further exacerbated the situation, leading to a significant increase in the number of peasants abandoning their farms. Japan found itself on the brink of internal collapse and faced the looming threat of national bankruptcy during this challenging period.

Japan initiated its invasion of the Chinese mainland in 1937, preceded by the occupation of Manchuria in 1931. Subsequently, Japan entered World War II against the United States, Great Britain, and the Allies in 1941. This shift in Japanese colonial policy had a detrimental impact on the lives of Korean workers and peasants.

The demand for war materials and munitions during the war effort exacerbated the plight of these individuals. Already in a disadvantaged position, the workers and peasants experienced a further decline, transitioning from a state of poverty to complete bankruptcy and from being underprivileged to unprivileged.

The Increased Exploitation of the Korean Peasantry

The Depression had a significant impact on the economic landscape of Korea, as Korean farmers bore the brunt of sacrifices made for Japan to navigate through its economic crisis. This crisis resulted in a steep decline in the prices of agricultural products, particularly grain, leading to a reduction in the income of households across the board.

To illustrate, a rice bag (1/2 sŏk) that was valued at 11.04 yen in 1925 plummeted to a mere 4.63 yen by 1931. The peasants faced hardships due to the disparity between the prices of their products and manufactured goods. This gap, created by Japanese industrialists and fueled by their monopolistic approach, left the Korean peasants vulnerable. They lacked the means to shield their interests, while the industrialists could exercise market control; resisting significant price reductions, while the Korean agricultural community suffered.

The Koreans found themselves in a challenging situation where they had to purchase manufactured goods at elevated prices and sell rice at reduced prices. This imbalance arose as the wholesale prices of rice experienced a significant 55% decline, while the prices of manufactured goods increased by 38% in 1931. Adding to the burden, the Japanese authorities implemented the inspection of rice and grains in 1932, necessitating additional energy and time investments from the farmers.

Moreover, Korean farmers were compelled to sell cotton in specified areas to cater to the preferences of Japanese cotton capitalists. The Japanese silk manufacturers were granted the authority to implement a tenant system for acquiring cocoons, allowing them to engage in usury practices. Meanwhile, Japan faced a decrease in agricultural production, as farmers were conscripted to the war front—the number of productive farms decreased while the number of needy mouths to feed only continued to grow—further impacting the overall agricultural scenario.

Table I:
Average Acreage Per Farm Household

(In chŏngbo)

During	Rice Paddy	Dry Land	Total	Index
1918	0.58	1.05	1.63	100
1920	0.56	1.02	1.58	96

During	Rice Paddy	Dry Land	Total	Index
1922	0.56	1.02	1.58	96
1924	0.57	1.02	1.59	97
1926	0.57	1.01	1.58	96
1928	0.57	0.99	1.56	95
1930	0.56	0.96	1.52	93
1932	0.56	0.94	1.50	92
1934	0.55	0.92	1.47	90
1936	0.55	0.89	1.44	88

Source: Hisama Kenichi, Choson Nosei no Kadai (*The Problematic Issues for the Farm Policies in Korea*), 1943, Tokyo, p. 210.

As seen in Table I, the increasing amount of Japanese regulation led to a decrease in usable agricultural land for Korean households.

Japan faced a compelling need to acquire Korean rice forcibly at arbitrary prices to meet the heightened demand for the Japanese army at the war front. This approach, known as "the delivery system," was initially enforced in 1940. However, within two years, Japan resorted to more severe measures to exploit Korean farmers. A comprehensive list of over 40 agricultural products, including grain, cotton, linen, vegetables, pine resin, and rosin oil, was established for this purpose; this list allowed for these other crops to face the same arbitrary and unfair prices as rice.

Armed forces were deployed to enforce the delivery on Korean farmers, with the delivery quota typically set at 70% of the total crops. In response, Korean farmers actively resisted Japanese quota collections and atrocities in various ways. They engaged in acts of sabotage, such as disrupting tillage, hiding crops, deserting farmland, burning collection points, and even assaulting or beating officials in charge. The impact and motivational causes of these actions is evident in the sharp decrease in farm production, as farmers were unwilling to increase yields during the five years of the system. The subsequent tables illustrate the decline in the average number of farm households and the reduction in the number of large landowners.

Table II:
Number of Independent and Tenant Farmers

(In thousands)

During	Independent Households	Independent and Tenant Households	Tenant Households	Fire-fields Households	Employed Households	Total Households
1914	569.5	1,056	911.3	----	----	2,592.2
	22.0%	41.1%	35.1%			100

During	Independent Households	Independent and Tenant Households	Tenant Households	Fire-fields Households	Employed Households	Total Households
1929	507.4	885.6	1,284	34.2	----	2,813.2
	18.0%	31.5%	45.6%	1.2%		100
1937	549.6	737.8	1,581.4	72.9	117.0	3,058.8
	18.0%	25.1%	51.7%	2.4%	3.8%	100
1938	552.4	729.3	1,583.4	71.2	116.0	3,052.4
	18.1%	23.9%	51.9%	2.3%	3.8%	100
1939	539.6	719.2	1,583.4	69.3	111.6	3,023.1
	17.9%	23.7%	52.4%	2.3%	3.7%	100
1940	550.9	711.4	1,616.7	66.0	101.6	3,046
	18.0%	23.3%	51.3%	2.2%	3.3	100

Source: Toyo-Keizai-Sinposha (ed.): Choson Sangyo Nenpo (*The Industrial Annual Book of Korea*), 1943, Tokyo, p. 57.

Table III:
Landownership by Nationality

(As of the end of 1937)

	Less than 5 danbo	5 danbo to 1 chŏngbo	1 to 3 chŏngbo	3 to 5	5 to 10	10 to 50	50 to 100	100 & over	Total	Land
Korea	1,905,635	722,253	711,373	191,666	107,162	43,632	1,891	476	3,684,118	4,011,974
Japan	49,340	14,608	20,296	7,623	6,457	6,412	782	596	106,114	423,125
Other Foreign	884	166	220	82	69	95	8	3	1,527	3,146
Total	1,955,859	737,027	31,889	199,311	13,718	50,139	2681	1,075	3,791,759	4,438,244

(In percentage)

Koreans	97.4	98.0	97.2	96.1	94.2	87.0	70.5	44.3	97.2	90.4
Japanese	2.5	2.0	2.8	3.8	5.7	12.8	29.2	55.4	2.8	9.5
Other Foreigners	0.1	0	0	0.1	0.1	0.2	0.3	0.3	0	0.1
Total	100.0	100.0	100.0	100.0	100.0	100.0	100.0	100.0	100.0	100.0

Source: Himeno Mineru, Choson Keizai Zuhyo, p. 320.

Table IV:
Number of Big Landowners

(In chŏngbo)

		1921	1927
More than 200	Korean	66	44
	Japanese	169	192
More than 160	Korean	94	80
	Japanese	108	122
More than 100	Korean	266	210
	Japanese	213	239
Total	Korean	426	334
	Japanese	487	553

Source: Hosokawa Karoku Shokuminshi (The Colonial History) Gendai Nippon Bummeishi (*The Modern History of Japanese Civilization, Vol. 10*), 1941, Tokyo, p. 340.

The Korean farmers experienced extremely challenging times, commonly referred to as "spring poverty." During these years, farmers were restricted to consuming grain only during the winter, enduring prolonged spring seasons marked by hunger, which was a recurring phenomenon. The table below presents the official statistics detailing the number of food-deprived Korean farm households in 1930.

Table V:
The Number of Farm Households in "Ch'ung'ung" (Spring Poverty)

(In thousand households)

Area	Independent ¾ Households	Partial Owner ¾ Households	Tenant ¾ Households	Total ¾ Households
S. Korea	5022.4	22040.0	62172.8%	89155.5
N. Korea	4214.5	10332.8	21661.3	36136.0
Total	9218.4	32337.5	83768.1	1,25248.3

Source: Bureau of Agriculture and Forestry, Choson Government-General (ed.), Choson ni okem Kosako nikansuru Sanko Jiko Tekiyo (*Reference Materials for Tenancy in Korea*), 1932.

The data reveals that nearly half of Korean farmers faced a lack of grain, with approximately two-thirds of tenant farmers hovering on the brink of starvation. The extent of poverty is further depicted in the subsequent table.

Table VI:
Average Main Grain Consumption by a Person

(In sŏk)

Average in 5 Years	Rice	Millet	Soybeans	Barley	Wheat
1912–1916	0.7188	0.2711	0.1825	0.4233	0.1119
1917–1921	0.6860	0.3231	0.1831	0.4394	0.1098
1922–1926	0.5871	0.3642	0.1772	0.4088	0.1280
1927–1931	0.4964	0.3564	0.1563	0.3876	0.1145
1932–1936	0.4010	0.2885	0.1486	0.4434	0.1063
1937	0.5679	0.2671	01525	0.4036	0.0840

Source: Choson Keizai Zuhyo, p. 207.

As seen in Table VI, as the years passed, there is a clear decrease in the average grain consumption, showing the increasing poverty.

Table VII:
Imports and Consumption of Chinese Millet

(In sŏk)

Consumption Per Person

During	Imported Millet	Millet	Rice	Combined
1912	15,000	0.245	0.774	1.957
1917	205,000	0.317	0.680	2.021
1923	1,270,000	0.366	0.603	1.916
1930	1,717,000	0.354	0.450	1.694
1932	1,584,000	0.303	0.411	1.607
1933	1,046,000	0.318	0.411	1.627

Source: Hosokawa Karuka, Shyokuminishi, p. 284.

These findings underscore the dependence of Korean farmers on imported cereals, considering that the per capita consumption of rice was declining despite the country producing an ample supply of rice. The impact of modern capitalism did not bring significant benefits to Korean farmers, as semi-feudal lords, landowners, and moneylenders exploited their situation.

Moneylenders played a central role in this exploitation, collecting farm products from farmers and selling them to Japanese capitalists at a profit. Additionally, moneylenders derived profits from the sale of inflated farming tools and daily necessities, further exacerbating the economic challenges faced by Korean farmers.

Table VIII:
Comparison of Domestic Expenses of Korean and Japanese Farm Households

(In yen)

	Korean Amount	**Japanese Amount**
Essential:		
Housing	10,142.3	20,353.7
Food	268,560.7	2,328,342.4
Clothing	26,376.0	42,977.8
Light and heat	39,028.8	33,206.1
Furniture	5,071.1	14,392.6
Subtotal	3,491,578.9	3,437,462.6
Secondary:		
Mental Training	260.1	6,541.2

	Korean Amount	Japanese Amount
Education	15,013.4	8,761.6
Social Relations	23,265.3	46,868.5
Hobby	8,531.9	27,235.0
Recreation	880.2	3,780.7
Sanitation	6,241.4	31,265.7
Marriage/funeral, etc.	23,115.2	35,496.5
Others	16,223.6	45,398.2
Subtotal	93,512.1	2,053,137.4
Grand Total Per Person	44,866,100,068.20	54,905,100,086.05

Source: Hisama Kenichi, Choson Nosei no Kadai (*The Problematic Issues for the Farm Policies in Korea*), 1943, Tokyo, p. 426.

Table VIII shows the disparity in the expenses able to be afforded by the Japanese compared to the Koreans. The amount spent on essentials was basically the same, though a doubling is seen in the Japanese spending on personal luxury expenses.

A startling comparison emerges when examining a Korean farmer who owned 2.5 chŏngbo in 1931 with a Japanese counterpart owning 1.2 chŏngbo. This insight is drawn from the "Survey of

Korean Farm Households" (1930-32) conducted by Choson Nakai (The Choson Agricultural Association) in collaboration with the Ministry of Agriculture and Forestry (MAF) in Japan.

According to the survey, the Korean farmer invested one-third more than the Japanese farmer but generated less than half of the latter's income. This substantial disparity resulted in a deficit for the Korean farmer that was five times greater than that of the Japanese farmer.[134]

Table IX:
Comparative Average Income of Farm Household in Korea and Japan

(In yen)

Classification	Korea	Japan
Total Income	778.36	913.41
Farm Products	707.60	751.57
Subsidiary and home works	70.76	38.41/123.43
Total Expenditure	349.92	373.99
Farm Management	334.22	360.03
Subsidiary works	55.06	109.47

Classification	Korea	Japan
Net Income	428.44	539.42
Farm products	373.38	391.54
Subsidiary and home	-	38.41
Works	55.06	109.47
Domestic Expenses	473.25	549.05
Balance	-44.81	-9.63

Source: Ibid, p. 436.

Table X:

The Amount of Farmers' Debt by Region and Household

(In yen)

Region	Partial Owner		Tenant-Farmers	
	Household surveyed	Average for Indebted Household	Household Surveyed	Average Indebted Household

Southern Korea	124	195	78	111
Central Korea	136	251	72	119
Northern Korea	85	193	60	118
National	115	213	70	116

Source: Choson Government-General (ed.) *Naka Keizai no Gaikyo to sono Hensen* (*The Present Status and Historical Changes of the Farm Household Economy in Korea*), 1940.

Table XI:
Percentage of Farmers' Debt by Interest Rate

Interest Rate Per Month	Partial Owner	Tenant-Farmer
Less than 1%	61.8%	56.3%
2	22.5	20.1
3	8.1	13.4
4	3.9	5.2
Over 4	3.7	5.0

Source: Ibid.

The tables presented above illustrate the impoverishment and dire economic straits of Korean farmers; many had to resort to borrowing money at higher rates just for the sake of survival. Partial owners, on average, carried a debt of 115 yen, while tenant-farmers held a debt of 70 yen. The debt rate hovered around 12 to 50% per year, and in addition to this financial burden, they were obligated to pay other taxes.

This economic strain led to a significant exodus from villages, with individuals either becoming mine workers or relocating to Manchuria and Japan. The large number of Koreans moving is shown in the tables below. During this time hundreds and thousands of Koreans were moving; this movement was substantial, considering that the population of Korea was only 22 million in 1936. As discussed in Chapter Three, a previous wave of Korean migration to Manchuria, Mongolia, Siberia, and Japan occurred from 1920 to 1925 due to land-survey-related opportunity reasons. Now, a new wave of migration emerged in Korea, driven by factors such as debt and other economic/social hardships.

Table XII:
Increase in Korean Residents in Japan

Year	No. of Koreans
1931	310,000
1934	530,000

Year	No. of Koreans
1937	730,000

Source: Choson Keizai Zuhyo, p. 53.

Table XIII:
Increase in Korean Residents in Manchuria

Year	No. of Koreans
1931	630,982
1932	672,649
1933	673,794
1934	719,988
1935	807,506
1936	876,692

Source: Ibid, p. 58.

Table XIV:
Korean Residents in Foreign Countries

(As of October 1, 1937)

Manchuria	777,749
Republic of China	11,480
Hawaii	6,501
Other Countries	5,569
Total	801,299

Source: Ibid, p. 57.

As previously detailed, after leaving the villages some individuals resorted to burning areas for farming, while others chose to become farm laborers. The number of those who chose to burn land to farm amounted to 52,445, constituting 1.7% of the total, and those who partially burned land numbered 195,511.[136] Additionally, the count of individual farm households increased to 130,377, 4.3% of the total, with more than one-third residing in Chola-do.

It's noteworthy that Korean migration out of the country predates the Japanese presence. During the Gojong administration, a consumer economy developed in the southern provinces, leading to increased peasant distress. However, Gojong provided no central guidance and focused on augmenting his private treasury through the unrestricted sale of rail, mining, and other concessions to the highest bidders. With little protection from the king (now emperor since 1895), some Koreans simply opted to leave the country, while others sought refuge in Western religion, particularly Protestantism.

Between 1895 and 1905, missionary activity played a significant role in increasing the number of Protestant converts from 528 to over 12,500. Under missionary influence, the first migrants to the United States departed for plantation work in Hawaii in early 1903.[138]

The Development of Mining and Manufacturing Industries and the Living Standard of the Working-Class Population

Following the outbreak of the Sino-Japanese War (S-JW) in 1937, Japan intensified mining activities in Korea to fulfill the demands of the war. Notably, Japan focused its efforts on specific mineral resources, prioritizing gold, silver, and smokeless coal. Gold and silver were sought after for monetary purposes, particularly for meeting Japan's foreign obligations in Europe and America. Smokeless coal was sought after because it served as an essential fuel for the Japanese navy.[139]

The exploration of mineral resources in Korea wasn't limited to military and government agencies; significant participation also came from successful capitalists in Japan. By 1925, there were a total of 29 mines in Korea, each with a net capital value exceeding 100,000 yen. With the exception of one gold mine that was Korean-owned, the rest were operated by the military, government agencies, or prominent Japanese businessmen associated with the Japanese government.

As early as 1920, the G-G altered the business regulation laws in Korea. Under the new regulations, the establishment of a company no longer required permission or a permit; instead, it only needed to be registered. However, this change was not intended to encourage capital investment by Koreans; rather, it aimed to foster a lucrative market in Korea for Japanese capital investment. Japan, with its economic prosperity, sought to supply the Allied nations and also sell finished Japanese goods in the Korean market.

The cost of employing cheap Korean laborers was notably lower than that of Japanese workers, being less than half, creating favorable conditions for Japanese investors. This economic advantage, coupled with the potential for abundant and affordable hydroelectric power, served as a significant attraction for Japanese investment in Korea.

In response to this opportunity, in 1926, the Choson Hydroelectric Power Company (CHPC) was established with the aim of developing the Pujon River plant in Hamgyong province. Additionally, the Choson Nitrogenous Fertilizer Company (CNFC) was founded in Hungnam for the benefit of Japan. This company played a pivotal role in developing nitrogen fertilizers, a technological advancement that had not yet been introduced in Japan at that time.

The substantial Japanese capital investment in Korea gained momentum with the outbreak of the Manchurian incident and the establishment of a Japanese puppet state, Manchukuo, with complete Japanese control over Manchuria. As Japan transformed it into a so-called national defensive state, there was a pressing need to develop Korea to support the Japanese munitions industry. Consequently, major Japanese Zaibatsu conglomerates competed to build factories in Korea, resulting in a rapid growth in the proportion of manufacturing industries within Korea's industrial market.

Between 1925 and 1939, there was a notable shift in Korea's economic landscape. In 1925, manufacturing industries constituted 17.7% of Korea's gross commodity product, a figure that increased to 22.7% in 1931, 31.3% in 1936, and further rose to 39% in 1939. Conversely, agricultural productions, which accounted for 72.7% of the total commodity product in 1925, witnessed a decline to 63.1% in 1931, 51.8% in 1936, and 42% in 1939.

When the 6% mining output is added to the 39% figure for manufacturing industries in 1939, the combined output of mining and manufacturing surpassed that of agriculture, marking a transition in Korea's economic structure. Some Korean areas, particularly Hamgyong province, became focal points for the concentration of new industrial plants, strategically serving as a new avenue for Japanese access to Manchuria.

Within the realm of manufacturing industries, the chemical industry played a significant role, accounting for 34% of the total output. When including contributions from the metal industry (9%) and machine-tool trades (4%), the manufacturing industry's overall share reached 47% in 1939. This distribution highlights the singular emphasis in Japan's development plans, underscoring the heavy focus on establishing a munitions industry in Korea. The development endeavors were not oriented towards benefiting the Korean people; instead, they were strategically aligned with Japan's war effort.

This approach allowed Japan to position Korea as a crucial supply base for its aggression against China. Leveraging the ideal location and abundant manpower in Korea, Japan implemented plans for mining and development, specifically tailored to support its wartime endeavors.

Table XV:
Mineral Products in Amount

(In thousand yen)

Year	Gold	Iron	Coal	Copper	Tungsten	Graphite	Others	Total
1911	5,076	165	539	---	---	169	238	6,185
1916	8,909	386	819	309	279	395	2,981	14,078
1921	3,938	6,546	3,192	18	---	209	1,634	15,537
1926	8,968	8,079	4,993	539	---·--	354	1,206	24,130
1931	10,137	5,413	5,190	260	7	232	502	21,741

Year	Gold	Iron	Coal	Copper	Tungsten	Graphite	Others	Total
1933	31,301	6,893	7,205	954	117	466	1,880	48,301
1935	51,911	15,376	11,925	1,546	1,389	1,208	4,684	88,039
1936	68,727	15,829	13,301	3,331	2,294	1,011	5,936	110,429

Source: Ibid, p. 254.

Japanese mining efforts in Korea were primarily focused on the exploration of mineral resources. The mining output in 1936 amounted to 24,654,000 yen, and this figure escalated significantly to 445,422,000 yen by 1942.[141] Gold played a substantial role, constituting 6,207,000 yen or 25% of the output in 1937.[142] The peak was reached in 1939, with 25,579 tons of gold mined, translating to nearly 99,175,000 yen.[143]

However, as the war progressed, coal, iron, tungsten, graphite, magnesium, and molybdenum became more crucial than gold. Korea emerged as the sole source for these minerals that Japan needed for its wartime endeavors.

The Koreans themselves didn't invest that much. Korean investment in coal was relatively modest, amounting to only 54 million yen, or less than 5%. In contrast, the Japanese invested a substantial 634,614,000 yen in coal. This stark difference in investment results in the fact that 94% of the total investment of 669,102,000 yen came from the Japanese, while Koreans contributed only 6%.[144]

Table XVI:
Tonnage and Price of Principal Mineral Products

Minerals	1930		1940		1944	
	Tonnage	Price (in 1000 yen)	Tonnage	Price (in 1000 yen)	Tonnage	Price (in 1000 yen)
Iron	532,497	2,808	1,185,426	7,015	3,331,814	41,147
Coal (soft)	405,661	2,503	2,587,766	30,128	2,518,513	30,776
Coal (smokeless)	478,477	2,824	3,153,175	32,669	4,530,263	53,014
Tungsten	11	6	4,218	24,166	8)33	44,514
Graphite	20,073	432	94,581	5,628	103,306	9,396
Magnetite	---	----	73,540	362	157,745	2,279
Molybdenum	28	28	195	1,745	760	6,494

Source: The Bank of Korea; Choson Kyongje Yonbo (*The Annual Report of the Korean Economy*), 1948, Seoul.

Table XVII:
Percentage of Principal Industries

(In thousand yen)

During	Agriculture	Manufacturing	Mining	Forestry	Fishery	Total
1911	330,369	43,528	6,182	19,795	9,417	409,294
1921	957,138	200,535	15,537	56,905	71,369	1,302,484
1930	724,227	280,963	24,654	63,360	82,882	1,176,086
1936	1,203,911	728,693	110,439	118,065	164,003	2,325,101

Production of Principal Industries By %

1911	80.8	10.6	1.5	4.8	2.3	100.0
1921	73.6	15.4	1.2	4.3	5.5	100.0
1930	61.6	23.9	2.1	5.4	7.0	100.0
1936	51.7	31.3	4.8	5.1	7.1	100.0

Source: Choson Keizai Zuhyo, p. 145.

Table XVIII:
Mining Production by Nationality

(In thousand yen)

Year	Korean	Japanese	Others	Total
1911	296	1,401	4,488	6,185
1916	1,042	3,623	9,413	14,078
1921	75	11,341	4,121	15,537
1926	3,752	17,219	3,159	24,130
1931	2,343	19,934	2,732	25,009
1933	7,809	35,935	4,557	48,301
1935	11,438	68,892	5,249	85,579
1936	9,871	84,353	6,399	100,623

Percentage

1911	4.8	22.7	72.5	100.0
1916	7.4	25.7	66.9	100.0

1921	0.5	73.0	26.5	100.0
1926	15.5	71.4	13.1	100.0
1931	9.4	79.6	11.0	100.0
1933	16.2	74.4	9.4	100.0
1935	13.4	80.5	6.1	100.0
1936	9.8	83.8	6.4	100.0

Source: Ibid, p. 325.

The major Japanese Zaibatsu that poured substantial amounts of capital into Korea included:

Table XIX:
Name of Firms (Zaibatsu) Paid-in Capital Date of Establishment

(In thousand yen)

Choson Brewery Co., Ltd. (Mitsui)	6,000	August 1933
Choson Onoda Cement Mfg. Co. (Mitsui)	500	October 1934

Hokusen Paper Chemical Co. (Mitsui)	20,000	April 1935
Tashito Railway Co. (Mitsui)	3,000	July 1935
Showa. Kirin Brewery Co. (Mitsubishi)	3,000	December 1933
Choson Rentan Co. (Mitsubishi)	2,000	November 1935
Choson Smokeless Coal Co. (Mitsubishi)	20,000	December 1935
Choson Hydro-Electric Co. (Noguchi)	20,000	May 1934
Choson Power Distribution Co. (Noguchi)	15,000	June 1933
Nippon Magnesite Metal Co. (Noguchi)	4,200	June 1933
Choson Coal Industrial Co. (Noguchi)	10,000	March 1935
Choson Nitrogenous Dynamite Co. (Noguchi)	1,000	April 1935
Funei Hydro-Electric Co. (Dentaku)	10,000	August 1936

Choson Electric Power Co. (Denryoku Renmei)	20,000	July 1935
Sanseki Railway Co. (Denryoku Renmei)	5,000	April 1936
Choson Cement Mfg. Co. (Ube Cement)	6,000	February 1936
Choson Weaving Co. (Ito Tada)	1,000	November 1932
Choson Ushi Co. (Nissan)	1,500	October 1933
Choson Seiren Co. (Shokugin)	10,000	February 1935
Toyokuni Seifun (Ito Chu)	2,000	December 1933[145]
Choson Seishi Co.	1,000	May 1936
Nippon VHP Heavy Industrial Co.	10,000	January 1936
Nippon Hard Pottery Co.	3,750	October 1939

Source: Cho Ki-Jun: *The Korean Economic History*, pp. 419–20.

The Koreans faced significant challenges in competing with the major Japanese companies. In 1936, there were 128 companies with a paid-in capital of more than 1 million yen, but only 19 of them were under Korean ownership. Among these, only two were industrial companies: the Kyongsong (Seoul) Textile Company and Choson Flour Company.

Following the commencement of the Sino-Japanese War in 1937, Japanese companies expedited their operations in Korea, particularly those involving industries that faced challenges in development within Japan. Mitsubishi Mining (MM) established an iron refinery in Ch'ongjin, Nippon, VHF Heavy Industrial Company (NVHFHIC) constructed the Songjin plant, Choson Nitrogenous Fertilizer Company (CNFC) built the Hungnam plant, and Choson Riken Metal Company (CRMC) established a plant in Inch'on. Notably, the majority of these industries were situated in northern Korea.

The table below illustrates the growth in manufacturing from 5,927 to 14,856 and the corresponding increase in the number of employees from 188,250 to 549,751, along with a rise in output from 730,806 yen to 2,050,000 yen during the period of 1936–1943. The distribution of industries is detailed as follows: textiles accounted for 13%; metallic 9%; machinery and tools 4%; pottery 3%; chemicals 34%; sawing, wool, and cork 1%; printing and bindery 1%; foodstuff 22.9%; gas and electricity 2%; and others for 11%. Large industries hiring more than 200 persons shared 61.8% of the total production, while small and medium-sized ones employing less than 200 employees contributed 38.2% to the total production.

Table XVIII:
Industrial Development After 1930s

During	No. of Factories	No. of Employees	Output in 1,000 yen
1936	5,927	188,250	730,806
1939	6,952	270,439	1,498,277
1943	14,856	549,751	2,050,000

Source: Suzuki Takeo, Choson no Keizai, pp. 233–35.

Table XIX:
Percentage of Distribution of Factories by Industry and Employees

(end of 1939)

Industries	Small		Medium		Large	
	Factory	Employees	Factory	Employees	Factory	Employees
Textile	68%	10%	25%	22%	7%	67%
Metallic	82	34	15	23	3	43

Machinery & tools	74	20	23	35	3	44
Pottery	73	19	24	44	3	37
Chemicals	79	22	19	39	2	38
Sawing, wool, & cork	82	41	17	50	0.8	8
Printing & bindery	83	43	16	38	1	14
Food-beverage	91	49	8	37	0.6	13
Gas-electricity	73	26	6	52	0.8	22
Others	79	26	19	41	2	33
Total	81.7	26.1	16.3	34.6	2	39.3

Large industries, constituting 2% of the total number of factories, employed a significant share of the workforce, amounting to 39.3% of the total factory employees. On the other hand, small and medium industries, representing 98% of the factories, employed 60.7% of the factory workforce. The concentration of employees in larger industries, particularly in the heavy chemical sector to meet war requirements, contributed to an economic imbalance.

During the war, some of these larger industries were hastily developed without due consideration for their internal relationships with other industries, this lead to the large imbalance seen and mentioned above (Table XIX). This rush for development further worsened the challenges and imbalances within the industrial landscape during this period.

Table XX:
Percentage of Major Machines and Tools Supplied Within Korea (1940)

Boiler and parts	3.7%
Engine	7.1
Machine tool	0
Processing machine	19.6
Locomotive	0
Railway car, ship, motor car, and parts	29.5
Watches, telegraph, & experimental tool	6.2

Note: The table includes those with paid-in capital of 1 million yen or more.

Source: The Bank of Korea, Chason Kyongje Yonbo, 1948, pp. 1–101.

There existed a notable disparity in industrial development between Japan and Korea. By the end of 1940, Japan had achieved a relatively well-proportioned industrial structure, with the metallic and machinery industries accounting for 45% of the total, a figure comparable to more advanced countries where it constituted 50%. In contrast, Korea's industrial structure at the end of 1943 depicted a significant imbalance, with the metallic and machinery industries making up only 20% of the sector. This disparity underscores the inferior position of Koreans under Japanese rule.

The fact that Koreans invested only 6% of the total further emphasizes the deliberate reshaping of industrial structures and policies imposed by Japan to suppress the Korean population. This restructuring had dire consequences, including the liquidation of small and medium industries in Korea. Korean entrepreneurs found themselves in a precarious situation, with non-wartime industries essentially gone. Even worse, they were unable to participate or invest in wartime industries.

The inability of Korean entrepreneurs to actively engage in large war industries can be attributed to various factors, with a significant obstacle being the lack of capital, as illustrated in Table XXI.

Table XXI:
Distribution of Industry Capital by Nationality (end of 1940)

Industry	Korean		Japanese	
	Capital in 1,000 yen	%	Capital in 1,000 yen	%
Chemicals	1,000	0	276,250	100
Metallic	6,100	2	373,000	98
Machinery & tool	61,500	42	85,050	58
Textile	14,000	15	76,600	85
Pottery	---	---	53,245	100
Wood and cork	5,500	10	47,000	90
Printing and bindery	1,500	43	2,000	57
Food and beverage	5,250	7	73,800	93

Industry	Korean		Japanese	
	Capital in 1,000 yen	%	Capital in 1,000 yen	%
Gas and electricity	---	---	553,030	100
Others	7,000	8	83,500	92
Total	101,850	6	1,623,475	94

Note: The table includes those with paid-in capital of 1 million yen or more.

Source: The Bank of Korea, Chason Kyongje Yonbo, 1948.

Table XXII:
Industrial Company Ownership by Nationality, 1938

Industry	No. of Companies			Paid-in Capital in 1,000 yen		
	Korean	Japanese	Total	Korean	Japanese	Total
Textile	37	39	76	6,075	23,103	29,178
Metals, machine, & tools	58	95	153	1,852	23,654	25,506

Industry	No. of Companies			Paid-in Capital in 1,000 yen		
	Korean	Japanese	Total	Korean	Japanese	Total
Beverage & materials	321	128	449	12,054	13,772	25,826
Pharmacy	33	25	58	1,676	934	2,610
Earthenware & product	12	40	52	432	15,791	16,223
Grain polishing & flour milling	94	70	164	2,526	9,860	12,386
Food	17	75	92	217	9,621	9,838
Wood & cork	19	82	101	594	10,553	11,147
Printing	44	42	86	625	1,461	2,086
Chemicals	37	75	112	2,954	100,736	103,690
Others	68	133	201	1,193	5,220	6,413
Total	740	804	1,544	30,198	214,703	244,903

Percentage

Textile	48.7	51.3	100.0	20.8	79.2	100.0
Metals, machine, & tools	57.9	62.1	100.0	7.3	92.7	100.0
Beverage & materials	71.5	28.5	100.0	46.7	53.3	100.0
Pharmacy	56.9	43.1	100.0	64.2	35.8	100.0
Earthenware and products	23.1	76.9	100.0	2.7	97.3	100.0
Grain polishing and flour milling	57.3	42.7	100.0	20.4	79.6	100.0
Food	18.5	81.5	100.0	2.2	97.8	100.0
Wood and cork	18.8	81.2	100.0	5.3	94.7	100.0
Printing	51.2	48.8	100.0	30.0	70.0	100.0
Chemicals	33.0	67.0	100.0	2.8	97.2	100.0
Others	33.8	66.2	100.0	18.6	81.4	100.0

| Total | 47.9 | 52.1 | 100.0 | 12.3 | 87.7 | 100.0 |

Source: Choson Keizai Zuhyo, p. 330.

Few Koreans were granted positions of responsibility in the lucrative metallic or heavy industries. According to a statistical survey, the number of Korean technicians was only 1,632, constituting 20% of all technicians by the end of 1944. However, this number saw a significant increase due to the expansion of war industries during this period.

The workforce composition also witnessed notable changes. The number of Koreans working in factories and mines surged from 142,676 in 1931 to 732,751 in 1943. To economize on wages, there was a substantial presence of juvenile and female workers. Among mine workers, 8% were women in 1943, and 30% of factory workers were also women. Juvenile workers constituted 48% of the workforce, with 109,000 individuals under the age of 19.[146]

While there was an increase in the number of workers over the years, the wages of Korean workers did not see an increase at all. For mine workers, the daily wage was 0.763 yen, while juvenile or child workers received only 0.15 yen, as per statistics from 1937. A survey conducted in June 1931 revealed that 34% of mine workers in 213 mines worked for more than 12 hours a day, and 81% worked 10 hours or more per day.

Comparing the working hours of Japanese textile workers (0.4%) to 82.2% of Korean workers who worked for more than 12 hours a day, the table below illustrates the exploitation of Korean laborers by Japanese capitalists.

Table XXIII:
The Number of Mines and Factory Workers

During	Mine Workers	Factory Workers	Total
1931	35,895	106,781	142,676
1937	161,954	207,003	368,957
1999	222,876	270,439	493,957
1943	183,000	549,751	731,751

Source: The Bank of Korea, Choson Kyongje Yonbo, 1948.

Factory workers in Korea were subjected to demanding conditions, being required to work more than 12 hours a day. In 1937, the average wages for a Korean worker were 50% less than those of Japanese workers, underscoring the significant wage disparity between the two groups.[148]

Eventually there was a slight improvement in the working conditions of Korean workers, who were now earning about 70% of the Japanese rate. Though many workers, especially in textiles, wood, and cork factories, still had to endure workdays exceeding 12 hours. A significant portion of factory workers, totaling 46.9%, were subjected to these demanding work hours.[149]

The table below provides a stark comparison of working hours between Korea and Japan. A mere 0.3% of Japanese workers were required to work for more than 12 hours, in stark contrast to 46.9% of Korean workers facing such demanding conditions. Worse in the textile industry, only 0.4% of Japanese textile workers worked more than 12 hours a day, while a staggering 82.2% of Korean textile workers endured such extended work hours.

Indeed, the stark contrast underscores how Japanese capitalists exploited Korean laborers, extracting significant profits, and subjecting them to grueling work hours for the sake of the war effort, all while securing tidy profits for themselves.

Table XXIV:
Comparison of Working Hours in Korea and Japan

Working hours	Korea	Japan
Less than 8 hours	0.8%	1.4%
9–10 hours	28.7	45.3
11–12 hours	11.9	43.6
More than 12 hours	46.9	0.3

Source: Hosokawa Karo-cu, Shokuminshi, 1841, Tokyo, p. 353.

Foreign Trade—Government Finance and Financial Institutions

In the rural sector, the Kabo tax reform rapidly transformed the economy. It changed "payment in kind" to "payment by cash" and played a pivotal role in boosting the commercialization of agriculture. As a result, rice exports experienced rapid expansion from 1895 onward. While this development benefited larger landowners and native merchants who continued to prosper from trade with Japan, the mass of smaller farmers did not experience significant improvements in their economic situation.

The flourishing trade during this period served as an indicator of Korea's economic development in the colonial era. Historical evidence supports the view that, even before the colonial period, Korea had established a trade relationship with Japan.[150]

Further substantiating this perspective is the fact that Korea's trade increased substantially during the three-and-a-half decades between opening and annexation. Available data illustrates that trade with Japan (exports and imports) grew from 2.5 million yen in 1879–81 to 36.3 million by 1907–1909. The annual average for Korea's total trade increased from 16 million yen to 55.3 million in the same period. The real volume of trade continued to expand rapidly during the colonial period, with trade rising more than tenfold by 1939–41 compared to 1910–12 (Table XXV).[151]

Table XXV:
Volume, Distribution, and Relative Importance of Foreign Trade 1910–12 to 1939–41

Percent Distribution (b) Volume (a)

Period	In million yen	Exports to			Imports from			Trade
	Prices in 1936	Japan	China (c)	Others	Japan	China (c)	Others	Ratios (d)
	(1)	(2)	(3)	(4)	(5)	(6)	(7)	(8)
1910–12	380.1	73.7	16.8	9.5	62.4	10.1	27.5	13.8
1914–16	567.4	79.9	13.0	7.1	67.5	12.9	19.6	17.6
1919–21	961.6	89.9	8.8	1.3	64.4	23.7	11.9	28.7
1924–26	1,593.3	93.1	6.6	0.3	68.0	24.3	7.7	39.9

Period	In million yen	Exports to			Imports from			Trade
	Prices in 1936	Japan	China (c)	Others	Japan	China (c)	Others	Ratios (d)
1929–31	2,073.5	91.4	8.2	0.4	76.4	15.9	7.6	51.7
1934–36	3,813.6	87.7	11.6	0.7	84.8	10.8	4.4	57.2
1939–41	4,174.4	77.4	21.2	0.4	88.3	4.8	6.9	53.5

Sources: Distribution and trade ratios: Suh Sang-Chui, *Growth and Structural Changes in the Korean Economy Since 1910*, tables 11-11 and 11-14; Bank of Choson, Economic Review, 1949, table 56 and pp. 426–34.

Note: Foreign trade here includes only commodity exports and imports.

Key:

(a) Three-year totals, deflated by the Seoul wholesale price index.

(b) Three-year averages based on current values.

(c) Includes Manchuria and areas in the north occupied by the Japanese.

(d) Exports plus imports divided by commodity product plus imports.

The growth of trade in Korea reached levels that surpassed international standards. Professor Suh indicated that trade ratios, calculated as exports plus imports divided by commodity product plus imports, increased from 14% in 1910–12 to more than 50% during the 1930s (Table XXV). This exceeded the 1938–39 average of 38% for the world's small countries, indicating that Korea's trade ratios were notably high during this period.[152]

While it's acknowledged that Korea's trade ratios were influenced by an upward bias (noting that the denominator omits services for which no data are available), they were deemed too high and exhibited a significant and sharp increase to be dismissed as mere statistical omissions. The remarkable ratios were so impressive that some observers characterized the growth during this period as "export-led" growth.[153]

Japan considered Korea not only as a supplier of food grains but also as a crucial market for Japanese industrial products. The reinforcement of Japan's monopolistic market position in Korea was marked by the elimination of all duties on exports from Korea in 1929 and the open entry for most imports from Japan by 1923. By 1931, a staggering 95% of Korean exports were directed towards Japan, and during that same year, a substantial 80% of all of Korea's imports originated from Japan. The significance of the Korean market for Japanese goods was evident in the proportion of Japan's total exports absorbed by Korea, reaching 34% in 1939.

In 1919, the imports of manufacturing products constituted 79.1%, maintaining the same level thereafter. These products included clothing, yarn and thread, alcoholic beverages, sugar, tobacco products, and paper goods, indicating that many daily items were routinely imported from Japan. Conversely, Korean exports to Japan primarily comprised foodstuffs and rice; though starting in 1930, raw materials and semi-finished goods also began to play a significant role. From the 1930s onward, Japan solidified its role as Korea's exclusive trading partner, and the growth of exports to Japan reflected a typical colonial relationship.

There was also an increase in the export of Korean manufactured products to Japan, reaching half of Korean exports in 1939 compared to only 10.4% in 1929. This trend steadily progressed through 1935. While the export of foodstuffs, mainly rice, decreased from 72% in 1919 to 57.2% in 1925 and further dropped to 27.9% in 1939, it did not signify a transformation in the colonial status relationship. Instead, it indicated an increase in Japanese investment in Korea and a shift in the direction of Japan's colonial policy. The fundamental structure of Japanese trade with Korea remained consistent, with Korean exports to Japan accounting for 78.6% of all exports, while imports from Japan constituted 86.3% of all Korean imports. This illustrates the extent of Korean dependence on the Japanese market, as depicted in the table below.

Table XXVI:
Volume of Trade With Japan and Other Countries

	1910–1919	1920–1931	1932–1936	1937–1939
Exports				

To other countries	16.2%	8.3%	12.2%	21.4%
To Japan	83.8%	91.7%	87.8%	78.6%
Total	100.0%	100.0%	100.0%	100.0%

Imports				
From other countries	33.8%	30.5%	15.7%	12.7%
From Japan	66.2%	69.5%	84.3%	86.3%
Total	100.0%	100.0%	100.0%	100.0%

Source: Choson Boeki Kyokai (ed.) Choson Boeki Shi (*The History of Trade in Korea*), 1943, Seoul, pp. 81–82.

Table XXVII:
Principal Exports of Korean Products to Japan

(As of the end of 1941)

Products	Quantity (in 1,000 yen)
Rice	152,776

Products	Quantity (in 1,000 yen)
White soybeans	11,565
Fishery products	55,080
Soap	11,926
Raw Chinese medicine and chemical products	16,709
Raw silk	23,680
Coal	23,216
Iron and metals	193,400
Fish Powder	15,966
Ammonium sulfate	14,772
Grand Total	519,000

Source: Toyo Keizai Shinposha (ed.): Nenkan Choson (*The Annual Book of Korea*), 1942, p. 71, Tokyo.

The table illustrates that while rice remained the leading item (percentage wise of Japanese need), iron and metals emerged as the largest export. This reinforces the notion of the significant role Korea played as a supplier of foodstuffs to Japan. On the other hand, secondary industrial products constituted 56.7% of all imports. The primary import category was cloth and related goods, followed by machine and tool metal products, which gained importance for mining and manufacturing purposes. This further emphasizes the intricate economic relationship with Korea serving as a source of both agricultural and industrial goods for Japan.

Table XXVIII:
Principal Products Imported From Japan

(As of the end of 1941)

Products	Quantity (in 1,000 yen)
Food	80,908
Medicine materials and chemical products	61,102
Cloth and related goods	229,712
Dress and related goods	105,965
Coal	40,463
Metal products	117,556
Machine and tools	227,779
Grand Total	863,485

Source: Ibid.

The subsequent table demonstrates a 96% increase in rice exports between 1929 and 1938. Interestingly, the exports escalated more rapidly than production. However, it's noted that rice export data after 1939 was classified as secret, while rice production data remained public. This suggests a deliberate move to conceal specific information related to rice exports, possibly due to strategic or economic considerations during that period.

Table XXIX:
Korean Rice Production and Exports to Japan

(In 1,000 sŏk)

During	Production	Export to Japan	Index (100 in 1929)
1931	24,129	8,412	150
1932	19,968	7,586	134
1933	20,563	8,074	144
1934	28,886	9,501	169
1935	21,080	9,001	160
1936	22,499	9,513	196
1937	19,411	7,202	128

During	Production	Export to Japan	Index (100 in 1929)
1938	26,797	10,997	196
1939	24,139	Not published	
1940	14,356	Not published	
1941	21,527	Not published	
1942	24,886	Not published	

Source: Ibid, p. 40.

The table indicates that raw materials, semi-finished, and finished foodstuffs comprised 83.5% of the total exports (Table XXX). Simultaneously, products of secondary industries constituted 55.7% of all imports. This highlights the colonial nature of the economic relationship between Japan and Korea, where Korea primarily served as a supplier of raw materials and foodstuffs while relying heavily on Japanese imports for manufactured goods. The economic dynamics between the two countries were deeply rooted in an almost mercantilist colonial framework during this period.

Table XXX:
Movement of Trade Composition of EXPORTS

(In thousand yen)

During	Raw Material	Semi-finished Materials	Semi-finished Food	Finished Food	Metallic Goods	Misc.	Total
1911	3,257	2,147	11,002	151	149	1,113	17,819
1921	24,250	28,025	139,077	3,707	5,564	15,366	215,989
1930	32,166	39,157	146,609	8,667	18,374	20,306	265,279
1936	96,298	98,899	298,871	18,849	54,178	24,163	591,258

Percentage

1911	18.3	12.1	61.8	0.8	0.8	6.2	100.0
1921	11.2	13.0	64.4	1.7	2.6	7.1	100.0
1930	12.1	14.8	55.3	3.3	6.9	7.6	100.0
1936	16.3	16.7	50.5	3.2	9.2	4.1	100.0

Movement of Trade Composition IMPORTS

(In thousand yen)

1911	4,337	7,452	1,593	5,584	30,033	5,083	54,082
1921	33,427	15,753	7,808	16,130	117,972	40,286	231,376

| 1930 | 47,787 | 40,765 | 55,461 | 21,300 | 183,801 | 16,950 | 366,064 |
| 1936 | 163,146 | 50,673 | 76,527 | 46,421 | 397,624 | 25,932 | 760,323 |

Percentage

1911	8.0	13.8	3.0	10.3	55.5	9.4	100.0
1921	14.4	6.9	3.4	7.0	50.9	17.4	100.0
1930	13.1	11.1	15.2	5.8	50.2	4.6	100.0
1936	21.5	6.7	10.1	6.0	52.3	3.4	100.0

Source: Himeno Mineru (ed.): Choson Keizai Zuhyo (*The Statistical Charts of Korean Economy*), 1940, Seoul, p. 150.

Korean trade was predominantly with Japan and, to a lesser extent, with other Yen Block member countries. The Yen Block comprised Manchuria and parts of Northern China that were occupied by Japan. Notably, Korea exported a higher proportion to Japan than it imported. This peculiarity is characteristic of an economic condition where the colonial power sends more exports to the colony. In the case of Korea, it primarily sent most exports to its colonial master, Japan, while Japan imports were less concentrated and tended to come from a broader range of countries.[154]

In the 1930s, there was a noticeable increase in the relative shares of manufacturers, industrial crude materials, and semi-finished materials. Although finished products continued to dominate imports, their share declined in the late 1920s and early 1930s. During this period, there was a rise in the import of crude food, industrial materials, and semi-finished manufactured goods. In the 1920s, the increase in food imports, including millet and inexpensive foreign rice, helped counterbalance domestic shortages resulting from population growth and the export of high-quality Korean rice to Japan. The abolition of the Corporation Law led to a surge in imports of semi-finished products and industrial materials, indicating the growing expansion of Korean industries. Initially, imports of finished products primarily consisted of consumer goods, with a focus on machinery and other investment goods required for heavy industries.

Table XXXI:
Commodity Composition of Trade, 1915–41

(Percent distribution: from current price data)

Exports

Period	Crude Materials			Manufacturers			
	Food	Other	Total	Food	Semi-finished	Finished	Total
1915–19	48.7	20.5	69.2	1.0	7.6	22.2	30.8
1920–24	63.0	11.1	74.1	1.7	11.0	13.2	15.9

Period	Crude Materials			Manufacturers			
	Food	Other	Total	Food	Semi-finished	Finished	Total
1925–29	64.2	8.7	72.9	2.5	12.2	12.4	27.1
1930–34	59.1	15.6	74.7	3.8	15.6	5.9	25.3
1935–39	41.8	15.2	57.0	3.5	21.0	18.5	43.0
1940–41	25.8	14.5	40.3	4.7	26.8	28.2	59.7

Imports

Period	Food	Other	Total	Food	Semi-finished	Finished	Total
1915–19	7.0	6.4	13.2	7.1	14.9	64.6	86.6
1920–24	11.6	14.7	26.3	5.9	20.2	47.6	73.7
1925–29	18.3	11.7	30.0	5.8	17.1	47.1	70.0
1930–34	10.3	21.9	31.2	6.7	12.6	48.5	67.8
1935–39	7.2	13.5	20.7	4.6	13.2	61.5	79.3
1940–41	8.1	8.8	16.9	3.6	9.9	69.6	83.1

Source: Suh Sang-Chui, *Growth and Structural Changes in the Korean Economy Since 1910*, table 11-13.

Several noteworthy elements emerged in the export and import of food grains; the persistent deficit in Korea's commodity accounts;

and the transition within finished imports from consumer goods to producer's goods. There was a strange simultaneous import and export of the same product, which was rationalized based on national differences in consumer tastes and transport costs. In reality, as previously shown, Korean agriculture was exploited for the benefit of the Japanese consumer, given the high value of rice in the Korean diet. Trade, therefore, served as the primary source of exploitation in this economic dynamic.[155]

One positive aspect of the trade was that, unlike Taiwan (Formosa), which consistently ran a trade deficit, Korea had greater access to resources within the Yen Block than it might have had as an independent state.[156]

The Second Sino-Japanese War in 1937 marked a turning point in China, leading to increased legitimacy for the Communist Party, broader intellectual support, and eventual communist state control in October 1949. The war revealed that Japan was not suited to lead the union of East Asia. For Korea, the war hastened independence more rapidly than anticipated by cultural nationalists or others. The conflict resulted in a reduction of foreign presence, with half of the 60,000 Chinese residents departing in 1937 as the war began.

During this time, Western companies were heavily involved in mining and petroleum products; they also played significant role in gold production. This troubled the Japanese as gold production had recently reached 90 million yen in 1936, with a concerning 10% of mines being owned by foreigners.

However, Japanese restrictions were on the rise after 1931. The American Oriental Consolidated Mining Company (OCMC) was compelled to sell its exports to a government agency at significantly low prices. As new regulations tightened import supplies, by mid-1939, the company decided to dispose of its Korean mines.[157]

U.S. firms had been dominant in the oil market since the 1890s, with the Standard-Vacuum Oil Company (SVOC, modern Exxon) being a pioneer in the early kerosene business. The Texas Oil Company (TOC) had offices in Seoul by 1937. The British Royal Dutch Shell Company (BRDSC) also operated in Korea through the Rising Sun Petroleum Company (RSPC).

Though in May 1935, foreign profits stated to wither as the government established the Choson Petroleum Company (CPC) with refineries set to compete with the foreign companies to meet Korean needs.[158] The Japanese decided to fix the CPC stockpile to maintain a six-month supply. The Japanese government's decision was driven by defense concerns and the increasing war consumption. It also acted as a deterrent to foreign companies by giving CPC an edge over their competition. This was because such stockpiling was against business law for foreign corporations.

The war brought benefits to Korea's commerce and industry as it disrupted Japanese labor and shipping. The war allowed the gaps between Manchukuo and North China to be filled by an increased flow of Korean goods. The "My Pet" brand of 12.5 million Korean cigarettes, exported to Northern China, was hailed by the official Keijo Nippon newspaper as a "military strike," stating "Thus Choson Tobacco (CT) is ready to march upon the field in North

China this spring and deliver a strong blow to the British and American tobacco trusts."[159]

The rising trade, coupled with the absence of competition from non-Yen Block goods, resulted in high employment, and the trade imbalance turned around by 1938. Chemicals and textiles were rapidly expanded for the war effort, while machinery, machine tools, and heavy vehicles saw rapid development in the Ch'ongjin area in the northeast and the Seoul-Inch'on area. The rural labor surplus was depleted as labor was directed into heavy industry, and from 1939 to 1941, more than 50,000 individuals per annum volunteered for jobs in mines, engineering, and factories, both in Korea and Japan. Between 1944 and 1945, around 500,000 Koreans went to Japan, either under central directive or voluntarily, when labor conscription was introduced in 1942.[160]

The number of women in the workforce was reduced as there was a move from light industries to heavy, war-related industries (i.e., iron and tungsten mining).

The forced rationalization implemented from 1941 had a profound impact on the economic landscape, leading to the closure of many weaker companies. This economic shift made the Korean economy closely resemble that of Japan. The rationing of rice and petrol in mainland Japan started in 1938. Meanwhile, new regulations also greatly affected Korea, with price controls and a shortage of petrol for freight cars slowing down trade.

Governor-General Minami played a crucial role in leading various initiatives, including the Feminine Question Research Society (FQRS). These efforts aimed at simplifying clothing, reducing consumption (eating less and cooking fewer meals), and curbing the purchase of various commodities like paper, wool, rubber, and metals. The rationing measures extended to lifestyle choices, including reducing smoking and drinking.

Moreover, there was an emphasis on changing Korean attitudes towards time, promoting the appreciation, saving, and efficient utilization of time. The directive included strict observance of schedules for movement, starting activities, and meetings. These measures were part of broader efforts to manage resources efficiently and align with the demands of wartime conditions.[161]

The wartime period saw a redirection of human resources and capital towards war efforts, prompting a renewed focus on expanding agriculture. Despite a bumper crop in rice and cotton in 1937, the subsequent year (1938) faced challenges with crop blight, leading to decreased cultivated land between 1937 and 1944. This decline in agricultural output was further exacerbated by authorities requisitioning livestock and crops at minimal prices, thereby reducing overall productivity.

To mobilize public support for the war, the governor-general (G-G) established an information committee with branches in provinces. Various forms of media, including newspapers, films, radio broadcasts, lectures, and mass-produced pamphlets in Korean, were utilized to disseminate information to every household. Dissent against these efforts was met with strict measures, leading to arrests of individuals, including Korean Christians Chang Tok-su and Yun Chi-ho, for unlawful activities in 1937–38.

The suppression of dissent extended to religious activities, with the sale of Bibles being banned in one district as a warning. Additionally, "banned" groups were forced to visit Shinto institutions to receive Shinto instructions.

To suppress the possibility of labor or rural agitations, anti-communist bodies were established, and various social and occupational groups were placed under official control. Starting in 1940, associations of ten-family units were formed with specific roles such as visiting Shinto shrines, raising Japanese flags, collecting war donations, maintaining security, distributing food, and disseminating official instructions. These units served as a means for the authorities to mobilize the Korean population under their control.

Militarization in Korea, particularly in schools, was directly overseen by the Japanese authorities. Teachers wore khaki uniforms, and the school uniforms designed by the Japanese were military in style, featuring black army-style uniforms for boys and sailor suits for girls. Morning parades were conducted in army barracks, and schoolroom maps depicted the Japanese army marching across China. Class songs were dedicated to Japanese military victory, and children were required to create their own wooden rifles for the school's "armory."

G-G Minami had a vision of completely reconstructing Korean identity to prove to Asia Japan's leadership prowess. He saw Korea as a test case, comparing Japanese and Western imperialism—considering the former as constructive and the latter as destructive. Minami supported the idea of Korean representation in the Japanese parliament and aimed to exert control over various aspects of Korean identity, including language, education, and religion.

In March 1938, a significant step was taken to align the Japanese and Korean educational systems. Both were put on the same levels of "elementary," "middle," and "girls' high." As part of this integration, all education was mandated to be conducted in Japanese. Furthermore, schools and government offices were instructed to prohibit Korean-language papers. This policy had severe consequences for Korean media, leading to the forced closure of Dong-a Ilbo and Choson Ilbo, two prominent Korean-language newspapers.[162]

Colonial restrictions on languages were indeed widespread during the imperialistic era. Similar policies were observed in various colonies, including New Zealand's adoption of language restrictions in Cook Islands and British prohibitions on Welsh language.

In November 1939, General Minami took a step further by encouraging Koreans to adopt Japanese names. This assimilation policy aimed to erase Korean identity by replacing Korean names with Japanese ones. The process was described vividly by Richard Kim in his autobiographical novel *Lost Names*. Kim recounted an incident where an aged Korean was invited to choose a new name in a police station. The Korean detective presented a list of names, and the old man, resigned to the situation, expressed indifference, saying, "It doesn't matter. No one's going to call me by that name anyway—or by any other name."[163]

Some Koreans had taken the "invitation," but in official records listed their original names anyway. Minami didn't like this, and he wanted to destroy the personal historical line and start from a metaphorical year zero. Despite the coercion and arrests associated with such policies, there was still deep-seated resentment among Korean; the name policy is one of the most bitterly remembered Japanese initiatives since 1875. Despite Japan's intimidation, many arrests, and constant hatred of Japanese policies, the Koreans also respected Japanese strength.

Even during this difficult time, some individuals, like Ch'oe Namson, sought to navigate the complex political landscape. While retaining nationalist ideals, Ch'oe Namson advocated for unity between China and Japan against Western imperialism. He even urged Korean students to participate in the "holy war" alongside Japan.[164]

The British consular report on Korea in 1937 provides insight into the atmosphere prevailing in Korea during the undeclared warfare in China. The report notes the disciplined enthusiasm of the Japanese, which had permeated into Korea. Instances of troop trains being greeted by schoolchildren and adults carrying Japanese flags, public prayers for victory at Shinto shrines with large crowds in attendance, and reports of wealthy Koreans making donations to patriotic funds were highlighted. However, the report suggests a nuanced perspective, indicating that these displays of support were either dictated by self-interest or actively controlled by the police, with backing from the Japanese ex-Service Men's Association (e-SMA) throughout the peninsula.

The report says about the deeper feelings of the Koreans as follows:

> The older people, who have seen their country and Manchuria swallowed, can hardly be enthusiastic over the present developments, but the younger generations attending Japanese schools have never known independence and are moreover never permitted to hear the other side of any case, accepted the Japanese propaganda and follow the line of least resistance. It is the opinion of a competent observer that Japan's successful defiance of the League of Nations (LN) in Manchuria and of the Western powers in China have stimulated many of the younger Koreans and implanted in them a thrill of pride in their citizenship in a conquering nation. There is nowhere any unrest or apparent dissatisfaction, but times are good, and the people have money in their pockets. A return of the lean years may spoil the picture.[165]

The decision in February 1938 to allow Koreans to become special army volunteers, followed by a similar ordinance for the navy in 1943, marked a significant development. According to the information provided, in the first two years after this decision, 15,000 Korean youths responded to the call. The numbers increased substantially in 1940 and 1943, with an additional 800,000 individuals volunteering. However, it's noted that in reality, only 17,500 were actually present in the army.[166]

The appeal of engaging in a war against Western empires initially succeeded, drawing in numerous Korean youths. Some individuals joined the army involuntarily, sent there due to unacceptable behavior by Japanese authorities, sometimes later labeled as volunteers by historians. Similar to Ch'oe Namson, many embraced Japan's cause as an all-Asian cause and felt more at ease in the Japanese army than in the Korean army.[167]

The administrative relationship between Korea and Japan underwent a significant change with the onset of the Pacific War. In 1942, Japan's Home Ministry integrated Korea as an essential part of the Japanese empire. Subsequently, the appointment of the governor-general was determined by the prime minister, leading to policies affecting the Korean population becoming more distant. Conscription into the Japanese army was enforced in Korea, with approximately 187,000 men recruited in 1944 before the war's conclusion. Over 150,000 Koreans were mobilized to the battlefield between 1941 and 1945, serving as transport and construction workers for the construction of roads and airfields in the war zone. Tragically, young Korean women, some barely more than children, were forcibly taken by the Japanese army to serve as prostitutes for their troops. Disturbing rumors circulated about the extraction of body oil from Korean teenage girls to supplement diminishing supplies.[168]

The exploitation of Korean industries and labor reached unprecedented levels of harshness, and the living conditions for Korean workers, both at home and on the battlefield, rapidly worsened. Many succumbed to diseases, accidents, allied bombings, or even brutal executions. In a factory in North Korea involved in military production, Korean workers were ruthlessly shot to prevent any revelations as Japan faced collapse in the latter stages of the Second World War. The grim realities of their plight reflect the severe hardships faced by the Korean workforce during this tumultuous period.

The representation of Koreans in Japan's Parliament was severely limited, with only one Korean appointed to the Upper House (JPUH) and one elected to the Lower House of Representatives (LHR). In 1944, the Japanese Diet passed a bill extending Japan's constitution and election laws to Taiwan and Korea, with the provision that Koreans over 25 years of age, having paid 15 yen in taxes, could elect 23 representatives. The civil administration under the G-G expressed optimism about the future, envisioning a day when Koreans would hold seats in the cabinet, and even the governor-general position would be occupied by a Korean.[169]

The plans for Korean representation and potential changes in governance came too late, occurring as the war was reaching its end. In mid-1944, preparations were made to defend Korea from potential invasions by the United States in the south and the Soviet Union in the north. Fortifications were established on Cheju-do, an island on the south coast, and troops were concentrated to counter potential threats from both the Russians and the Americans. Thousands of Koreans were mobilized for the defense of Korea. However, the use of nuclear weapons at Hiroshima and Nagasaki, along with the Soviet Union's declaration of war on Japan, ultimately saved Korea from further humiliation, torture, and continued Japanese control.

Korea underwent industrialization and modernization during Japanese colonialism, but the Korean people were passive participants in this process, manipulated according to Japanese objectives, and primarily contributing to Japanese profits. While

Koreans were introduced to city life, modern schools, and factory work, they did not experience these changes positively. This pattern reflects a common theme in the history of imperialism, though the more recent nature of Japanese imperialism brought about more systematic and ambitious socio-economic planning than seen in earlier Western imperial endeavors. Korean society bore the direct impacts of colonialism, particularly during the brief period of Japanese empire. Following the Second Sino-Japanese War, social upheavals accelerated, leading to a doubling of the urban population between 1935 and 1940, from 7% to 14%. In 1925, the urban-agricultural ratio was 1:22, which shifted to 1:6 by 1944. All of this reflects a rapid and substantial growth of large cities between 1930 and 1940.

Table XXXII:
Growth of Large Cities Between 1930 and 1940

	1930	1935	1940
Seoul	394,240	444,098	935,464
Pusan	146,098	182,503	249,734
P'yongyang	140,703	182,121	285,965
Taegu	93,319	107,414	178,923
Inch'on	68,137	92,997	171,165
Kaesong	49,520	55,537	72,062

Wonsan	42,760	60,169	79,320
Hamhung	43,851	50,571	75,320
Chinnamp'o	38,296	50,512	68,656
Mokp'o	34,689	60,734	64,256
Kwangju	33,023	54,607	64,500

Source: Yunshik Chang, 1977, p. 70.

The development of Ch'ongjin, particularly its connection to the new port development of Najin in northeast Korea, was highly noteworthy. Ch'ongjin transformed from a small town with a population of 20,000 in 1925 to 55,000 in 1935. Within five years, its population surged to 197,918, establishing itself as a crucial military-industrial center during the war. However, the impact of colonialism wasn't limited to the internal dynamics of Korean society. Millions of Koreans were dispersed across China, Manchuria, Japan, the Soviet Union, and the South Pacific during this period.

Following the end of Japanese domination, many Koreans faced decisions about returning home, while others adopted a wait-and-see approach to assess the unfolding developments in the country. According to Marxist analysis, "Imperialism changed the society by reducing the authority of traditional elites, but the imperial power had not obliterated themselves entirely, and the new Cold War Imperialism (CWI) was to prevent the Korean classes from resolving their differences in isolation. So, the collapse of the

Japanese domination was not an end entirely in itself, and the respite from foreign intrusion was to be very brief."[170]

Ultimately, Korea finally achieved sovereignty, but the outcome was a bitter division into two separate entities: South Korea, officially known as the Republic of Korea (ROK), and North Korea, officially known as the Democratic People's Republic of Korea (DPRK).

This chapter illustrated Japan's struggle during the Depression of the 1930s, leading to its departure from the gold standard and facing the brink of internal collapse and national bankruptcy. In response, Japan expanded its aggressive colonial policies, invading the Chinese mainland in 1937 and Manchuria in 1931, ultimately entering World War II against the United States, Britain, and the Allies in 1941. The impact on workers and peasants, especially in Korea, was severe. Peasants were compelled to sell their produce, including cotton, at designated locations to Japanese colonial capitalists. With Japanese farmers sent to fight in the war, Korean farmers faced challenges in agricultural production, leading to protests, crop hiding, and desertion of farmland. These hardships were compounded by "spring poverty," forcing the Korean peasantry to consume less grain during the winter. Tenant-farmers also had to pay additional taxes, prompting some to seek employment in mines or migrate to Japan and Manchuria for jobs.

In 1937, driven by the Sino-Japanese War, Japan initiated the development of mines in Korea, specifically targeting gold, silver, and smokeless coal, crucial resources required for the war effort. The extraction of mineral resources became a focus, with Japanese government entities, military agencies, and prominent Japanese capitalists actively involved in exploring and exploiting Korean mines. Only one mine belonged to a Korean capitalist, as Korean investment was not encouraged. During this period, cheap labor and hydroelectric power attracted Japanese investors, while Japan's big Zaibatsu competed with each other to build factories in Korea. Manufacturing was also expanded, and heavy factories were built because of the expansion of the war. Women and juveniles were working at lower wages. Even regular mine workers got low wages and long working hours, as the Japanese capitalists took advantage of the Korean working class and burdened them with the war effort. The Korean wages at their fairest were still 70% of the Japanese workers. Japan's trade with Korea increased tenfold between the opening and annexation of Korea, as Korea already had trade relations with Japan even before the colonial period. The Korean economic growth in the colonial period is termed by many as "export-led" growth.

Korea played a dual role during this period, serving not only as a crucial supplier of food grains but also as a market for Japan's burgeoning industrial products. The rural surplus labor in Korea was depleted as a significant number were mobilized into heavy industries and mines, while others were compelled or volunteered to work in Japan. Unfortunately, Korean industries and their labor force faced exploitation and harsh conditions, both at home and on the battlefield, leading to numerous casualties due to diseases, accidents, allied bombings, and brutal acts of violence.

In the later stages of Japanese colonial rule, the political landscape in Korea underwent significant changes. Only one Korean representative was appointed to Japan's Parliament Upper House (JPUH), and one to the Lower House of Representatives (LHR).

This period also witnessed common colonial practices such as language restrictions. The Japanese authorities attempted to reshape the Korean historical line, aiming to establish a new beginning, metaphorically termed as "year zero." As World War II intensified, some Korean patriots aligned themselves with Japan in the fight against Western powers for the greater cause of Asia.

In 1942, Japan's Home Ministry took direct control of Korea, integrating it as an integral part of the Japanese Empire. The appointment of the governor-general of Korea was now determined by the Japanese prime minister, leading to policies affecting Koreans becoming more remote. The scope of conscription expanded, with Korean workers not only recruited for military service but also deployed in construction and transport roles. Shockingly, young Korean women, some barely more than children, were forcibly taken to serve as prostitutes for Japanese troops, and there were disturbing rumors about the extraction of oil from the bodies of Korean teenage girls due to an oil shortage.

As preparations were made to repel potential invasions by U.S. forces in the south and Soviet Union forces in the north, Korea faced the harsh realities of exploitation and deteriorating conditions. The end of World War II in 1945 marked the occupation of U.S. forces in the south and the USSR's forces in the north. Only in 1948 did a semblance of independence appear when the US and the USSR left Korea. However, instead of a unified Korea, two distinct countries emerged: The Republic of Korea in the south and The Democratic People's Republic of Korea in the north.

This chapter delved into the intensified exploitation of Korean peasants by the Japanese government, traders, and landowners. The acquisition of land from Korean peasants saw an increase, accompanied by Japanese investments in Korean farmland. The Oriental Development Company (ODC), utilizing the emerging banking system and rail lines, took the lead in land grabbing under the guise of reform. The agricultural policies enforced by the governor-general (G-G) were detrimental to Korean farmers, aiming to boost rice production primarily for the benefit of Japan.

As previously discussed, the export of high-quality rice to Japan placed a heavy burden on Korean farmers, who often faced severe conditions, including periods of starvation lasting for almost half of the year. The agricultural focus remained predominantly on crops, neglecting the development of livestock, fertilizer, and silk production. The land survey, intended to benefit Japanese landlords, further marginalized Korean peasants. Irrigation projects, rather than aiding Korean peasants, contributed to a large number of them becoming destitute.

The manufacturing sector in Korea during this period primarily favored Japanese interests, with control over larger companies remaining in their hands. However, it's important to note that the available data may not always be accurate. Japanese workers enjoyed better pay and shorter working hours, creating a stark contrast with Korean workers who faced longer hours and lower wages. This challenging situation made it difficult for Korean workers to support their families and providing education for their children seemed like an unattainable dream.

Despite these hardships and the pervasive control exerted by the Japanese, some dedicated Korean entrepreneurs managed to establish companies using their own capital and hard work. Notable examples include An Hui-je's Paekan Trading in Pusan, which not only contributed significant funds to the Korean independence movement but also played a role in promoting education and the cooperative movement in Korea.

All in all, Japan's economic domination of Korea through 1932–45 had significant negative effects that reverberated damagingly throughout Korea. These horrendous effects leave the realm of economic and show the horrible cultural and humanitarian oppression suffered by Koreans under Japanese colonialism. The long lasting impacts of Korea's economic domination can even still be felt in the present world today.

CHAPTER 6:

Development of Foreign Trade

Government Finance

Japanese Control of Finance

In August 1904, as per the Korean agreement, a Japanese fiscal adviser, Megata Tanetaro, was appointed, giving him virtual control over the Korean fiscal administration. In 1905, he initiated the reformation of the Korean currency, which at that time primarily comprised of yopchon brass and nickel coins. Megata replaced the currency with a new one minted by Daiichi Ginko, a Japanese bank, as many of the existing coins were made of substandard metals. In exchange, the old coins were categorized into three grades based on their intrinsic worth. The A-grade coins were valued at 2.5 cents (sen), B-grade as 1 cent, and C-grade declared as valueless and non-exchangeable. The C-grade coins, which represented two-thirds of the nickel in circulation, caused a significant loss for Korean businessmen.

Before the new Japanese currency was introduced, many Korean merchants were skeptical about its value and preferred to invest in the old coins. However, after the exchange went into effect, they had to bear significant losses as they had no capital left to finance their businesses. As a result, Japanese businessmen made huge profits from the currency reform, which paved the way for the economic growth of Japanese commercial interests. Furthermore, it allowed Japanese banks to dominate the financial sector.

Once the ports of Korea were opened, Japanese financial institutions started to appear. In the early 1900s, many Japanese banks, including Daiichi Ginko, established their branches or agency offices in Korea. These banks played a significant role in the financial activities of Korea. In 1905, Daiichi Ginko was authorized to issue currency and act as a central bank in Korea. It performed various central banking activities, such as buying gold and silver bullion, giving loans to the government, and collecting customs duties in the ports. When the Bank of Korea (BK) was established in 1909, it took on these responsibilities, and the manager of Daiichi Ginko's general offices in Seoul was appointed as the governor of the new bank.

Following the annexation of Korea in 1911, the Bank of Korea was transformed into the Bank of Choson (BC). The name BC was derived from the Japanese pronunciation of the word "Choson," reflecting Japan's historical reference to Korea. This bank was given the responsibility of functioning as a central bank. Additionally, the Industrial (Shokusan Ginko) Bank was formed in 1906 to aid in the agricultural and industrial development of Korea. However, after the annexation, its primary purpose shifted towards supporting Japanese businessmen and farmers.[171]

During the Protectorate period, the Korean government had to borrow money from Japan to support the activities of Japanese R-G, such as establishing banks, improving roads, and employing Japanese officials. The Japanese government and banks provided loans through the R-G, and Daiichi gave a loan of 3,000,000 yen for currency reform and made a huge profit. This policy of borrowing from Japan to finance Japanese activities in Korea continued aggressively until annexation, and Korea's debt had reached 45,000,000 yen by 1910. This debt burden made the Korean government dependent on Japan, and to redeem the debt, a nationwide movement collected contributions from the Korean people. After annexation, the Japanese G-G repaid the debt by collecting taxes from the Koreans.

Government Finance

Korea's colonial status was evident in its economic dependence on Japan. Since 1910, the Japanese government had funded Korea's economic development, with Korea relying on subsidies from the general funds in Tokyo. As time passed, the subsidies decreased, and tax collections in Korea increased. However, after the Sam-Il Movement, the need for occupational expenditures, such as an expanded police force, led to a continued need for subsidies from Japan.

The Japanese government kept their army stationed in Korea and had a budget for military and administrative expenses. This budget was increased significantly after the Sam-Il Movement and even further during the worldwide depression in the 1930s. It continued to rise during the Japanese invasion of Manchuria and the Sino-Japanese War (S-JW).[172]

Increase in Japanese Expenditures

From 1911 to 1937, the expenditure of the G-G in Korea grew tenfold. The majority of this budget was spent on communication and transportation, which accounted for a significant 56.3% of the overall expenses. The rest of the budget was spent on bond repayment, public works, and industry promotion.

Table I:
Japan's Budget for Colonization of Korea

(In thousand yen)

During	Military Operation	Administration	Total
1907	10,626	16,701	27,328
1908	15,229	15,679	30,909
1909	10,358	10,848	21,207
1910	10,193	15,643	25,836
1911	9,052	12,350	22,002

During	Military Operation	Administration	Total
1912	8,984	12,350	21,334
1913	8,233	10,000	18,233
1914	7,069	9,000	16,069
1915	6,971	8,000	14,971
1916	8,737	7,000	15,737
1917	10,536	5,000	15,533
1918	11,189	3,000	14,189
1919	15,838	---	15,838
1920	17,857	10,000	27,857
1921	24,587	15,000	39,587
1922	19,551	15,600	35,151
1923	17,369	15,017	32,387
1924	15,238	15,021	30,260
1925	15,769	16,554	32,324
1926	15,716	19,445	35,162

During	Military Operation	Administration	Total
1927	15,441	15,000	30,441
1928	15,873	15,000	30,873
1929	18,559	15,000	33,559

Source: Himeno Mineru (ed.): Choson Keizai Zuhyo (*The Statistical Charts of Korean Economy*), 1940, Seoul, p. 141

Table II:
(Budget) Expenditure of the Government-General of Choson

(In thousand yen)

During	Admin	Police	Education	Public Works	Business Encouragement	Gov't Enterprise	Bond Repayment	Others	Total
1911	6,466	6,550	825	13,326	2,469	10,068	1,733	7,304	48,741
1914	7,237	6,716	1,237	4,291	2,778	22,683	5,202	9,268	59,412
1917	7,408	6,960	1,654	4,660	2,351	27,098	5,471	7,040	62,642
1920	13,987	22,736	4,595	7,108	5,865	33,570	7,441	19,015	114,317
1923	18,321	29,220	5,996	10,627	10,627	51,241	12,798	11,622	146,007
1926	16,473	26,992	6,212	9,433	16,333	94,264	15,121	9,660	194,488

During	Admin	Police	Education	Public Works	Business Encouragement	Gov't Enterprise	Bond Repayment	Others	Total
1929	18,875	29,676	8,567	14,197	20,541	122,930	19,447	12,619	246,852
1932	13,778	19,740	7,598	10,620	10,362	112,495	23,090	21,703	219,381
1935	10,660	20,926	12,079	15,994	17,861	152,805	27,027	32,915	290,267
1937	12,952	25,280	14,989	26,260	26,161	239,332	29,764	50,385	425,123

(Budget) Expenditure of the Government-General of Choson by Percentage

1911	13.3	13.4	1.7	27.3	5.1	20.7	3.5	15.0	100.0
1914	12.2	11.3	2.1	7.2	4.7	38.2	8.8	15.6	100.0
1917	11.8	11.1	2.6	7.4	3.8	42.3	8.7	11.3	100.0
1920	12.2	19.9	4.0	6.2	5.1	29.4	6.5	16.4	100.0
1923	12.5	20.0	4.1	4.2	7.3	35.1	8.8	8.0	100.0
1926	8.5	13.9	3.2	4.8	8.4	48.4	7.8	5.0	100.0
1929	7.7	12.0	3.5	5.7	8.3	49.8	7.9	5.1	100.0
1932	6.3	9.0	3.5	4.8	4.7	51.3	10.5	9.9	100.0
1935	3.7	7.2	4.2	5.5	6.1	52.7	9.3	11.3	100.0

| 1937 | 3.0 | 5.9 | 3.5 | 6.2 | 6.2 | 56.3 | 7.0 | 11.9 | 100.0 |

Source: Ibid, p. 99.

Government Revenues

In 1937, the Japanese government relied heavily on monopolies and property rights as their primary sources of revenue, which made up 54.6% of the total revenue (as shown in Table III). The majority of their revenue came from railway, postal, telephone, and telegraph companies, as well as monopolies in tobacco, ginseng, salt, and opium (as depicted in Tables IV and V).

Table III:
(Budget) Revenues of the Government-General of Choson

(In thousand yen)

1911	12,440	863	---	11,791	11,791	10,000	12,350	4,163	677	52,284
1914	16,685	1,857	---	16,299	16,299	7,640	9,000	9,639	927	62,047
1917	22,679	4,224	---	18,592	18,592	12,830	5,000	10,639	940	74,903

1920	34,839	8,848	---	26,736	26,736	22,355	10,000	32,776	10,789	146,343
1923	34,392	9,391	5,179	40,360	45,539	26,595	15,017	14,247	7,542	152,713
1926	41,947	11,798	12,729	91,238	103,967	13,383	19,761	13,137	7,715	211,708
1929	45,987	11,372	15,710	108,416	124,126	13,747	15,423	20,461	9,463	240,579
1932	41,166	11,760	17,892	103,136	121,023	23,035	12,913	17,171	3,227	220,300
1935	64,364	18,700	21,022	154,905	175,927	20,922	12,826	32,593	3,887	330,219
1937	72,524	18,693	30,686	227,528	233,551	65,000	12,914	22,182	2,789	427,653

(Budget) Revenues of the Government-General of Choson by Percentage

1911	23.8	1.7	---	22.5	22.5	19.1	23.6	8.0	1.3	100.0
1914	26.9	3.0	---	26.3	26.3	12.3	14.5	15.5	1.5	100.0
1917	30.3	5,6	---	24.8	24.8	17.1	14.2	1.3	1.3	100.0
1920	23.8	6.0	---	18.3	18.3	15.3	6.8	22.4	7.4	100.0

1923	22.5	6.1	3.4	26.5	29.9	17.4	9.8	9.3	5.0	100.0
1926	19.8	5.6	6.0	43.2	49.2	6.3	9.3	6.2	3.6	100.0
1929	19.1	4.7	6.5	45.0	51.5	5.2	7.4	8.2	3.9	100.0
1932	18.7	5.3	8.1	46.8	54.9	10.5	5.9	3.2	1.5	100.0
1935	19.4	5.7	6.4	46.9	53.3	6.3	3.9	9.9	1.5	100.0
1937	17.0	4.4	7.2	47.4	54.6	15.2	3.0	5.2	0.6	100.0

Source: Ibid, p. 102.

Table IV:
Revenue of Taxation of the Government-General of Choson

(In thousand yen)

1911	---	---	6,648	190	260	---	4,061	1,275	12,440
1914	---	---	10,100	365	477	---	3,893	1,848	16,685
1917	404	---	10,225	849	1,472	---	7,295	2,430	22,679
1920	1,598	---	11,453	645	3,767	614	9,747	7,011	34,830
1923	953	---	15,226	487	7,750	1,483	7,145	1,391	34,392

1926	1,091	---	15,348	516	9,460	2,325	12,202	1,004	41,947
1929	1,199	1,516	14,819	619	13,229	3,095	10,716	787	45,987
1932	1.006	1,233	15,422	744	11,366	2,379	7,966	1,027	41,166
1935	9,202	1,848	13,768	1,797	19,590	3,077	13,266	1,816	64,364
1937	1,659	2,580	13,827	2,567	24,067	12,801	12,801	5,551	81,590

Revenue of Taxation of the Government-General of Choson by Percentage

1911	---	---	---	55.4	1.5
1914	---	---	60.5	2.2	2.9
1917	1.8	---	45.1	3.7	6.7
1920	4.6	---	32.9	1.8	10.8
1923	2.8	---	44.3	1.4	22.5
1926	2.6	---	36.6	1.2	22.6
1929	2.6	3.3	32.2	1.4	28.8
1932	2.4	3.0	37.5	1.8	27.6
1935	14.3	2.9	21.4	2.8	30.4

| 1937 | 20.3 | 3.2 | 16.9 | 3.2 | 29.5 |

Source: Ibid, p. 105.

Table V:
Revenue from Government Enterprises and Properties

(In thousand yen)

During	Tobacco	Salt	Ginseng	Opium	Total
1911	---	18	121	---	139
1914	---	106	1,275	---	1,381
1917	---	448	2,070	---	2,518
1920	---	291	2,548	12	2,851
1923	16,928	567	2,225	65	19,785
1926	27,591	1,313	2,568	---	31,742
1929	34,319	1,603	2,481	---	38,403
1932	33,108	4,594	2,099	284	40,085
1935	43,190	6,641	1,704	492	52,027

1937	55,758	6,968	1,812	1,215	65,754

Table V continued:

Railway	Post/Telegrams/Telephones	Other	Total
5,757	2,593	3,300	11,791
7,734	3,149	4,032	16,299
4,730	4,492	6,851	18,592
4,921	7,642	11,318	26,736
7,478	11,017	7,259	45,539
518,111	12,324	8,357	103,967
63,038	14,409	8,276	124,126
59,009	14,393	7,541	121,028
90,470	19,371	1,409	175,927
12,639	24,680	19,112	235,939

Revenues from Government Enterprises and Properties by Percentage

1911	---	0.2	1.0	---	1.2	48.8	22.2	28.0	100.0
1914	---	0.7	7.8	---	8.5	47.5	19.3	24.7	100.0
1917	---	2.4	11.1	---	13.5	25.4	24.2	36.2	100.0
1920	---	1.1	9.5	0.1	10.7	18.4	28.6	42.3	100.0
1923	37.2	1.3	4.9	0.1	43.5	16.4	24.2	15.9	100.0
1926	26.5	1.3	2.5	---	30.3	49.8	11.9	8.0	100.0
1929	27.6	1.3	2.0	---	30.9	50.8	11.6	6.7	100.0
1932	27.4	3.8	1.7	0.2	33.1	48.8	11.9	6.2	100.0
1935	24.5	3.0	1.0	0.3	29.6	51.4	11.0	8.0	100.0
1937	23.6	3.0	0.8	0.5	27.9	53.6	10.4	8.1	100.0

Source: Ibid, p. 105.

According to information from 1934, the amount of Japanese government and private capital that flowed into Korea between 1910 to 1933 was 3.016 billion yen. During the same period, there was an outflow of capital from Korea to Japan, which amounted to 1.803 billion yen. This means that the net inflow of Japanese funds was almost 1.213 billion yen.

Table VI shows that the Japanese investment in Korea was 1.888 billion yen between 1910 and 1923. The outflow of profit and interest from Korea was 363 million yen, which equates to a return of 18% on the actual investment.

Table VI:
Money Flow to and from Japan for Reasons Other than Trade (1910–23)

(In thousand yen)

	Incoming
Public bonds	361,519
Private bonds	559,919
Corporation investment from main offices in Korea	222,917
Corporation investment from main offices in Japan	313,556
Loans for banks and corporation	430,378
Total	1,888,286
	Outgoing
Payment of interest for private bonds and loans	179,375

Profit for investment from Japan by firms in Korea	76,109
Profit for investment by firms in Japan	107,479
Total	362,964

Source: Hosokawa Karoku, pp. 333–34.

Banks and Other Financial Institutions

As previously mentioned, during the period between 1910 and 1937, various financial institutions operated in Korea. BC was responsible for banking, while the Industrial Bank of Choson (IBC) and the ODC financed long-term industrial and agricultural activities. The Savings Bank of Choson (SBC) provided savings bank functions. Several commercial banks, including the Choson Trust and Insurance Company (CTIC), Financial Co-operatives (FC), the Co-operative Financial Company (Mujin) (CFC), and usurers, also controlled banking. The Commercial Banks (CB) consisted of six Korean-owned banks, such as Hansong, Tongil, Korea Commercial, Taegu Commercial and Industrial, Kyongsang United, and Honam, and branches of three Japanese banks, namely Daiichi, Yasuda, and Sanna.

Between 1910 and 1937, the Korean deposit ratio remained constant, while the Japanese ratio gradually increased. Loans given to Koreans increased from 28.9% in 1910 to 39.8% in 1937. At the same time, the loans given to the Japanese decreased from 68.7% to 60.1% (as indicated in Table VII).

Table VII: Bank Deposits and Loans by Nationality

(In thousand yen)

During	Korean		Japanese		Other Foreigners		Total	%
	Actual Amount	%	Actual Amount	%	Actual Amount	%		
				Deposits				
1910	3,899	21.8	11,980	67.2	1,975	11.0	17,855	100.0
1916	6,931	19.1	26,118	71.9	3,246	9.0	36,296	100.0
1921	17,799	14.6	99,326	81.8	4,511	3.6	121,636	100.0
1926	26,506	16.9	124,103	79.1	6,251	4.0	156,866	100.0
1931	35,081	19.0	144,626	78.6	4,371	2.4	184,078	100.0
1936	80,659	23.9	250,099	74.1	6,641	2.0	337,405	100.0
1937	78,185	20.9	289,637	77.3	6,954	1.8	374,776	100.0

Loans

| 1910 | 6,631 | 28.9 | 15,797 | 68.7 | 561 | 2.4 | 22,990 | 100.0 |

1916	14,259	28.2	35,966	70.6	675	1.2	50,899	100.0
1921	85,556	38.4	135,003	60.1	3,232	1.5	223,792	100.0
1926	105,438	36.6	179,588	62.3	3,356	I.I	288,382	100.0
1931	179,899	49.5	181,560	50.0	1,783	0.5	363,242	100.0
1936	301,475	44.5	371,420	54.9	3,807	0.6	676,702	100.0
1937	322,518	39.8	486,211	60.1	843	0.1	809,572	100.0

Source: Himeno Mineru; Choson Keizai Zuhyo, 1940, Seoul, p. 379.

Foreign Capital in Korea, Development of Foreign Trade, Government Finance

Developing countries often relied on foreign capital to supplement their domestic capital for industrialization. In BC, ownership of deposits was distributed to Japanese and Koreans at a ratio of 95:5, while loans were given at a ratio of 98 to 2 (as shown in Table VIII). This resulted in a monopoly of deposits and loans for the Japanese.

Table VIII:
Deposits and Loans of "The Bank of Choson" by Nationality

(In thousand yen)

During	Deposits			Loans		
	Korean	Japanese	Total	Korean	Japanese	Total
1909	923	5,506	6,429	81	3,519	3,600
1912	710	11,270	11,980	3,450	10,314	13,764
1914	902	13,991	14,893	3,851	14,151	18,002
1916	733	15,162	15,895	3,275	17,374	20,649
1918	734	27,776	28,501	3,562	47,344	50,906
1920	557	13,704	14,261	6,477	38,473	44,950
1922	410	18,542	14,952	6,084	37,009	43,093
1924	719	19,122	69,841	5,147	57,859	64,006
1926	621	10,351	10,972	6,601	35,824	41,885
1928	1,598	15,913	17,511	5,287	21,646	26,933

1930	1,095	33,211	34,306	2,501	28,733	30,784
1932	1,613	22,803	24,416	4,672	50,369	55,041
1934	1,857	33,158	35,015	5,193	59,907	65,100

Source: Bureau of Finance, Choson Government-General (ed.): 1939 Nen Shirabe Choson Kinyu Jika Sankosho (An Extensive Study on the Financing System concluded in 1939).

Table IX:
Percentage of Deposits and Loans of "The Bank of Choson" by Nationality

During	Deposits			Loans		
	Korean	Japanese	Total	Korean	Japanese	Total
1909	15	85	100	2	98	100
1912	6	94	100	26	74	100
1914	6	94	100	30	70	100
1916	5	95	100	16	84	100
1918	8	92	100	6	94	100
1920	4	96	100	15	85	100

During	Deposits			Loans		
	Korean	Japanese	Total	Korean	Japanese	Total
1922	2	98	100	14	86	100
1924	2	98	100	10	90	100
1926	6	94	100	15	85	100
1928	10	90	100	20	80	100
1930	4	96	100	7	93	100
1932	5	95	100	9	91	100
1934	6	94	100	8	92	100

Source: Ibid.

The IBC enjoyed several privileges, which allowed it to issue debentures equal to 15 times its paid-in capital. This bank played a significant role in Korea's colonization and resource exploitation. In 1934, IBC distributed ownership of deposits between the Japanese and Koreans in a ratio of 76:22, whereas the loan distribution was 38:61 (as illustrated in Table X).

Table X:
Private Deposits and Loans of "The Industrial Bank of Choson" by Nationality

(In thousand yen)

Year	Deposits				Loans			
	Korean	Japanese	Foreigners	Total	Korean	Japanese	Foreigners	Total
1918	3,759	11,042	407	15,245	13,248	14,833	446	28,528
1921	4,777	30,532	622	35,932	48,392	42,362	722	91,476
1925	5,672	36,752	631	43,057	56,244	79,560	1,924	137,729
1926	7,584	38,562	852	46,999	59,867	81,282	1,671	142,821
1928	11,532	45,047	1,190	57,771	103,999	73,504	2,466	179,969
1930	6,073	29,190	1,155	36,418	117,814	74,985	2,407	195,206
1932	7,766	33,256	566	41,588	130,635	88,551	882	220,068

Year	Deposits				Loans			
	Korean	Japanese	Foreigners	Total	Korean	Japanese	Foreigners	Total
1934	11,949	39,707	525	52,181	150,629	97,551	2,259	250,439

Source: Ibid.

Percentage

Year	Deposits				Loans			
	Korean	Japanese	Foreigners	Total	Korean	Japanese	Foreigners	Total
1918	24	72	4	100	45	53	2	100
1921	13	85	2	100	53	46	1	100
1925	13	85	2	100	40	58	2	100
1926	16	82	2	100	41	57	2	100
1928	19	78	3	100	57	40	3	100
1930	16	80	4	100	60	39	1	100
1032	19	79	2	100	59	40	1	100

Year	Deposits				Loans			
	Korean	Japanese	Foreigners	Total	Korean	Japanese	Foreigners	Total
1934	22	76	2	100	61	38	1	100

Source: Ibid.

According to Tables XI and XII, the growth rate of Korean deposits in SBC was slower than that of Japanese deposits. However, the Korean loans increased at a faster pace compared to the Japanese loans. Between 1929 and 1935, Korean deposits saw an 85% increase, while their loans increased by 248% during the same period.

Table XI:
Deposits and Loans of "The Savings Bank of Choson" by Nationality

(In thousand yen)

During	Deposits				Loans			
	Korean	Japanese	Foreigners	Total	Korean	Japanese	Foreigners	Total
1929	6,636	14,588	128	21,352	2,675	3,297	38	6,010
1930	5,928	18,416	102	24,446	2,730	3,629	22	6,381

During	Deposits				Loans			
	Korean	Japanese	Foreigners	Total	Korean	Japanese	Foreigners	Total
1931	6,044	20,038	60	20,142	2,252	3,387	12	5,651
1932	6,327	21,835	37	28,199	2,578	4,438	7	7,023
1933	6,676	23,113	24	29,813	3,053	5,467	---	8,520
1934	7,989	26,003	30	34,022	4,551	6,644	3	11,198
1935	12,352	30,949	70	43,371	9,308	10,207	10	19,525

Source: Ibid.

Table XII:

Indices of Deposits and Loans of "The Savings Bank of Choson" by Nationality (1929 and 1935)

During	Deposits				Loans			
	Korean	Japanese	Foreigners	Total	Koreans	Japanese	Foreigners	Total
1929	100	100	100	300	100	100	100	300
1935	185	212	54	203	203	348	309	324

Source: Ibid.

Table XIII:
Private Deposits in Commercial Banks by Nationality by Percentage

(In thousand yen)

During	Korean	Japanese	Total	Korean	Japanese	Total
1908	5,508	6,612	12,120	46	54	100
1912	1,816	6,866	8,672	21	79	100
1916	3,360	13,274	16,634	20	80	100
1921	12,261	57,210	69,471	20	80	100
1926	18,301	75,058	93,359	20	80	100
1928	21,780	159,333	181,113	12	88	100
1930	25,750	95,966	121,716	21	79	100
1932	27,984	97,994	125,978	21	79	100

Source: Ibid.

Table XIV:
Private Loans of Commercial Banks by Nationality by Percentage

(In thousand yen)

During	Korean	Japanese	Total	Korean	Japanese	Total
1908	1,406	12,004	13,410	10	90	100
1912	3,991	12,564	16,555	21	79	100
1916	5,420	14,711	20,131	26	74	100
1921	30,174	52,263	82,437	39	61	100
1926	39,508	62,326	101,834	39	61	100
1928	41,849	60,595	102,444	41	59	100
1930	50,602	58,569	109,171	47	53	100
1932	53,539	60,714	114,243	41	59	100

Source: Ibid.

The deposits of the Japanese continued to increase while those of the Koreans decreased until 1932. The ownership of deposits was distributed between Koreans and Japanese at a ratio of 2:8, as shown in Table XII. The ratio of loans to Koreans compared to total loans increased, but for the Japanese, it decreased. In 1931, 1932, and 1937, approximately 40% of all loans extended to Koreans by IBC, ODC, and other banks were secured by real estate, as shown in Tables XIV, XV, and XVI. Therefore, a significant portion of Korean real estate was used as collateral for loans provided by financial institutions.

Table XV:
Amount of Hypothecation held by "The Industrial Bank of Choson"

(In thousand yen)

Year	Real Estate	Others	Total
1918	9,995	19,844	29,839
1921	49,141	82,042	131,183
1925	95,523	101,570	197,093
1928	123,869	129,244	253,113
1930	147,533	150,923	298,456
1932	141,748	196,590	338,338

Percentage

Year	Real Estate	Others	Total
1918	33	67	100
1921	37	63	100
1925	48	52	100
1928	49	51	100
1930	50	50	100
1932	41	59	100

Source: Ibid.

Table XVI:
Amount of Hypothecations Held by Banks (December 1931)

(In thousand yen)

Kind	Bank of Choson	Industrial Bank of Choson	Savings Bank of Chosen	Commercial Banks	Total	Percent
Security	5,165	4,178	59	5,143	14,546	2.97%

Kind	Bank of Choson	Industrial Bank of Choson	Savings Bank of Choson	Commercial Banks	Total	Percent
Merchandise	19,613	16,055	---	10,972	10,972	9.54%
Land & Building	23,176	145,451	591	44,307	213,887	43.72%
Incorporate fund	5,103	5,374	---	705	11,182	2.29%
Mineral Right	105	---	---	---	105	0.02%
Fishery Right	---	467	---	3	471	0.10%
Credit	8,318	138,186	4,640	19,367	170,512	34.85%
Other	4,022	2,645	---	25,177	31,845	6.51%

Source: Choson no Kinyu (Finance of Choson) pp. 90–91.

Table XVII:

Amount of Choson Hypothecations Held by Banks & "Oriental Development Company" (June 1937) (in thousand Yen)

Kind Bank	Security	Merchandise	Land & Building	Incorporate Fund
Bank of Choson	26,822,039	25,899,490	30,431,653	14,853,624
Industrial Bank of Choson	33,872,235	23,897,493	224,784,990	4,492,023
Commercial Banks	16,988,936	11,175,431	79,434,024	1,697,795
Savings Bank of Choson	1,526,609	---	2,605,913	---
Oriental Development Company	1,096,390	5,444,299	37,794,806	1,148,270
Total	80,309,209	66,416,713	375,051,386	22,191,712
Percentage of Total	8.65	7.15	40.40	2.39

Kind Bank	Security	Merchandise	Land & Building	Incorporate Fund
Total in December 1936	73,843,848	95,697,757	354,416,556	14,586,344
% of Total in December 1936	7.86	10.18	37.70	1.55

Kind Bank	Mineral Right	Fishery Right	Credit	Other	Total
Bank of Choson	---	---	29,850,554	18,025,089	145,882,429
Industrial Bank of Choson	---	566,000	193,774,820	2,417,372	483,804,933
Commercial Banks	---	1,060	23,545,043	44,204,265	177,046,454
Savings Bank of Choson	---	---	16,691,334	5,866,481	26,690,337
Oriental Development Company	3,694,249	24,345	45,611,169	---	94,813,528

Total	3,694,249	591,405	309,472,920	70,513,087	928,237,681
% of Total	0.39	0.06	33.34	7.59	100
Total in December 1936	2,807,208	492,454	362,163,409	35,986,780	939,994,356
% of the total in December 1936	0.30	0.05	38.53	3.83	100

Source: Choson Shokusan Ginko Chosabu (Industrial Bank of Choson): Choson Kinyu Jigyo Gaikyo (*The Present Status of the Financing System in Korea*), 1937.

Interest rates were lower for the Japanese than for the Koreans, and the rate of interest on loans secured by real estate ranged between 19.3% and 12.9% per month for the Japanese while among the Koreans the rates ranged between 21.8% to 14.3% (Table XVIII).

Table XVIII:
Interest Rates of Real Estate Hypothecation Loans

Highest

	1928	1929	1930	1931	1932	1933	1934	1935
Between Koreans	2.79	2.67	2.61	2.60	2.55	2.46	2.28	2.18
Between Japanese	2.53	2.50	2.37	2.31	2.24	2.16	2.02	2.93
Between Korean & Japanese	2.67	2.64	2.57	2.55	2.47	2.35	2.20	2.13

Lowest

1.83	1.80	1.80	1.79	1.71	1.64	1.50	1.43
1.70	1.69	1.63	1.57	1.50	1.45	1.35	1.29
1.81	1.78	1.77	1.73	1.65	1.57	1.47	1.47

Median

2.22	2.17	2.13	2.12	2.05	1.98	1.87	1.75
2.08	2.05	1.95	1.90	1.83	1.76	1.66	1.58
2.19	2.15	2.12	2.08	1.99	1.88	1.82	1.72

Source: Choson Shokusan Ginko Chosabu (Choson Industrial Bank): Fudosan Teito Kojin Kan Taishaku Kinri Shirabe (The Survey Report on the Interest Rates of Private Loans on Mortgage of Real Estate, as summarized from the first, third, and seventh surveys).

The survey on usurious loans showed that the highest monthly rate for the Japanese was 30%, while for the Koreans it was 39% (as presented in Table XIX).

Table XIX:
Interest Rates on Usurious Private Loans (monthly)

Year	Transactions Between Koreans			Transactions Between Japanese		
	Highest	Lowest	Median	Highest	Lowest	Median
1911	60	25	38	48	22	31
1912	52	24	34	44	23	31
1913	94	18	35	78	15	30
1914	93	18	37	73	17	32

Year	Transactions Between Koreans			Transactions Between Japanese		
	Highest	Lowest	Median	Highest	Lowest	Median
1915	82	17	39	73	14	29
1916	49	22	31	39	19	27
1917	46	21	30	37	18	26
1918	42	20	28	36	17	25
1919	47	22	30	38	19	28
1920	47	24	32	44	22	31
1921	45	22	32	42	20	30
1922	49	22	34	42	21	30
1923	46	21	31	38	19	27
1924	46	23	32	39	19	27
1925	44	21	31	38	18	26
1926	44	22	30	37	18	26
1927	45	21	31	37	18	26
1928	44	21	30	36	17	25

Year	Transactions Between Koreans			Transactions Between Japanese		
	Highest	Lowest	Median	Highest	Lowest	Median
1929	43	21	30	35	17	25
1930	42	20	28	33	16	24
1931	42	20	29	33	17	23
1932	42	21	29	32	16	23
1933	41	20	28	32	16	23
1934	39	18	27	30	15	22
1935	39	18	26	30	14	21

Source: Bureau of Finance, Choson Government-General (ed.): 1937 Nen Shirabe Choson Kiniyu Jiko Sankosho (An Extensive Study on the Financing System in Korea conducted in 1939).

The Difficulties Faced by the Native Korean Enterprises

During the late nineteenth century, Korean entrepreneurs started to invest in modern commercial and industrial activities with their capital. Private Korean companies took steps to establish themselves in various fields of business. The modern merchants' associations at the ports were organized similarly to chambers of commerce. In 1895, the government introduced the "Regulations

Governing Chambers of Commerce." By 1905, a businessman's association called the Hansong (Seoul) Chamber of Commerce (CC) was established. However, this was a challenging time for Korean businessmen due to the Russo-Japanese War (R-JW) and Japan's tightened political hold on Korea. Additionally, they were struggling financially due to Megata's currency reforms.

The Hansong Chamber of Commerce (CC) was established by Korean businessmen to save themselves from financial disaster. Their main goal was to overcome the shortage of capital they faced. However, when their proposals to the government were not heard due to Japanese obstruction, they decided to found their own bank, the First Bank of Korea (Hanil Unhaeng-FBK). The Hansong CC also had a display hall and published a monthly commerce and industry bulletin, which provided a wide range of information on domestic and international economic trends to fellow businessmen. Unfortunately, the Hansong CC was dissolved after Korea became a Japanese colony, and Korean businessmen were absorbed into the Japanese-dominated Keijo (Seoul) CC.[173]

Starting from 1897, Korean entrepreneurs became interested in modern industries and began building modern manufacturing facilities. They believed that they could compete successfully with Japanese businesses by producing quality goods. They focused mainly on textiles and established several well-known mills, such as An Kyong-su's Korea Textile Works (1897), the Chongno Textile Company (1900), which was founded by the old government-licensed cotton cloth shop in Chongno, and the Kim Tok-ch'ang Textile Company (1902), which modernized its antiquated factory. Alongside textiles, there were also factories for ceramics, rice cleaning, tobacco products, and milling.

During a time when foreign powers were competing for concessions to build railways in Korea, it was decided that Korean capital would be used to construct the railways. This led to the establishment of the Pusan and Southwest Perimeter Railway Company in 1898, led by Pak Ki-jong, intending to link Pusan with the Naktong River region. In 1899, the Korea Railway Company was formed to build railway lines connecting Seoul to Uiju, Seoul to Wonsan, and from Wonsan northward to the Hamgyong province. There were other railway companies established as well, but due to inadequate capital, the government decided to directly undertake the construction of these railway lines and established a railway bureau in 1900. A new government agency was then created to manage the Seoul-Uiju line, and its construction was initiated in 1902 by its director, Yi Yong-ik. However, when the R-JW broke out in 1904, Japan took control of the right to build the rail link.

In regard to shipping, a joint venture between the government and private sector operated in the early 1890s. However, after it ceased to function, it took until 1897 for a purely private shipping industry to begin emerging. In 1900, several cargo-carrying lines were established, such as Korea Joint Mail and Shipping, Inch'on Mail and Shipping, and Inhan Steamship Company. Subsequently, full-service freight forwarding and shipping companies came into existence.[174]

The commercial and industrial activities carried out by Korean capital were negligible compared to those of the Japanese. This was because opportunities for the development of enterprises by Korean capital were more limited after the annexation in 1910. A law was enacted by the R-G to regulate all business companies, and in 1911, this law was strengthened to give the Japanese G-G complete control over the formation and dissolution of business houses. The Japanese companies were also restrained in their freedom to develop by the Japanese, and companies operating with Korean capital faced even more serious problems. This is evident from the statistics on industrial output in 1917 by nationality of factory owner (as presented in Table XX). There were not significantly fewer Korean-owned factories than Japanese-owned ones, yet the Korean companies had only one-eighteenth the capital of the Japanese, and their output was barely one-tenth. As a result, Korean industrial companies were mostly small-scale and had almost insignificant operations.

Under the Japanese colonial regime, Korean-owned companies were underdeveloped because Japanese banks controlled access to capital in Korea. Additionally, after a currency reform, there was a shortage of finance, making it difficult for Korean entrepreneurs to obtain enough capital to survive. Although some Korean banks, such as the FBK, were established by wealthy Seoul merchants with the support of previous Korean government officials, these were small-scale efforts that could not compete with Japanese banks. In 1903, the Korean government circulated an ordinance to create a central bank, but even their plans for their own central bank did not materialize.

Table XX:
Factories by Industry and Nationality of Owner (1917)

Industry	Owner	Number of Factories	Capital (in yen)	Production (in yen)
Cotton Cloth, Dyeing	Korean	70	236,390	612,073
and Weaving	Japanese	36	6,894,989	6,230,739
Paper, Pulp	Korean	51	15,886	58,022
	Japanese	4	15,000	144,116
Hides and Tanning	Korean	37	52,900	299,139
	Japanese	8	1,991,036	3,531,663
Ceramic Products	Korean	115	137,720	169,350
	Japanese	67	506,500	631,944
Soap, Fertilizer	Japanese	20	474,200	763,627
Metalworking	Korean	106	202,250	378,695
	Japanese	57	279,270	1,590,729
Lumber, Wood-	Korean	22	33,917	80,529

Industry	Owner	Number of Factories	Capital (in yen)	Production (in yen)
working	Japanese	43	544,010	1,344,906
Milling, Rice Cleaning	Korean	154	546,420	5,855,153
	Japanese	152	3,682,906	41,685,923
	Others	1	500	4,500
Noodles, Confectionary	Japanese	36	170,250	350,974
Tobacco Products	Korean	5	211,880	539,627
	Japanese	21	2,214,413	6,016,332

Note: Factories with less than five employees and government-owned enterprises are not included.[175]

Between 1911 and 1919, the non-agricultural industry in Korea was concentrated on traditional areas like mining, garment and food preparation, and papermaking. However, things changed after 1916. Due to the World War, Western Europeans became more involved in Europe than in East Asia; thus, there was less competition. Additionally, there was a relaxation of the CL, which led to a rapid increase in small household factories with five or more workers, and the industrial workforce rose to over 40,000, quadrupling the previous figure. New technology arrived with new businesses, and skilled Japanese workers came to train and supervise Korean workers. The production values more than doubled in all major sectors of the economy between 1916 to 1918, except for forestry. However, food preparation, textiles, alcohol, and tobacco were still tied to agriculture. As a result, agriculture declined as a percentage of overall production value while industries became the major beneficiary (Table XX).[176]

Table XXI:
Percentage of Total Korean Production by Industry (1920 to 1930)

	Agriculture	Forestry	Fisheries	Mining	Industry
1920	80.6	1.8	3.7	1.5	12.4
1930	61.6	5.4	7.0	2.1	23.9

Source: Kaneko Furnia, "1920 nendal ni okeru Choson sangyo seisaku no Keisei," ed. Hara Akira, Kindai Nihon no Keizai to seiji, Tokyo 1986, p. 179, 197.

The government played a major role in driving modern industry inside the centrally controlled economy of colonial Korea, even more so than in Meiji, Japan. The G-G railway works was the largest industrial establishment in the country, employing around one thousand laborers in Seoul alone. The workers were responsible for building passenger and freight cars, as well as repairing locomotives and cars. In addition, depots in Pusan and P'yongyang employed another 450 individuals for minor repairs. The G-G's success led to the establishment of other industries, including the Onoda Cement Factory, built by Mitsui near P'yongyang in 1920. This factory employed 600–700 individuals, with 80% of the workforce being Koreans.[177]

It was clear that Korea's finances were under complete control of the Japanese, whether through the G-G or private companies. Although Koreans owned more factories than the Japanese, the result was that the Japanese invested more capital, resulting in higher production in their factories (as shown in Table XX). Often, Koreans and Japanese had joint ventures, which benefited the Japanese more so than their Korean counterparts. Loans and deposits were also higher on the Japanese side, resulting in Koreans suffering from higher interest rates on loans. The interest rate on real estate loans was between 19.3% to 12.9% per month for Japanese, while for Koreans, it was between 21.8% to 14.3% (as presented in Table XVIII).

During the colonial period, rice exports from Korea to Japan reached their peak in the Import and Export section. Between 1929 and 1938, rice exports increased by 96% (as shown in Table XXVII). However, the G-G did not publish any export data for rice after 1939, although production data was made public. Primary products such as raw materials, semi-finished, and finished foodstuffs constituted 83.5% of exports, while secondary industrial products made up 55.7% of imports (as indicated in Table XXVIII). This reflects the colonial economic relationship between Japan and Korea. Additionally, Japanese investment from 1910 to 1923 totaled 1.888 billion yen, with the outflow of interest and profit from Korea to Japan amounting to 363 million yen, constituting an 18% return on the net investment (as depicted in Table VI).

The G-G of Choson relied on revenues from Korea to cover its expenses. This dependence arose from the fact that the Choson government held monopolies over various sectors, including railways, postal services, telephones, telegraphs, tobacco, ginseng, salt, and opium. A significant portion of these funds went towards sustaining the Japanese army in Korea, particularly after events like the Sam-Il Movement, the Great Depression in the 1930s, the Japanese invasion of Manchuria, and the S-JW. The majority of banks in Korea were Japanese owned, with only a few in Korean hands, contributing to Japan's economic gains. Consequently, Korea was financially exploited by Japan in every possible way.

CONCLUSION

Korea was a "hermit kingdom" and was not open to outside people, though there was Chinese influence, and the country had trading relations mainly with China, Japan, and some other countries. It was after the turn of the nineteenth century that the corruption, internal conflicts among the ruling factions, and exploitation of the poor peasantry by the feudalistic society of the Choson Dynasty reached its peak. It was then that the Western capitalistic nations began to knock at the door of the "hermit nation." Even before the nineteenth century, foreign vessels visited Korean shores for different purposes, such as for trade or missionary work. Japan was the first East Asian country that successfully overthrew its feudalistic rulers and achieved capitalism. Now, it was going out of the country to expand trade. For that, Japan wanted to have a trade relationship with Korea, and at first, it was unsuccessful. But Japan did not retreat and ventured to use military force against Korea to open its ports to Japan, and Korea had to sign a treaty of "friendship," following some ports being opened to the Japanese traders. Japanese goods flowed to Korea without any obstacle of customs, and the Korean government also signed similar treaties with other foreign nations.

Several years after the signing of the "friendship" treaty, Korea became an exclusive market for Japanese goods. A military revolt (1882) made the position of China better in Korea, and Japan and

China competed with each other for hegemony in trade in Korea. There was a failed attempt by the Korean Min faction to invite Russia to check China and Japan. Instead of taking advantage of the conflicts among the foreign powers, the Korean political leaders engaged in an internal power struggle, and that paved the way for the Japanese invaders, who were more ambitious than the other nations.

Japan's capitalism developed under the leadership of the landowners, bureaucrats, and feudal lords who ruthlessly suppressed the peasants and civil rights leaders. Japan's domestic market became too narrow for her expanding capitalism, and so the country had to seek foreign markets (i.e., China and Korea). Korea had to give up control of telegraphs and railways and also open more ports to Japan under an agreement following the S-JW (1894–95). Korea became more powerless in the competition among the foreign powers to capture the Korean market. Japan made the greatest penetration into Korea and also won the R-JW, and Korean exports, primarily consisting of agricultural products and gold, were directed to Japan under compulsion until the Japanese occupation of Korea.

Before and after the annexation, Japan had to face Korean resistance, as the RA was organized by the Korean literati with the peasantry and the disbanded Korean army (1907). The Korean army fought the Japanese forces in the streets of Seoul, and in some places in central Korea, they defeated the Japanese army. The RA or the guerrilla bands retreated to the mountainous areas, supported by the local people, and they knew the area. Their activities declined after the annexation, and they shifted to Manchuria and RMT to continue to fight the Japanese.

Japan developed the existing transportation system for its own benefit, and the railway was expanded with forced cheap labor and land forcibly taken at lower prices. But these modern communications were cursed by the Koreans as those were used later against them. Education was also controlled by the Japanese, and the Japanese language was made compulsory even in traditional Korean schools. Gradually, the Koreans were allowed to enter into the Japanese schools in Korea. It is ironic that the Koreans learned more progressiveness in Japan than in Korea, as they had to go to Japan for higher studies. Rich Koreans used to go to Japan even for elementary education, and there was no bar for that. As in Japan, the Koreans were not interested in the education of girls, especially in the rural areas. But more girls began to attend schools in the later part of colonialism and achieved self-confidence and participated in sports and politics. They participated in national protest movements against the Japanese on numerous occasions.

Japan began to dominate the economy of Korea after the appointment of R-G in 1906. For that, they made a land survey to grab the Korean lands by the Japanese individuals and companies. Japan or the G-G (R-G became G-G after the annexation in 1910) became the largest landowner in Korea and tortured the peasantry to the extreme. Thus, Korea as a colony was exploited by Japan and the Japanese people in Korea. The resistance of the RA and the sacrifice of life by patriotic people was a failure. Though the Koreans did not give up their country without a fight, due to the works of the treacherous faction of the Koreans, they had to face defeat. There were still organizations at home and abroad to free Korea from the clutches of Japanese domination. The Koreans had to wait until 1945, after the end of World War II, to become free from Japanese aggression, and another three years passed before becoming independent and becoming a developed country or a member of G8.

The Japanese government, traders, and landowners seized more and more land from the Korean peasants. With that, the Japanese people started to invest money in Korean farmland. The Oriental Development Company, with the advent of the banking system and the rail line, took the lead in land grabbing in the name of reform. The agricultural policy of the G-G was also harmful to Korean farmers. It was to increase rice production for the benefit of the Japanese in Japan. Korea had to export better quality rice to Japan, and the Korean farmers had to starve for nearly half of the year (at times limited to one meal a day). Crops were the main production, and less emphasis was given to livestock, fertilizer, and silk production.

The land survey made the Japanese big landlords and benefitted the Japanese companies, not the Koreans. Even the irrigation project did not help the Korean peasants, and many of them became destitute. The land survey widened the gap between the farmers and the landlords; independent farmers and partial landowners became tenant-farmers. Manufacturing was also a part of Japanese colonialism. Most industries were built in North Korea, and when the country was divided, both North and South Korea had problems as the economy of both parts was complementary to the other in manufacturing and agriculture. Most of the industries were owned by the Japanese, as they had more capital and had to pay less interest on loans (see Chapter 2). The Japanese also monopolized the Korean resources, and the

Japanese workers used to get more wages than the Koreans, and the Koreans had to work longer hours than the Japanese.

Christianity and Protestantism had an influence on politics and education in Korea and also led campaigns against drinking and smoking and for equality of sexes, strict monogamy, ethics, and simplicity of popular ceremonies. Protestantism was welcomed by Korean intellectuals and businessmen, leading to economic development in some provinces. Religious movements also instilled national consciousness. Confucian leaders, though conservative, wanted to reform Confucianism to adapt to the changing conditions. A reform movement within Buddhism, albeit also conservative, had strong nationalistic ideals. The G-G supported Buddhism and Confucius, learning to counterbalance the other religious movements. There was a state attempt to develop Shintoism but without much success.

There was an effort to rediscover old Korean textbooks and standardize the Korean language and spelling. Old Korean texts were reprinted, and the history of the nation-building of other countries was a model to the Koreans, and biographies of heroic figures were read by them. There arose many organizations like the SYMCA, MAS, NKYA, KNA, AKP, NPA, KYIG, KYIC, KIG, PGRK, LKLF, TFMAS, KPA, RPU, CLU, CCP, RA, CI, CP, ID, IP, CG, and RS. All these organizations supported the restoration of Korean independence in their own way. Some of them were working from abroad, even from Tokyo, Japan.

The Korean nationalists fled to Manchuria and RMT when Korea became a Japanese colony, and from there started movements for independence of Korea. While inside Korea, the nationalists had contact with patriotic elements abroad. There were organizations with the goal of restoring the country's freedom by force of arms. Popular disturbances took place all over Korea. The MFM started with a peaceful Declaration of Independence. It was crushed ruthlessly by the Japanese military force; many were killed, injured, and arrested, and houses, churches, and schools were demolished by fire. The movement failed to have the support of the Western powers and failed to achieve its goal.

The Koreans were completely controlled by the Japanese. The independent farmers became tenant-farmers and faced starvation. There were sporadic revolts by the farmers against the landlords. In the industrial sector, the Korean workers had to work longer hours with low wages, and discontent was expressed in increasing strikes. Korea was waiting for the right time to revolt against Japan. The opportunity came at the end of World War II in 1945.

In 1937, because of the S-JW, Japan developed mines in Korea for gold, silver, and smokeless coal as it needed them. Not all the national resources were extracted or mined, and the Japanese government and military agencies, big capitalists of Japan, explored the Korean mines. Only one belonged to a Korean capitalist, as Korean investment was not encouraged. Cheap labor and hydroelectric power attracted Japanese investors, and Japan's big Zaibatsu competed with each other to build factories in Korea. Manufacturing was also expanded, and heavy factories were built because of the expansion of the war. Women and juveniles were working at lower wages. Even mine workers used to get low wages with long working hours, as the Japanese capitalists took advantage of the Korean working class and burdened them with the war effort. Wages were 70% less than those of Japanese workers in

Japan. Japan's trade increased tenfold between the opening and annexation of Korea. The Korean economic growth in the colonial period is termed by many as "export-led" growth.

Korea was not only a supplier of food grains but also a market for Japan's expanding industrial goods. The rural labor surplus was exhausted as thousands of them were sent into heavy industries and mines, and others went to Japan under compulsion or voluntarily. Korean industries and the labor force were exploited with harshness, and the conditions at home and on the battlefield were deteriorating. Many died of diseases, accidents, allied bombing, or brutal murder.

Only one Korean was appointed in the JPUH and one in the LHR. Language restrictions in colonies were very common. The Japanese also tried to change the Korean historical line. In World War II, Korean patriots fought against the Western powers for Asia. Japan's Home Ministry took over Korea as an integral part of the Japanese empire in 1942, and the Japanese G-G of Korea was to be appointed by the Japanese PM. Conscription was applied to Korean workers who were not only to fight but be used for construction and transport also. Young Korean women, some hardly more than a child, were taken to the war front to serve as prostitutes for the Japanese troops. Rumors were there that the Japanese used to extract oil from Korean teenage girl's bodies as there was a shortage of oil for the machinery. The Koreans were being prepared to repel an invasion by the U.S. forces in the south and the Soviet Union's forces in the north. Korea finally got independence in 1948 after it was evacuated by the U.S. Army in the south and the USSR's government in the north after occupying them in 1945. Two countries emerged from a united Korea: The

Republic of Korea in the south and The Democratic People's Republic of Korea in the north.

The finance of Korea was totally controlled by the Japanese, either by the G-G or by the Japanese private companies. Sometimes, it was also seen that the Koreans owned more factories than the Japanese, but the end result was that the Japanese invested more capital, which resulted in the Japanese having more production in their factories (Table XX in Chapter 6). Often, the Koreans and the Japanese had joint ventures, again for the benefit of the Japanese. The loans and deposits were also higher on the Japanese side than for the Koreans. One of the reasons the Koreans were suffering was that the interest rates of the loans for the Koreans were higher than for the Japanese. Even the rate of interest on loans for real estate of the Japanese was between 19.3% to 12.9% per month, while the interest for the Koreans was between 21.8% to 14.3% (Table XVIII in Chapter 6).

In the Import and Export section, rice exports to Japan increased to a maximum during the colonial period. They increased by 96% between 1929 and 1938 (Table XXVII in Chapter 6), and the governor-general did not publish the export data of rice after 1939, although the production data were made public (Table XXVII in Chapter 6). Primary products (raw materials, semi-finished, and finished foodstuffs) amounted to 83.5% of the exports, and secondary industrial products comprised 55.7% of the imports (Table XXVIII in Chapter 6). It shows the colonial economic relationship nature between Japan and Korea. The Japanese investment in 1910–1923 was 1.888 million yen, and the outflow of interest and profit from Korea to Japan was 363 million yen, i.e., 18% return on the net investment (Table VI in Chapter 6). The G-

G of Choson's expenditure was met by revenues from Korea as the Choson government had monopolies of the railway, postal, telephone, and telegraph companies and also on tobacco, ginseng, salt, and opium. Some of the expenditures were for keeping the Japanese army in Korea, as it was increased after the Sam-Il Movement and also after the Great Depression in the 1930s, the Japanese invasion of Manchuria, and the S-JW. The banks all belonged to Japan and a few to the Koreans, which were also a source of profit to Japan. Thus, Korea was financially robbed by the Japanese in every way.

Thus, finance, trade, land, industries, banks, mines, and in fact, all the infrastructure were in the hands of the Japanese. The Japanese were resisted by the Koreans, but it was unfortunate that they did not get any external help to get freedom from Japan. Even after WWI, the Allied powers did not react to the brutal atrocities of the Japanese in Korea, as they needed Japan's cooperation and raw materials, etc. Just due to a handful of treacherous politicians, Korea was handed over to Japan, and Japan took full advantage to become the supreme power in Korea. In fact, Japan wanted to rule the whole of Asia and started by defeating Russia in Manchuria, and China was also held back, and some areas of China were taken away by Japan.

The Japanese, as a colonial power, did not train the Koreans in any field, and almost all the industries, banks, and other offices were run or manned by the Japanese. The Koreans were ordinary workers, and when Japan had to leave Korea after WWII, there were nearly no trained people to run any of the offices. Everywhere, there was chaos and confusion to run the offices when the country was taken over by the Americans in the south and by the USSR in the North. The Koreans got their final independence in 1948 but with a division of Korea into South and North. But we can say that it took only 35 years for the Koreans to get rid of the Japanese and another three years to get final independence through the declaration of the two Republics. And we should remember that the Japanese did not go willingly but had to leave as they were defeated very badly in World War II and had to surrender to the Allied powers.

WORKS CITED

Primary Sources

Agriculture in Korea: 1936, Seoul.

Bank of Choson, *Economic Review:* 1949. Same scholar placed the share of the agricultural sector at about 85% of Korean GDP in 1910-12 (B.H. Lee 1948: 352–53).

Bank of Choson: Economic Review, 1949.

British Consular Report

Bureau of Agricultural Forestry, Choson Government-General (ed.):

Bureau of Agriculture and Forestry, Choson Government-General (ed.): *Choson Kosaku Nenpo Dai L Shi* (The Korean year book on Tenancy) 1 Sept. 1937.

Bureau of Agriculture Forestry, Choson Government-General (ed.): Choson ni okeru *Kosaku ni Kansuru Sanka Jlko Tekyo* (Reference Material for the Tenancy in Korea), 1932.

Bureau of Education, Choson Government-General (ed.): *Kojyo oyobi Kosanni okeru Rodosha Jyokyo Chosa* (The Survey Report on the Factory and Mine Laborers), 1933, Seoul.

Bureau of Education: Choson Government-General (ed.): *Kojyo Ayobi Kasan Niokery Rodosha Jokyo Chosa* (The Survey Report on the Working Condition of Factories Mineral Laborers), 1933.

Bureau of Finance, Choson Government-General (ed.): 1939 *Nen Shirabe Choson Kinyu Jiko Sankosho* (Extensive Study on the Financial System concluded in 1939).

Bureau of Internal Affairs, Choson Government-General (ed.): *Kapsha oyobi Kojioni okeru Rdosha nee Chosa* (The Survey Report on the Company and Factory Laborers), 1923.

Bureau of Land Survey (Provisional) Choson Government-General (ed.): *Choson Dachi Chosajigyo Hokokusho* (Report of the Land Survey in Korea), 1918, Seoul.

Choson Boeki Kyoki (ed.): *Nenkan Choson* (The Annual book of Korea), 1942, Tokyo.

Choson Government-General (ed.): *Choson Slokufu Takai Nenpo* (The Statistical Year Book of the Choson Government-General) March 1933.

Choson Government-General (ed.): *Naka Keizai no Gaikyo to sono Hensen,* (The Present Status and Historical Changes of the Household Economy of Korea) 1940.

Choson Government-General: *Shishei 30 Nenshi* (The 30 Years History of the Choson Government-General.

Choson no Kenyo: (Finance of Choson).

Choson No Nogyo (Agriculture in Korea).

Choson Shoko Shimbun: 13 Aug. 1938 in O. Gaylord Marsh (Seoul)· of United States, 25 Aug. 1938, U.S. State Dept. records, item 895.5017/1.

Choson Shokusan Ginko Choshabu (Choson Industrial Bank); *Fudasan Taito Kojin Kan Taishaku Kinri Shirabe* (The Survey Report on the Interest Rates on Private Loans on mortgage of real estate, summarized from the 1st, 3rd, and 7th surveys).

Choson.Dachi Kairyu Kabushiki Kaisha Shi: (The History of the Land Improvement Co, Ltd.), p. 3.

FO 371/22190, British Consulate-General, Seoul, *Annual Report on Korea/or 1937,* dated 24 Dec. 1937.

Government-General of Choson, 1837.

Grajdanzev 1944: 1720. 62.

Japan Year Book, 1930.

Japan Year Book, 1940–41.

Keijyo Imperial University Hobungakukai: Choson Shakai Kaizaishi kenkyu (The Study of the Korean Socio-Economic History), Tokyo, 1933.

Korean Land Economy Research Center: *A Study of the Land Tenure System in Korea*.

Quotation and Replies from the United States Consultant General Leo Bergholz to Secretary of State, 17 and 23 April 1919, 22 May 1919, records of the Dept, relating to internal Affairs of Korea 1910-129, document 895.00/622, 895.00/628, 895.00/1639.

Quoted from Official translation presented to President Woodrow Wilson by the Korean National Association, 7 April 1919 in records of the State Dept., relating to the Internal Affairs of Korea, 1910-29, documents 895.01/2.

Ranford S. Miller, United States Consul-General, Seoul, to the State Dept. 29 May 192, item 895.00/705.

Reports from Gaylord Marsh, United States Consul (Seoul) to Sect. of State, 4 and 25 Feb. 1937, US State Dept. Report, 895.114.

Schumpeter (ed.): *The Industrialization of Japan and Manchukuo, 1930-40*, NY 1940.

The Bank of Choson, Research Dept. (ed.): *The Annual Report of the Korean Economy*, 1948, Seoul.

The Choson Government-General (ed.): *The Statistical Year Book*, March, 1936, Seoul.

Toyo Keizai Sinposha (ed.): *Choson Sangyo Nenpo* (The Industrial Annual book of Korea), 1943, Tokyo.

Toyo Keizai Sinposha (ed.): *Choson Sungyo Nenpo* (The Industrial Year Book of Korea), 1943, Tokyo.

Toyo Takushoko kabushi Kaisha Zo Nenshi: (Twenty years history of the Oriental Development Company), Tokyo, 1928.

United States State Dept. O. Gaylord Marsh, Consul (Seoul) Item 895.60/2: United States State Dept., item 895.63.

United States State Dept. records, V. Alex John, Vice-Consul (Seoul) to Sect. of state, Dec. 1937.

United States State Dept. records, W, R. Langdon, Consul (Seoul) to Edwin Neville, Charge d' Affairs (Tokyo) 29 Oct. 1935, item 895.6363/5; U. Alexis Johnson, Vice-Consul (Seoul) 'Present Position and Future Prospects of American oil firms operating in Choson,' 26 Jan. 1938, item 6363/13.

Zenkoku Keizai Chosakikan Rengikai Chisen Shibu (ed.): *The Annual Report of the Korean Economy, 1939.*

BOOKS, ARTICLES, NEWSPAPERS, AND OTHER DOCUMENTS

NEWSPAPERS

Choson Ilbo Newspaper Imperial Post

Independent News Hanson Sunbo, 1883

Keigo Nippon Newspaper Capital Gazette

Korea Self-strengthening Society Monthly Dong-a Ilbo

Korean Daily News, 1905.

BOOKS

Andrew Jonah Grajdanzev, Modem Korea, Korea under Seize, New York: International Secretariat, Institute of Pacific Relations, 1944 (B.M. Lee 1948: 352-53, New York, Octagon Books), 1978.

Ban Sung-whan, *Growth Rates of Korea in Agriculture,* Korean development Institute, 1973, Seoul, 1918-71, Korean Development Institute Press Review, Seoul, 65, 1974.

Bruce F. Johnson, Masaburo Hosoda and Yoshio *Kusumi, Japanese Food Management in World War II,* Stanford, Stanford University Press, 1953.

Chicago, Chicago University Press, 1936.

Cho Kijun: *The Korean Economic History,* Tonga Publishers, Seoul, 1962.

Cho Kijun: *The Korean Economic History.* (Colonial History- theory of modernization), 1974, Seoul.

Cho Kijun et al., 1971: Transformations in Twentieth Century Korea (2006) Routledge, 270 Madison Avenue, New York, NY 10016.

Cho Kijun et al., *flche ha wi minjok saenghwalsa.* Seoul, 1971. Kajimura Hideki, 'Shokuminchi Choson de no Nihonjin', ed.

Choe Tae-Ho; *Hwqjionmin e kwanhan Yon'gu:* (The Study on the Burnt-field Cultivators): The Journal of the College of Economics and Commerce, Chun-ang University, Seoul, vol. 8.

Choi Ho-chin: An Outline of Korean Economic History, Seoul, 1962.

Chon Sok-Tam and two others, *Choson Kyongji-Sa* (The Korean Economic History), Seoul, 1949.

Chong Sok-Tam and three others: *The Economic History under the Japanese Rule,* 1947.

Chong-sik Lee, *Japan and Korea- The Political Dimension.*

D.I. Steinberg: The Republic of Korea- Economic Transformation and Social change, West View Press Boulder and London, 1989.

David Brudnoy, *'Japan's Experiment in Korea', Monumuta Nipponica,* vol 25, Nomor ½, 1970, halama 158, 18 Eckert.

Han Shokwi, *Nihon no chosen Shihai to Shukyo Seisaku,* Tokyo, 1978.,

Hatada Takashi: *Choson Jin jido ni taisuru Choson solokufu no rekishi kyoiku* (ed.): Hatada Takashi, Nihom wa Choson de nani o oshieta na ka, Tokyo, 1987.

Henry Rosovsky, 'Japan's Transition to Modern Economic Growth, 1868-1885, in H. Rosovsky (ed), *Industrialization in Two System.*

Himeno Mineru (ed.): *Choson Keizai Zuhyo* (The Statistical Charts of Korean Economy), Seoul, Korea, 1940.

Himenu Mineru, *Choson keizpi Zuhyo* (The Statistical Charts of Korean Economy) 1940, Seoul. Hosokawa Karuko, *Shyoku Minshi.*

Himenu Mineru: *The Statistical Chart of Korean Economy.*

Hiroaki Takeuchi M.D., *Metronidzole Neoropathy-A* Case Report-Department of Internal Medicine, Kagawa Medical School-Miki-cho Kita-gun, Kagwa, Japan, 1988. See also Tak-geneli Regula of Melanocyte Differentiation-Biological Institute, Toheku University, Aoba-yama, Sendai, Japan.

Hisama Kenichi, *Choson Nosei no Kadai* (The Promatic Issues for the Farm Politics in Korea), 1943, Tokyo.

Hochin Choi, The Economic History of Korea -from earliest times to 1945-The Freedom Library, Seoul, Korea, 1970.

Hoon K. Lee: *Land Utilization and Rural Economy in Korea.*

Ki-baik Lee, A New History of Korea, translated by Edward W. Wagner with Edward J. Shultz, Ilchokak Publishers, Seoul, Korea, 1948.

Kim Pyong T'ae: *Mosum e Kwanhan Yon'gu* (The Study on Farmland in Korea), 'Economy', The Korean Economic Association vols. 4-5, Seoul.

Kimbara Samon, *Chihobunka no Nihonshii to senso,* Tokyo, 1978.

Kimijima Kazuhuko, *Choson ni okeru senso doin taisee noten Kai Kati/* (eds.): Fujiwara Akira/Nozawa Yataka, *Nikonfashizumu to Higashi Ajia,* Tokyo, 1977.

Lee Chang: *Labor Movement and Political Development in Korea,* Seoul, 1971.

Lee See-jae, *The Odyssey of Korean Democracy: Korean Politics,* 1987.

Park Soon Won: *'The Emergence of a Factory Labor Force in Colonial Korea',* A Case Study of the Onoda Cement Factory, (Ph.D. Dissertation, Harvard University), 1985.

Paul W. Kuznet, *Economic Growth and Structure of the Republic of Korea:* (New Haven and London, Yale University Press), 1977.

Ramos H. Myers and Adrienne Ching, *'Agricultural Development in Taiwan· under Japanese Colonial Rule.* ' Journal of Asian Studies: University of Colorado, 23, no 4, 1964. (Taiwan and Korea are said to have shared many similarities during the postwar period i.e. Japanese Colonial Legacy).

Ranford S. Miller, United States Consul-General, Seoul to the State Dept. 29 May 192, item 895.00/705.

Richard E. Kim, *Autobiography-Lost Names,* New York, Praeger, 1970.

Russell Anthony Vacante, Japanese Colonial Education in Korea 1910-45, An Oral History (Doctorial Dissertation), State University, New York at Buffalo, Wagner & W. Edward, 1987.

Samina Sultana, (Ph.D. Dissertation): Rajshahi University, Rajshahi, 2013.

Samina Sultana: The Role of the United States in the Development of the South Korean Economy-1945-1990. Itihas Academy Dhaka, Dhaka 2016.

Samuel P. S. Ho, *Agricultural Transformation Under Colonialism; A Case of Taiwan.'* Journal of the Economic History, Sept. 1968.

Simon Kuznets, *Six Letters on Economic Growth:* Journal of Political Economy, 1969 no 1 (Dec. 1971).

Sorensen, 1990.

Stamford, California, Hoover Institution Press, 1985.

Stewart Lone and Gavan McCormack - Korea Since 1850, (Longman Cheshire), St. Martin's Press Inc., New York, NY 10010. 1993.

Suh Sang-Chul, *Growth and Structural change in the Korean Economic Situations, 1910-45.*

Suzuki Masafumi: *Choson Keizaino Gendan Kai* (The Current Stage of Korean economy), 1938, Tokyo.

Suzuki Takeo, *Choson no Keizai.* A Comparative Study on Diaspora *in* Russia, China is more focused on the Economy: East Asian Regionalism and Korea in the 1940s. International Journal of Korean History 20/41: 101-125, the author stressed from the pre-war to post-war.

The Dong-A ilbo, Newspaper, originally published as daily, Seoul, *Korea under Japanese Colonial Rule:* Mishigan, Kalamazoo, 1973.

Y. Hon-Ku: *Choson Nongop Ron* (The Structure of the Korean Agriculture) 1935, Seoul.

Yoo Se Hee The North Korean Communists Leadership, 1945-65, Britannica Educational Publication, Carle Roberts (Doctorial Dissertation), 1974.

Young Hoon Ka g, 1977.

Zen Koku Keizie Chosakikai Rengokai Choson Shibu (ed.): *Choson Keizai Nenpo:* (The Annual Report of the Korean Economy), 1939, Tokyo.

ENDNOTES

........◆........

Introduction Sections

[1] Park Soon Won "The Emergence of a Factory Labor Force in Colonial Korea. A case study of the Onoda Cement Factory', Ph.D. Dissertation, Harvard University, 1985, p. I 08. Also see S. Lone & G. McCormack, p. 70.

[2] See Dallet. Traditional Korea and Hulbert, The Passing of Korea.

Remainder of Book

[1] The discussion is brief. Readers interested in more detail about the social, economic and political conditions are referred to Takashi Hatada's A History of Korea. About political relations see C. I. Eugene Kim and Han Kyo Kim, Korea and the Politics of Imperialism, 1876-1910.

[2] Samina Sultana, The Role of the United States in the Development of the South Korean Economy, ltihas Academy Dhaka, 2016, Dhaka, p. 5.

[3] Hochin Choi-The Economic History of Korea-From the Earliest Times to 1945, (The Freedom Library, Seoul, Korea), pp 89–90.

[4] Hochin Choi, The Economic History of Korea-From the Earliest Times to 1945- The Freedom Library Seoul Korea,1970, p. 191–193.

[5] Hochin Choi, op. cit., pp. 191–93.

[6] See M. Frederick Nelson, Korea and the Old Ordered in Eastern Asia. pp. 203–20.

[7] Paul W. Kuznets-Economic Growth and Structure in the Republic of Korea, (New Haven and London, Yale University Press,1977), p. 5.

[8] Chon Sok-Tam & three others: Ilche-ha ui Choson Kyong-je-Sa (The Korean Economic History under the Japanese Rule), p. 18, 1947. Seoul.

[9] Yi Hong-Chik and three other: Kuska Shingang (New Lectureon Korean History), p. 379, 1958, Seoul.

[10] Choi Ho-Chin: An outline of Korean Economic History. p. 336.

[11] M. F. Nelson, op. cit., p. 41.

[12] Scott S. Burnett, 1989, A Scholar--- influence in 1896-1905, South Korea's Minjung Movement-The culture & politics of Dissidence-Kenneth M. Wells, University of Hawaii at Manoa, Centre for Korean Studies--edited & with an introduction by Scott S. Burnett pp. 62-63, Allen to Sect. of State Hay, 23 Aug. 1900.

[13] S. Lone & G. McCormack, op. cit., p. 38.

[14] P. W. Kuznets. op. cit., p. 6.

[15] Ki-baik Lee-translated by E. W. Wagner and E. J. Shultz, A New History of Korea, (Ilchokak publishers, Seoul, Korea). p. 310.

[16] Ibid, p. 311.

[17] Ibid, p. 311.

[18] Ibid, p. 312.

[19] There were two views of the situation of the period; 1. The Japanese skillfully dealt with mutinous Koreans: 2. The Koreans had reasons to rebel against injustice & oppression. See Hilary Conroy, The Japanese Seizure of Korea, pp. 344–47; Hulbert, The Passing of

Korea, pp. 208–20; and Andrew J. Grajdanzev, Modern Korea, pp. 34–46. Disagreement is there between those impressed by Japan bringing civilization & reform to Korea and those saw the helplessness of relatively backward people at the mercy of the Japanese.

[20] Putnam Weale, 'The Corean Problem', North China Herald', 15 Dec. 1905.

[21] Ichikawa Masaaki (ed.), Nik-Kan gaiko shiryo, Tokyo, 1964, vol. 2, pp. 315–28. Regarding the Ilchinhoe amalgamation proposal, some observers acknowledged that it was designed to pre-empt a Japanese annexation. This was the view of Britain's Consul-General in Seoul, FO 410/55, Arthur Hyde Lay (Seoul) to Foreign Sect. Grey, 7 Dec. 1909.

[22] According to Conroy, op. cit.,pp.442-91, the Japanese trade with Korea was unimportant in Japan's total trade, and their ventures—the rail interests and the Oriental Development Company, an agricultural land development enterprise—were not successful prior to annexation. The Company failed to attract Japanese farmers and there was little emigration to Korea. "Japanese do not like to leave home and do not like to settle in cold climatic countries with resident people who have a lower living standard than their own."(E. B. Schumpeter, ed. The Industrialization of Japan and Manchukuo 1930-1940, p.66). The Japanese comprised less than 3% of the total Korean population even in the late 1930s and most of them were in govt. services, commerce and industry. Conroy has shown Japan had limited economic success in Korea before 1910, he failed to demonstrate that economic factors were insignificant in Japan's desire to annex Korea. Later it became the main factor for Japan in Korea

[23] A NEW HISTORY OF KOREA, Ki-baik Lee translated by Edward W. Wagner and Edward J. Shultz. Ilchokak Publishers, Seoul, Korea, 1984, p. 313.

[24] Ibid, p. 314.

[25] Ibid, p. 314.

[26] Ibid, p.16.

[27] Quoted in Grajdanzev, 1944; p. 269.

[28] S. Lone & G. McCormack, (Longman Cheshire), St. Martin's, New York, 1993, p. 65.

[29] Cho Kijun et al., 1971, p. 585.

[30] Hatada Takashi, 'Chosenjin jido ni tai suru Choson sotokufu no rekishi kyoiki', ed. Hatada takashi, Nihom wa Choson de nani O osh{etd noka, Tokyo, 1987, p. 32.

[31] Yamanaka Seigo, 'Kyokasho kenkyu no kadai to hoko', in Hatada, 1987, pp. 20–21.

[32] Grajdanzev, 1944, op. cit., p. 266.

[33] Cho Kijun et al., 1971, op. cit., pp. 208–19.

[34] Government-General of Tiosen, 1937, p. 80.

[35] Anthony Vacante, Japanese Colonial Education in Korea 1910–45 An Oral History, (Doctorial dissertation), State University of New York at Buffalo), 1987 er, W. Edward, pp. 208–19.

[36] Lee Chang, Labor Movement and Political Development in Korea, Seoul, 1971, p. 178

[37] S. Lone and G. McCormack, op. cit., p. 60.

[38] Bureau of Land Survey (provisional), Choson Govt-General (ed); Choson Dochi Chosajigyo Hokokusho (Report of the Land Survey in Korea), 1918, pp. 1–24, Seoul.

[39] Cho Ki-Jun: The Korean Economic History, 1962, Seoul, p. 305.

[40] Ibid, pp. 305–6.

[41] Chongbo is approximately 2.45 acres.

[42] Ibid, p. 307.

[43] Source: Ibid, p. 58.

[44] Reports from 0. Gaylord Marsh, United States (US) Consul (Seoul) to Sect. of State, 4 & 25 Feb. 1937, US State Dept. records, 895, 114.

[45] A Korean farmer developed a lengthy irrigation channel that interfered with the water rights of Chinese farmers and boatmen, resulting in local riots. In retaliation, Chinese residents in Korea were attacked, with 37 killed at P'yongyang and some 10,000 fleeing to Manchuria in one week.

[46] S. Lone & G. McCormack, op.cit. p. 73.

[47] Keijyo Imperial University Hobungakukai: Choson Shakai Keizaishi Kenkyu (The Study of the Korean Socio-Economic History), p. 54, 1933, Tokyo. Hochin Choi, The Economic History of Korea-from earliest times to 1945, The Freedom Library, Seoul, Korea, 1970, p.210.

[48] Ki-baik Lee, .cit., p. 319.

[49] Choi Ho-chin: An outline of Korean Economic History, Seoul, 1962, pp. 340–350.

[50] Hochin Choi, op. cit., p. 212.

[51] Henry Rosovsky, 'Japan's Transition to Modem Economic Growth, 1868–1885, in H. Rosovsky. Ed. Industrialization in Two System, p. 93. The Japanese figures refer to employed population not households. He feels they overstate the agricultural population and

suggests the figure of 79% being more realistic than the published figure of 83%.

[52] Suh Sang-Chui, in "Growth and Structural Changes in the Korean Economy Since 1910," shows annual average product per worker in 1929–31 and 1939–41. It was 91% of the national average during the first period and only 74% in the second (this includes the poor rice crop in 1939). Grajdanzev shows that average gross output per capita was three times as high in Japan as in Korea in 1938 (Modern Korea, p. 84). Some of this difference was due to differences in the occupational structures of the 2 economies (in Japan a larger number of workers was concentrated in manufacturing and other productivity sectors), calculation of gross value of output per person in agriculture for 1938 indicates that output was two-thirds higher in Japan than in Korea. (sources: gross value of production [Grajdanzev, p. 84]: occupied population, [Schumpeter, The Industrialization of Japan and Manchu/aw, p.76: Bank of Choson, Economic Review, 1949, p. IV 18]).

[53] Choson Dochi Kairyo Kabushiki Kaisha Shi (The History of the Korean Land Improvement Co., Ltd), p. 22.

[54] Hochin Choi, op. cit., p. 214.

[55] Yoo Se Hee, The Northern Korean Communists leadership, 1945-65, Britannica Educational publication, carle Roberts (Doctoral Dissertation) 1974, p. 64.

[56] Ranford S. Muller, United States Consul-General, Seoul to US State Dept. 29 May 1925, item 895.00/705.

[57] Ibid.

[58] Discussion of the tenant movement is largely derived from Yoo Se Hee, 1974.

[59] Young Hoon Kang, 1977, p. 288. Also see Yoo Se Hee, pp. 114-16.

[60] United States State Dept. records, Ranford S. Miller (US Consul-General, Seoul) to State Dept, 31 AUG. 1929, 'the farmers and farmlands of Choson (Korea) in 1928', document 895.61/5; Grajdanzev 1944, p. 119.

[61] Government-General of Tyosen, 1937, pp. 213-16.

[62] Yoo Se Hee, 1974.

[63] Paul W. Kuznets, Economic Growth in the Republic of Korea (New Heaven, Yale University Press, 1977. pp. 14-15.

[64] Choson Government-General: Shisei 30 nenshi (The 30-Year History of the Choson Government -General), p.310-11, see also Hochin Choi, op. cit., p.213.

[65] Ki-baik Lee., op. cit., p. 349.

[66] Korean Land Economic Research Center. A Study of Land Tenure System in Korea, p. 151.

[67] Ban Sung-whan, 'Growth Rates of Korean Agriculture, 1918-1968,' pp. 26-28, 37-39. The partial productivities for land, labor and capital grew at annual rates of 4.23, 1.09 and 0.80% respectively from 1918, 1920-1938, 1940 and 1941 in South Korea and probably for all Korea as well. Allocation of output growth between increasing inputs and productivity as Ban notes is sensitive to choice of factor shares. So the figures in the text provide a rough approximation of the actual allocation.

[68] Tenancy estimates are shown in the Korea Land Economic Research Center's A Study of Land Tenure System, p.44. Japanese ownership shares are given in Suh, "Growth and Structural Changes," p. 11 1 79 and Grajdanzev, Modern Korea, p.106.

[69] Yi Hon-Ku: Chason Nongop Ron (The Study of the Korean Agriculture), p. 301, 1935, Seoul.

[70] Hochin Choi, op. cit., p. 222.

[71] Rents are discussed in Hoon K. Lee, Land Utilization and Rural Economy in Korea, p. 163. The Japanese investigation is cited in Grajdanzev, op. cit., p. 117.

[72] Schumpeter (ed.): The Industrialization of Japan and Manchulaw, p. 292: Johnson. Japanese Food Management in World War I, .p, 55; Korea Land Economic Research Center, A Study of Land Tenure System, p. 53; Suh Sang-chul, Growth and Structural Changes," p. IV 40. All the calculations shown in these sources suffer from accurate date on inventories and carryover. Suh notes the expansion of warehouse capacity in Korea during the early 1930s and the imposition of controls after 1937 to minimize consumption and increase commodity reserves in preparation for war suggests a possible decline in consumption levels (Ibid, pp. IV 139, IV 141).

[73] Johnston, op. cit., p. 54.

[74] Samuel P. S. Ho, "Agricultural Transformation Under Colonialism; The case of Taiwan." p. 315.

[75] Johnson, Japanese Food Management, p.51.

[76] Ho, op. cit., pp. 238–40.

[77] Ramos H. Myers and Adrienne Ching, 'Agricultural Development in Taiwan Under Japanese Colonial Rule." See P.W. Kuznets, op. cit., p. 18.

[78] P.W. Kuznets, p.19.

[79] For estimates of the shares of handicraft establishments and composition of factory output, see, Suh S g-Chul, op. cit., III 84 and table A-14.lf the output of modern factories were taken separately, growth rates would have been even higher.

[80] P. W. Kuznets, op. cit., p. 21.•

[81] Suh, 'Growth and structural Changes,' table III-II; Choi Ho-chin, 'The Process of Industrial Modernization in Korea,' p. 17.

[82] Ibid, tables V-4, V-8, and V-9.

[83] Grajdanzev, Modem Korea, pp. 230-34.

[84] Zenkoku Keizai Chosakikan Rengokai Choson Shibu (ed.); Choson Keizai Nenpo (The Annual Report of the Korean Economy), Appendix No. 2, p. 16, 1939, Tokyo.

[85] Ki-baik Lee, op.cit., p. 355.

[86] Ki-baik Lee, op., cit. p.356.

[87] Ki-baik Lee, op. cit., p. 359.

[88] Hochin Choi, op. cit., p. 241.

[89] Choe ehn-hyun, Population Distribution and Internal Migration in Korea, p. 20.

[90] Most of the Americans were missionaries, Japan Year Book 1930, p. 475.

[91] Cho Kijun et al., llche ha wi minjok saenghwalsa, Seoul, 1971, p. 498.

[92] Kajimura Hideki, 'Shokuminchi Choson de no Nihonjin', ed. Kimbara Samon, Chiho bunka no Nihanshi, vol 9; chihoDemokurashii to senso, Tokyo, 1978, p. 340.

[93] Government-general ofTyosen, 1937, pp. 88-89.

[94] Irene B. Taeuber, 'The Population Potential of Post-war Korea', p. 298.

[95] Ibid, p. 295.

[96] Ibid, p.306. Korea was not unique in this respect, since the same situation with similar causes occurred in Taiwan under Japanese

domination (see W. Barclay, Colonial Development and Population in Taiwan, chap. 10).

[97] Im Tae-bin gives the distribution of gainfully employed workers by sector in 1930 and 1940 and total for gainful workers by sex in 1944 (The Korean Labor Force and School Population, pp. 108-12). Im's figures agree with Sub's for 1930 and 1840, and both show that the number of workers declined by a half million between the two dates. Suh's information was obtained from G-G census data, Im's from an article by Park Chai-bin ('A Review of Korean Population Statistics', Economic Planning Board, Monthly Statistics of Korea, vol 4, nos. 1 and 2) Park's data for 1930 and 1940 came from the same source as Suh's. They show that the decline came mainly among women (gainful workers as a proportion of the total female population fell from 33% in 1930 to 22% in 1940 before rising to 30% in 1944). The 1930 census was probably taken in the fall, when a large number of farm women participated in the harvest, whereas the 1940 census came at a time of the year when the labor force and its composition reflected a seasonal low.

[98] P. W. Kuznets, op. cit., pp. 23–24.

[99] S. Lone & G. MacConnack, p. 53.

[100] Government-general of Tyosen, 1937, pp. 88–89.

[101] Grajdanzev, Modem Korea, p. 263.

[102] Ki-baik Lee, op. cit., p. 331.

[103] Ibid, p. 334.

[104] Ibid, p. 335.

[105] Ibid

[106] Sorensen, 1990.

[107] Han Sokhwi, Nihon no Choson Shihai to Shulcyo Seisaku, Tokyo, 1978, p. 340.

[108] Japan Year Book 1940-41, p. 879.

[109] Ki-baik Lee, op. cit., p. 336.

[110] Ki-baik Lee, op. cit., p.338.

[111] Ki-baik Lee, op. cit., p. 342.

[112] Ki-baik Lee, op. cit., p. 343.

[113] Ki-baik Lee, op. cit., p.338-46.

[114] Zenkoku Keizai Chosakikan Rengokai Choson Shibu, The Annual Report of the Korean Economy, 1939, Appendix No. 2, p. 8, 1939.

[115] Hochin Choi, op, cit., pp.244–45.

[116] Himenu Mineru: Choson Keizai Zuhyo (The Statistical Chart of Korean Economy), p. 258.

[117] Hochin Choi, op.cit., pp. 149–50.

[118] Chon Sok-Tam; Chason Kyongje-Sa (The Korean Economic History), 1949.

[119] Quotation and Reports from United States Consul General Leo. Bergholz to Secretary of State, 17 and 23 April 1919, 22 May 1919, records of the State Dept. relating to the internal affairs of Korea 1910-29, document 895.00/622, 895.00/625, 895.00/639... see also Stewart Lone and Gavan McCormack, Korea since 1850, (Longman Cheshire, St. Martin's Press, New York, 1993), p. 57.

[120] Ibid. p. 59.

[121] Hochin Choi, op. cit., p. 251.

[122] S. Lone & G. McConnack, op. cit., p.60.

[123] S. Lone & G. McCormack, op. cit., p. 60.

[124] Zenkoku Keizai Chosakikan Rengokai Choson Shibu (ed.), The Annual Report of Korean Economy, 1939, Appendix.

[125] Hochin Choi, op. cit., p. 253.

[126] Stuart Lone & G. McCormack, op. cit., p. 62.

[127] Ranford S. Miller, United Sates Consul-General, Seoul, to United States State Dept. 29 May 1925, item 895.00/705.see also Stewart & G. McCormack, op. cit., p. 62.

[128] S. Lone & G. McCormack, op. cit., p.64.

[129] Yoo Se Hee, 1974 provides a detailed analysis of the red Peasant Unions, See also Ibid, p. 64.

[130] Ki-baik Lee, op. cit., p. 362.

[131] Ibid, p. 362.

[132] Hochin Choi, op. cit., pp. 158-60.

[133] Hochin Choi, op. cit., p 263.

[134] Hisama Kenichi: Choson Nasei no Kodai (The Problematic Issues for the Fann Policies in Korea), 1943, pp. 424-27.

[135] Paul W. Kuznets, Economic Growth and Structure in the Republic of Korea, (New Heaven and London, Yale University Press, 1977), p.18.

[136] Choe Tae-Ho: Hwajononmin e k.11anhar: Yon'g-.1 (The Study on the Bumtfield Cultivators) The Journal of the College of Economics and Commerce, Chung-Ang University vol, 8, Seoul.

[137] Kim Pyong T'ae: Mosum e Kwanhan Yon'gu (The Study on Farmland in Korea), "Economics", The Korean Economic Association, vols. 4-5, Seoul.

[138] S. Lone & G. McConnack, p. 37.

[139] Samina Sultana, (Ph. D Thesis), p.30.

[140] Paul W. Kuznets, Economic Growth and Structure in the Republic of Korea, (New Heaven and London, Yale University Press, 1977), p.18.

[141] Zenkoku Keizie Chosalcikan Rengokai Choson Shibu (ed.): The Annual Report of the Korean Economy, 1942, Tokyo.

[142] Ibid.

[143] The Bank of Choson, Research Department (ed.):The Annual Report of the Korean Economy, 1948.

[144] Ibid.

[145] Cho Ki-Jun: The Korean Economic History, pp, 419-420.

[146] Chon Sok-Tam with 3 others: The Korean Economic History under the Japanese Rule, 1947, p. 121.

[147] Himeno Mineru: The Statistical Chart of Krean Economy, p. 258.

[148] Bureau of Education, Choson Government-General (ed.): Kojyo oyobi Kosan ni okeru Rodosha Jokyo Chosa (The Survey Report on the Working Conditions of Factory and Mine Laborers), 1933, pp. 36-40.

[149] Jbid., pp. 84-86.

[150] Samina Sultana: The Role of the United States in the Development of the South Korean Economy 1945-1990-A Historical Study. p.39.

[151] Paul W. Kuznets: Economic Growth and Structure in the Republic of Korea, (New Haven and London, Yale University Press), 1977.p.9-I0.

[152] Simon Kuznets, Six Lectures on Economic Growth, p. 96.h

[153] Suh, "Growth and Structural Changes," pp..11 59-11 61: Schumpetter, The Industrialization of Japan and Manchuria, pp.288-90 Grajdanzev, Modern Korea, p. 226.

[154] P.W. Kuznets, op. cit. ,p.11.

[155] Differences in income and in tastes might be justified the simultaneous rice export and import of cheaper grains. The exploitation revolves around the determinants of income rather than the trade process.

[156] P. W. Kuznets, op. cit., p.13.

[157] United States State Dept, O. Gaylord Marsh, Consul (Seoul), item 895.60/2; United States State Dept., item 895.63.

[158] Details from US State Dept. records, W.R. Langdon, Consul (Seoul) to Edwin Neville, Charged' Affairs (Tokyo), 29 October 1935, item 895.6363/5; U. Alexis Johnson, Vice-Consul (Seoul), 'Present Position and future prospects of American oil firms operating in Choson', 26 January 1938, item895.6363/1 3.

[159] Contained in United States State Dept. records, U Alexis Johnson, vice-consul (Seoul) to Secretary of State, 27 December 1937.

[160] Chong-sik Lee, 1985, pp. 16-17.

[161] Quoted from Choson Shoko Shimbun, 13 August 1938 in 0. Gaylord Marsh (Seoul) to Secretary of State, 25 August 1938, US State Dept. records, item 895.5017/1.

[162] E Lone and G. McCormack, op. cit., pp.84-86.

[163] Richard E. Kim, 1970, p. I 04.

[164] Takeuchi, 1988, pp. 232-53, 257.

[165] FO 371/22190 British Consulate-General, Seoul, Annual Report on Korea for 1937, dated 24 December 1937.

[166] Kimijima Kazihuko, 'Choson ni okeru senso loin taisei no tenkai katei', eds Fujiwara Akira/ Nozawa Yutaka, Nihon fashizumu to higashi Ajia, Tokyo 1977, 96.

[167] Dong, 1973, p. 160.

[168] Lee See-Jae, 1987, p. 9.

[169] Quoted in Brudnoy, 1970, p. 186.

[170] S. Lone and G. McConnack, op. cit., p.89.

[171] Ki-baik Lee, op. cit., pp. 322-23.

[172] Hochin Choi, op. cit., p.299.

[173] Ki-baik Lee, op. cit, p. 324.

[174] Ibid, p. 325.

[175] Ibid, p. 326.

[176] D.L. Steinberg, p. 69,

[177] Park Soon Won "The Emergence of a Factory Labor Force in Colonial Korea. A case study of the Onoda Cement Factory', Ph.D. Dissertation, Harvard University, 1985, p. I 08. Also see S. Lone & G. McCormack, p. 70.

www.ingramcontent.com/pod-product-compliance
Lightning Source LLC
Chambersburg PA
CBHW070136100426
42743CB00013B/2721